Praise for *Rethinking Africa*

'A healing for the world. Today our world is ailing, almost overcome by the poisons of greed, anger and foolishness which have penetrated deeply. This book is the resound of health and healing, illuminating and affirming the original feminine ways of being. The original ways of compassion, connection and wholeness are revealed within its pages. Written by seekers and knowledge keepers, is wisdom so greatly needed now. How wonderful!'
– LOREN BRAITHWAITE KABOSHA, SOKA GAKKAI, SOUTH AFRICA

'This book is a powerful reminder of the herstories and the knowledge produced by indigenous women. These stories must be told and become part of knowledge production. It is part of the process of renaming Memorial Hall to Sarah Baartman Hall and the establishment of the Khoi and San Unit at UCT. It is testimony to what is possible when higher education partners with the people of the land.'
– LORETTA FERIS, DEPUTY VICE CHANCELLOR: TRANSFORMATION, UNIVERSITY OF CAPE TOWN

'The best way to go into the depth of indigenous people's history is if they write about it themselves. They have the knowledge of their traditional ways of life and matricentric/matriarchal social forms from within, which have never been understood correctly by male researchers from the outside. This is especially valid if it is about women in indigenous societies of this kind, who have been ignored in general; this brought about a perfectly distorted picture of the egalitarian, peace-based, matricentric/matriarchal societies around the world.

Therefore, this book is a unique contribution to promote the understanding of women in these societies in present and past and to demonstrate their importance for profoundly changing the patriarchal disaster we are in today.'
– HEIDE GOETTNER-ABENDROTH, INTERNATIONAL ACADEMY HAGIA FOR MODERN MATRIARCHAL STUDIES, GERMANY

'Thank you to the editors, the contributors and the ancestors about whom you write. I have searched for this perspective – a book about indigenous people from the perspective of indigenous women in South Africa.

For so long we have been fed the perspective of the coloniser and his descendants – a perspective that normalised racist, corporate greed that ravaged the earth and humanity. Committing genocide while its conservationists lionised the "noble savage".

May these voices reshape how we see our world and our possibilities as human beings.'

– Pregs Govender, author of *Love and Courage: A story of insubordination*

'*Rethinking Africa* is an extraordinary, pioneering anthology that captures through words and images the wisdom of African feminist thought. Largely invisible in the centuries-old canon of feminist theory, this discourse makes an important scholarly contribution to Indigenous Studies, African Studies, Women's and Gender Studies, and Transnational Feminist Studies. A must read for scholars, activists, organizers, artists, this collection beckons readers to reimagine South African history, in particular, and the experiences of indigenous women across generations.'

Beverly Guy-Sheftall, founding director of the Women's Center at Spelman College, and editor of *Words of Fire: An anthology of African American feminist thought*

'The book features powerful narratives by women thinkers sharing similar histories and trajectories as descendants of indigenous people in Southern Africa.

The book is also an invitation to explore new methodologies that challenge the western cartesian paradigm and its fixation on the intellect, for approaches that are at once more intuitive and rigorous, while being less dismissive of the spirit and the sentient experience. In the process of rediscovering ways of knowing, it is only fitting to appreciate and validate the multiplicity of meanings and manifestations of the 'indigenous', and acknowledge how socio-political influences across centuries add new hues to present imaginings of the pre-colonial.'

Aditi Hunma, University of Cape Town

'This retelling by indigenous women comes at a critical time in our collective existence. It needs to experience indigenous femininity with all of its wisdom and expressions. I am proud of this initiative.'

– Lesle Jansen, CEO of Resource Africa

'This book represents a milestone for the academy. It embodies the decolonial scholarship we are working towards. It is an important manifestation of bringing our voices to the foreground. It is an example for scholars across the global south to follow. This book shows what is possible and necessary.'

– Shose Kessi, Dean of the Faculty of Humanities, University of Cape Town

'This book is an important project of surfacing and disrupting narratives that make indigenous women invisible and thereby robbing them of their equal humanity. It is therefore a recuperation of their stories and re-centring them as active agents of their own lives. Necessarily it also is a work of critique against patriarchal narratives that often further make women's lives and narratives subordinate. Re-presenting indigenous women, giving them a voice and agency makes the book a progressive work of empowerment. It enriches and diversifies narratives of suppressed humanity and provokes to critical self-reflection about our complicity in silencing. The way we see, think of and represent indigenous women and other marginalised subjects will never be the same. Finally, it continues the tradition of rethinking history as not a narrative of great man and events but ordinary people making history.'

TAWANA KUPE, VICE CHANCELLOR, UNIVERSITY OF PRETORIA

'Now that the death grip of Euro-Christian colonialism is loosening from around the world's throat, Indigenous peoples are reclaiming the stories of themselves to repair their worlds. The twelve contributors to *Rethinking Africa* are embarking upon precisely that journey, simultaneously occupying the past and the future. Importantly, they are recovering the sacred women's lore embedded in the soil of South Africa, drawing upon its still vital, if cruelly constricted, stories of matriliny. All indigenous themselves, the authors eschew Western-style "scholarship," with its prim and categorical isolation of information, in pursuit of the old, familiar and familial ways of knowing, being, and telling.'

– BARBARA ALICE MANN, SENECA BEAR CLAN, UNIVERSITY OF TOLEDO

'Today, 'Re-thinking' must be a prerequisite to thinking itself! As we reemerge from dark times to face the third decade of this stunted century, our actions must be fierce, forceful and never reactive. Therefore, let us look to the roots of our collective struggles – to Indigenous Africa, to matricentric herstories – as this important new book by Muthien and Bam so superbly does. Read *Rethinking Africa* with special seriousness, as we prepare to rebuild the world.'

– MATT MEYER, SECRETARY GENERAL, INTERNATIONAL PEACE RESEARCH ASSOCIATION

'This book is an exquisite demonstration of what it means to decolonise and re-shape knowledge. The writing weaves history, sociology and story-telling into a coherent collection of insight into the archive of matriarchies of southern Africa. The concept of 'rematriation' emerges as a strong conceptual anchor that cements this books distinctiveness in the intellectual lineages of books about African women.

I particularly identified with the life of Ma-Meneputo who describes "her carefree childhood, hunting small animals like rabbits and young buck with a bow and arrow, and making and playing with dolls. No Euroformed binaried colour-coded games for her." This is the life of many of us remember, raised in a peasant world with little access to consumer commodities where girlhood was as much about herding cattle with our grandmothers, as well as learning from that same grandmother how to weave mats. As it was about learning to weave reed mats surrounded by industrial capitalism.

The collection achieves "ukubuyiswa" (re-centering) of matricentricity as a wellspring of African sociology, giving context to the many permutations of African women's lives. The cadence of the book is non-linear because it is interspersed with poetry and recollections which are interwoven with conventional academic argumentation.

The chapter on indigenous women and their ecological knowledge reminds us of the depth of scientific-medical knowledge of the environment accumulated and passed down by Khoekhoe women through time into the present. This speaks through the epistemic erasure of Khoekhoe descendants in South African historiography and how these practices have continued through time and their matriarchies.

This book shows just how necessary it is for us to keep developing our own historical and sociological concepts, rooted in our many vernaculars, that can speak across the many kinds of African indigeneity that we emerge from and continue to live in the present.'

– NOMALANGA MKHIZE, NELSON MANDELA UNIVERSITY AND RHODES UNIVERSITY

'Long-overdue and long-awaited, this women-centred *Rethinking Africa* volume will reset discourses on and of the continent.'

– SHAILJA PATEL, AUTHOR OF *MIGRITUDE*

'This important collection of essays by African feminists is a gift to the growing matricentric women's movement South and North, which is shedding light on the cultures that came before and will come after the capitalist patriarchal system, which is now perpetrating the matricide of Mother Earth and all her human, animal and plant populations. The perspectives contained in this volume create a common ground of anti-colonial critique in terms of which that system can be understood, dismantled and at last replaced by a "rematriated" and egalitarian society.'

GENEVIEVE VAUGHAN, CO-FOUNDER, INTERNATIONAL FEMINISTS FOR A GIFT ECONOMY

'This exciting pathbreaking book seeks to herstoricise notions and epistemologies that challenge 'histories' and theories which have tended to exclude African and indigenous women's existence and the past. Offering exciting lenses, it allows the reader to consider and reconsider our received notions by providing pathways ways to study and envisage being and becoming. It adds to the growing body of decolonized global knowledge.'

– WANGUI WA GORO, KING'S COLLEGE AND SOAS, UNITED KINGDOM; UNISA, SOUTH AFRICA

Rethinking Africa
Indigenous women reinterpret
southern Africa's pasts

Edited by
Bernedette Muthien and June Bam

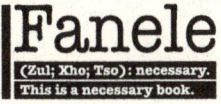

First published by Fanele, an imprint of Jacana Media, (Pty) Ltd, in 2021
Second impression 2023

10 Orange Street
Sunnyside
Auckland Park 2092
South Africa
+27 11 628 3200
www.jacana.co.za

© Bernedette Muthien and June Bam, 2021
All rights reserved.

This publication is Volume IV of the Rethinking Africa series in the Pre-Colonial Catalytic Project of the Centre for African Studies funded by the National Institute for the Humanities and Social Sciences.

ISBN 978-1-4314-3021-5

Cover design by publicide
Design and layout by Aimee Armstrong
Editing by Glenda Younge
Proofreading by Lara Jacob
Indexing by Christopher Merritt
Set in PSFournier Std 10/14pt
Printed and Bound by Creda Communications

Job no. 004003

See a complete list of Jacana titles at www.jacana.co.za

For our mothers and our sisters

Contents

    Foreword
    Lungisile Ntsebeza   xi

    I've come to take you home – A tribute to Sarah Baartman
    Diana Ferrus   1

    Introduction
    June Bam and Bernedette Muthien   3

1. Writing ourselves back into history: The liberating narrative of who we are
   Sylvia Vollenhoven   17

2. Rematriation: Reclaiming indigenous matricentric egalitarianism
   Bernedette Muthien   51
   green kalahari
   Bernedette Muthien   85

3. Gendering social science: *Ukubuyiswa* of maternal legacies of knowledge for balanced social science studies in South Africa
   Babalwa Magoqwana   87

4. Feminism-cide and epistemicide of Cape herstoriography through the lens of the ecology of indigenous plants
   June Bam   103

    The bones
    Diana Ferrus   121

Camissa
Khadija Tracey Carmelita Heeger   123

call to art
Shelley Barry   127

5. Valuing the increased and invisible workload: Indigenous women, labour and the COVID-19 pandemic
Sharon Groenmeyer   129

6. Decolonising the representation of indigenous women at the Cape during Covid-19
June Bam and Robyn Humphreys   147

7. Repositioning !uiki Ilnaosa/aia/
gertrude fester-wicomb   169

8. Ancestral letter to unborn descendants
Sarah Malotane Henkeman   183

9. The falling sky: Some notes about originary peoples in Brazil
Ana Lígia Leite e Aguiar   201

Conclusion
June Bam and Bernedette Muthien   209

one & many
Bernedette Muthien   213

Contributors   215

Captions for images   221

Index   225

Foreword

Lungisile Ntsebeza

The book *Rethinking Africa: Indigenous women re-interpret southern Africa's pasts*, is, as the Introduction shows, published under the auspices of the *Rethinking Africa* series. The latter is an initiative of the Centre for African Studies (CAS) at the University of Cape Town (UCT) since its relaunch during 2012. The main mission of CAS since 2012 has been to promote African Studies across departments and faculties at UCT and beyond, particularly, though not exclusively, within the African continent and the global South.

The *Rethinking Africa* series serves as a platform for engaged intellectuals within and outside academic institutions who are committed to inter-/trans-/multi-/non-disciplinary perspectives and are interested in the political, socio-economic, international, developmental, and other intersectional issues concerning Africa and its people.

Key questions raised in this series include: What is the meaning and significance of the study of Africa and its people? Who should study Africa and its people? Does it make sense for Africans to study themselves? What would be the implications for Africa and its people if 'others' undertook the study?

Contributions to this series can be in the form of occasional papers, research reports and books, some of which, as is the case with this book, are co-published with commercial publishing companies.

Key to the success of the *Rethinking Africa* series has been the publication of books that emanate from the catalytic project on the precolonial historiography of southern Africa. This is an initiative of the National Institute for Humanities and Social Sciences (NIHSS), which was established in 2012 to support and nurture research over the long term to promote the development of methodologies and studies that would advance the study of precolonial eras in southern Africa.

This volume is the fourth in the *Rethinking Africa* series published by CAS. It follows on the heels of the groundbreaking book, *Whose History Counts: Decolonising African pre-colonial historiography*, published in 2018. *Whose History Counts* focuses on epistemological and foundational questions about the writing of history and, as the title asks, whose history counts? It also explores methodologies for researching and writing history.

In many ways, the *Rethinking Africa* series, and the *Whose History Counts* volume, address the clarion call that emerged in the context of the student-led rebellion following the #RhodesMustFall campaign, which erupted at the University of Cape Town on 9 March 2015, but had simmered for decades. At the heart of the rebellion was the students' condemnation of what they referred to as 'colonial' education, in favour of a 'decolonised curriculum'.

The book, *Rethinking Africa: Indigenous women re-interpret southern Africa's pasts*, strikes me as a direct response to the central question posed in *Whose History Counts*. As the editors boldly point out in their Introduction, this is the first volume in the *Rethinking Africa* series to focus on indigenous women, who tell their own herstories in their own voices. The perspectives of indigenous women – and how they understand and narrate their pasts – have been and continue to be left at the margins of scholarship. This book shows us how this process of marginalisation, informed by colonial thinking, is robbing scholarship of developing new concepts and methodologies that are rooted in how indigenous peoples lived before colonial intrusions and disruptions, and continue to live today.

My heartfelt congratulations to the editors and contributors for producing this book during the COVID-19 pandemic. June Bam has been an integral part of the precolonial historiography project from the

Foreword

outset. She has now been joined by Bernedette Muthien, who comes with her own energy and insights.

We look forward to more volumes in this series!

LUNGISILE NTSEBEZA
SERIES EDITOR: RETHINKING AFRICA
A.C. JORDAN RESEARCH CHAIR IN AFRICAN STUDIES
NATIONAL RESEARCH FOUNDATION (NRF) RESEARCH CHAIR IN LAND REFORM
AND DEMOCRACY IN SOUTH AFRICA
EMERITUS PROFESSOR, CENTRE FOR AFRICAN STUDIES
UNIVERSITY OF CAPE TOWN

I've come to take you home
A tribute to Sarah Baartman

Diana Ferrus

I have come to take you home –
home! Remember the veld,
the lush green grass beneath the big oak tree?
The air is cool there and the sun does not burn.
I have made your bed at the foot of the hill,
your blankets are covered in buchu and mint,
the proteas stand in yellow and white
and the water in the stream chuckles sing-songs
as it hobbles along over little stones.

I have come to wrench you away –
away from the poking eyes of the man-made monster
who lives in the dark with his clutches of imperialism,
who dissects your body bit by bit,
who likens your soul to that of satan
and declares himself the ultimate God!

I have come to soothe your heavy heart,
I offer my bosom to your weary soul.
I will cover your face with the palms of my hands,
run my lips over the lines in your neck,
feast my eyes on the beauty of you
and I will sing for you
for I have come to bring you peace.

I have come to take you home
where the ancient mountains shout your name.
I have made your bed at the foot of the hill.
Your blankets are covered in buchu and mint,
the proteas stand in yellow and white.
I have come to take you home
where I will sing for you,
for you have brought me peace,
for you have brought us peace.

Glossary
buchu – a herb used by Khoekhoe people for medicinal purposes
mint – a herb also used for medicinal and cooking purposes
protea – the national flower of South Africa
veld – open vegetation

Introduction

June Bam and Bernedette Muthien

There is often the blatant assumption and statements by both academics and the South African public that the Khoe[1] and San people are largely extinct. The discourse on Khoe and San 'extinction' frequently gets entangled with DNA studies on who is who genetically, and who could claim authenticity based on physiology and genetic studies. This is an unfortunate legacy of colonial scholarship. A postgraduate student at a historically white Apartheid (Euro-Christian) university once shared that one of her professors claimed that there was no archaeological evidence on the Cape Flats of what one reads of the precolonial rituals and philosophies of the Khoe and San, as these people were confined to the Northern Cape. Anecdotal evidence that suggests the existence of archaeological evidence that may get us to rethink scholarship on the region is easily dismissed. This illustrates the limitations of existing Western-based research methods of the disciplines.

Such assertions on where evidence exists, and indeed where it does not, wipe out the multigenerational knowledge of indigenous women of the Cape in one dismissive stroke, foregrounding ongoing coloniality and its attempts to erase existing multigenerational knowledge (epistemicide) in our present-day scholarship. Inadvertently, this form of

---

1 The authors use 'Khoe' and 'Khoi' interchangeably in the text.

coloniality links to the well-known ubiquitous assertions in European male travellers' texts since the 1400s that the indigenous people of the Cape, especially the women, were the most savage of all savages in the world. In brutally affirming this colonial belief, the knowledge and philosophies of these women were erased and marginalised through genocide (massacres, with the hope for total extermination), linguicide (brutal suppression of indigenous language use), ethnocide (attempts to erase ethnicity and culture), ecocide (attempts to erase environmental, landscape and botanical knowledge), and epistemicide (attempts to erase deep intergenerational knowledge).

Today it is widely acknowledged that the indigenous people of the old colonial Cape colony suffered the most brutal colonial encounters as the 'first contact' people. This recognition was embraced in the 'I am an African' speech of then deputy president Thabo Mbeki, with the founding of the first democratic Constitution for the Republic of South Africa in 1996 under President Nelson Mandela.

> I owe my being to the Khoi and San whose desolate souls haunt the great expanses of the beautiful Cape – they who fell victim to the most merciless genocide our native land has ever seen, they who were the first to lose their lives in the struggle to defend our freedom... (Mbeki 1996)

Within this historical context, some Khoe and San activists today choose to speak of 'first nations' (a contentious concept in contemporary South Africa). The genocidal losses referred to by Mbeki in the 1996 'I am an African' speech were never meaningfully engaged with in both scholarship and dialogical public discourse. As a start, it could not be addressed by the Truth and Reconciliation Commission (TRC) because of the TRC's limited legal and political mandate confined to Apartheid's gross human rights violations and atrocities committed from 1960 to 1993. The TRC was a political process seeking a political settlement between the Apartheid state and its Apartheid legislature on the one hand, and former liberation movements and their allies on the other hand. It was not tasked with attaining restorative and cognitive justice (to know the truth of over 300 years of colonial oppression, enslavement, land dispossession, economic exploitation, violence and consequent losses over deep time).

Hitherto, scholarship has engaged only in limited ways with these 'losses' suffered and their further entrenchment in the Western disciplinary canons, with its Cartesian approaches to validation of knowledge, theorisation, and interpretation of evidence and objectivity. Vast scholarship exists on these 'erased' people, known as the Khoe and San and historically related Xhosa people, but from a largely 'exteriority' perspective. This perspective is limited and deficient, often exclusively focused on the Bleek and Lloyd archive of the turn of the last century, archaeological debates on 'who is who', and related vexing identity issues and debates on whether the massacre of the San was in fact 'genocide'. While these debates on terminology have been raging on in 'exteriority' mode in predominantly white academia, important voices of the people themselves and their descendants have been excluded. Although attempts have been made to bring in the personalities and agencies of //Kabbo and others, of Autshumao, Krotoa and even Sarah Baartman[2] in recent years, in the attempt to unmute their silences in the colonial archive, these attempts have remained predominantly captured within the paradigm of 'voicelessness', speaking on behalf of and for. Such scholarship, though important in its various archival contributions, remains deficient in a decolonial framework.

Community engagement on recovering and revalidating the lost knowledges of theory and interpretation has not yet become mainstreamed in higher education in South Africa. The establishment of the A/Xarra Restorative Justice Forum (with Khoe and San traditional structures, civic and rights bodies) at the University of Cape Town's Centre for African Studies in 2018 sets an important precedent in the higher education transformation landscape.

These attempted knowledge erasures were deep, multiple and varied, and took place in different locations and over several layered spatialities in the southern African landscape, as elsewhere with indigenous communities globally. In recognition of these multigenerational tangible losses (rights to the land and structural wealth) and intangible losses through significant invisibilisation (indigenous knowledge, culture, language), important social and civic movements have become more prominent since at least 2000 to reclaim and reposition marginalised indigenous knowledge and practices as mainstream, both historically and in contemporary times.

The decolonial Portuguese scholar De Sousa Santos (2016) speaks of 'ignorant ignorance', which comes to mind when critically engaging Eurocentric arrogance in contemporary times. The question therefore

---

2   Renowned San and Khoe figures, in especially the colonial archives.

begs in our time: How do we rethink Africa from an indigenous feminist perspective that critically engages 'ignorant ignorance', to produce knowledge of our precolonial past that is fuller, more complex, diverse, of immense value and, therefore, not dismissable? Where necessary, we critically engage the Eurocentric scholars who continue to study indigenous peoples as subjects. Because of ignorant ignorance (you don't know what you don't know), indigenous people are often labelled dismissively and with indifference as naïve or coy, as 'emotional', biased scholars. They are ridiculed in the Western disciplinary canons that obsessively seek 'scientific objectivity' through fixed terminologies, classifications, and other fixities, scholarship patronage and colonial patriarchies. In these canons there is little room for fluidity, for marginalised indigenous women's voices. To critically engage these masculinities in scholarship on the precolonial in southern Africa, the authors draw on feminist indigenous scholarship worldwide, but also on the important, often-overlooked, scholarship of indigenous female historians such as *Tara* Yvette Abrahams and *uMakhulu* Nomathamsanqa Tisani. Although they achieved their doctorates in historiography at historically white, Apartheid universities about 20 years or more ago, their voices have been decidedly muted by Eurocentric scholarship with little recognition of their major contributions in how we rethink historiography in Africa.

Indigenous feminist scholars carry intergenerational epistemic trauma, little recognised – as addressed in Chapter 8 by Malotane Henkeman. Some of this psychological trauma is unspeakable and best penned, as here, in a letter to unborn generations whose task will be to carry on with the work of cognitive justice. This trauma, which Malotane Henkeman names, has always remained largely hidden in the deep architecture of historically white universities. Hence, colonial writing of the static and frozen-in-time 'Peaceful Bushman', a trope that has carried through into contemporary times, even in liberal writings on the indigenous peoples. In all of this, indigenous women and their knowledge and deep pasts have been completely ignored by Western canons and their narratives of 'worthwhile knowledge'.

In the process of redress, we have to start by rethinking our methods and the kind of questions we ask within the suffocating Western canon of limiting disciplines of what we know and how we know it, of what counts and why.

The other vexing and relevant challenge in rethinking our methods, relates to the contentious issue of terminology. While the debate on 'genocide' rages on within predominant white scholarship globally, there are others we hope to engage with more authentically in this book. Contestations about terminology are not only confined to white scholarship, but come with the inclusive territory of rigour in scholarship and in mainstreaming this work. The words we are expected to define in discourse include 'indigenous', 'feminist' and 'feminism', the notion of divinity or deities, spirits or ancestors, as well as the erroneous yet deliberate colonial imposition of black–white, and South–North. Hierarchies of meaning through contestations about terminologies impede solidarity for recognition and the pertinent issues for redress among diverse indigenous peoples on all continents. Many are constructed within colonial contexts; others hold different and diverse meanings in various social and historical contexts. Terminologies like 'tribe' and 'First Nation' (see fester-wicomb, Chapter 7 in this volume) therefore have different meanings in different contexts. In southern Africa these terms are particularly contentious; the prior linked to colonialism, as critiqued by Mafeje (1971), and the latter to 'firstism', as criqued by Mellet (2020). Ugandan scholar Mahmood Mamdani (2020) argues therefore for deterritorialising ethnicity as an important step in the decolonisation of tribalisation.

Cognisant of the challenge in affirming decoloniality through scholarship rigour, all authors have been allowed to express and argue for themselves in terms of their identities and preferred terminologies. It is widely recognised in scholarship that identities, like terminologies, are context-based, fluid and changeable, and that in keeping with most indigenous traditions that foster diversities, this volume encourages polyvocality, since change is constant. We embrace these debates, even among ourselves, as we co-create new relevant African future scholarship that gives meaning to decoloniality.

For instance, whereas Groenmeyer problematises what she considers a lack of definition of 'indigenous', Muthien, without irony,[3] deploys the United Nations Declaration on the Rights of Indigenous Peoples.[4]

---

3   The very foundation of the United Nations, and its precursor the League of Nations, served as a stage for victorious post-war colonial powers to carve up the world and its peoples, often arbitrarily, as evinced by the San people who inhabit the Kalahari, which straddles six southern African countries.

4   United Nations Department of Economic and Social Affairs: Indigenous Peoples, United Nations Declaration on the Rights of Indigenous Peoples, Adopted by the General Assembly, 13 September 2007. Online at: https://www.un.org/development/

As South Africa is a comparatively young constitutional democracy, it is through law and its transformative potentials that many of us seek redress and even comfort. UNDRIP's Article 31 states that

- indigenous peoples have the right to *determine their own identity or membership* in accordance with their customs and traditions. This does not impair the right of indigenous individuals to obtain citizenship of the States in which they live.
- indigenous peoples have the right to determine the structures and to select the membership of their institutions in accordance with their own procedures.

Thus UNDRIP addresses the vastness of diversities and herstories, patriarchal colonisations, slaveries and dispossession, among indigenous peoples on all continents. This is the international legal definition of indigenous, with regions and states able to supplement and domesticate UNDRIP with their local, complementary laws and policies.

So when we speak of our mothers' healing herbs, and our people's matricentricity, it is our chosen identity or membership, in a moment, in all its heterogeneous, polymorphous, polyvocal, diverse shapes and many voices. We – indigenous – speak for and define ourselves.

In Chapter 7, fester-wicomb refers to the Charter of Feminist Principles for African Feminists (African Women's Development Fund 2016) a groundbreaking document developed by the African Feminist Forum, supported by the African Women's Development Fund, whose members are historically privileged in relation to the majority of 'ordinary' women on the continent. These trailblazing African Feminists define themselves in their preamble:

> We define and name ourselves publicly as Feminists because we celebrate our feminist identities and politics. We recognize that the work of fighting for women's rights is deeply political, and the process of naming is political too. Choosing to name ourselves Feminist places us in a clear ideological position. By naming ourselves as Feminists we politicise the struggle for women's rights, we question the legitimacy of the structures that keep women subjugated, and we develop tools for transformatory analysis and action. We have

---

desa/indigenouspeoples/declaration-on-the-rights-of-indigenous-peoples.html (Accessed 11 December 2020).

multiple and varied identities as African Feminists. We are African women when we live here in Africa and even when we live elsewhere, our focus is on the lives of African women on the continent. Our feminist identity is not qualified with 'Ifs', 'Buts', or 'Howevers'. We are Feminists. Full stop.

South Africa appropriately signed and ratified the Protocol to the African Charter on Human and Peoples' Rights on the Rights of Women in Africa, also known as the Maputo Protocol,[5] important international human rights legislation and policy effected by the African Union in 2005. Signed by 49 of 55 African member states by July 2020, and ratified by 42 member states, the Maputo Protocol guarantees comprehensive women's rights to equality, autonomy and justice, from the social and political to health and reproduction. This book is written by such Feminists, full stop.

Linda Tuhiwai Smith (1999:167–168) asserts that

> the very labelling of women demonstrates the pluralism within the feminist world, and the multiple directions from which feminist theory has emerged and to which it may be heading. These Other/ed women have argued that oppression takes different forms, and that there are interlocking relationships between race, gender and class which makes oppression a complex ... Condition ... This position intersects with Maori attitudes to research, and the writings of African-American women in particular have been useful for Maori women in legitimating, with literature, what Maori women have experienced.

So, too, does Magoqwana (Chapter 3 in this volume) at times draw inspiration from African-American feminist thinkers, and Muthien (Chapter 2) draws on diverse indigenous and African scholars like Barbara Mann and Ifi Amadiume. We hold various views reflective of our diversity, and at root we are indigenous, African and feminist, as well as women-centred, or matricentric, as Muthien discusses.

We use the language of divinity, of our ancestors and deities to simplify complex and ancient spiritual practices which are not

---

5   Protocol to the African Charter on Human and People's Rights on the Rights of Women in Africa, Adopted by the Second Ordinary Session of the Assembly of the Union, Maputo 11 July 2003. Online at: https://www.un.org/en/africa/osaa/pdf/au/protocol_rights_women_africa_2003.pdf.

patriarchal, dominating, hierarchical, vengeful and oppressive, as European or 'Western' organised religions might be. Several contributors discuss and define their spiritualities (often ancestral) in this volume.

After colonialism in South Africa, a government was founded on the violent, brutal, genocidal racial hierarchy of white over black, called Apartheid, which lasted for 50 years, and is codified as a 'crime against humanity' in the Rome Statute of the International Criminal Court. Thus we capitalise the term Apartheid, to highlight its significance in history and its continued impacts in South Africa and elsewhere.

The Apartheid state waged wars not only on its own citizens who were not 'white' (and were therefore 'black' – including the indigenous), but it also waged wars against neighbouring states whose citizens were majority black. It is in this particular context of Apartheid that contributors use the concepts of 'white' (as in historically white universities or white privilege) and 'black' (as in people who are not white; people who are of colour). In South Africa, privilege and structural economic benefit was determined largely by pigmentation. This stark pigmentation-based Apartheid discrimination may be somewhat different for our indigenous kin in Scandinavia (Sami) or North America (Haudenosaunee) or, indeed, in parts of North Africa (Berber). It is merely illustrative of our unique historic standpoint in South and southern Africa. Because of structural genocide (and we use this term with our authenticity of self-determination), exploitation and oppression, we consider all indigenous peoples, whether paler or darker, as not white and hence 'black'. We view other oppressed peoples, such as the Irish and Palestinians, similarly as 'black' and hence express solidarity with them.

Several contributors to this volume write of the 'in/visible' in their respective chapters. To the neocolonial and patriarchal gaze, the work of women is often unseen, unpaid and unacknowledged. Yet indigenous and other women witness and appreciate their and others' labours. The violences perpetrated by patriarchy and neocolonialism are made invisible by and to the structures of oppression, as Henkeman (Chapter 8) shows, yet the victims and survivors of these violences are very much aware of their/our own suffering. Thus it is important to acknowledge the various standpoints and reflections: in/visible for and by and to whom?

In reflecting on these contemporary issues, when the urge for decoloniality is increasing in a COVID-world of further marginalisation of the structurally oppressed and their voices in the various scholarly disciplines, this book sets out as a *deep listening* book. Interspersed with poems by indigenous women, it foregrounds 'knowing differently' and 'doing differently' in how we produce and understand relevant knowledge about the precolonial past and its ongoing presence, from an indigenous feminist perspective in South Africa. In its aim to open new pathways for critical decolonial scholarship and solidarity, and the reclamation of indigenous self-definition, this book concludes with a reflection from a scholar in Brazil with questions around what that decoloniality would entail in how we think about the precolonial, not only in southern Africa but also in the larger world. Brazil has the largest African-descendant population outside Africa – a legacy of enslavement. Brazil presents similar historical parallels to the Cape in terms of indigenous issues, as in a confluence of African enslaved and local indigenous communities, jointly oppressed by the brutality of colonialism and enslavement. In Brazil, the 'precolonial' necessarily presents a hybrid of African enslaved and Native American indigenous cultures. Indigenous Brazilians were also depicted as cannibals, and brutal genocide by the Portuguese followed, along with the concomitant ecocide and epistemicide. These similarities between Brazil and South Africa's Cape give rise to interesting and new complex questions within the global South and indigenous studies. Global South here simply means structurally marginalised peoples in the world, including indigenous and migrant peoples in the global North (such as the Haudenosaunee in North America, the Sami in Scandinavia and African-descendant peoples in the United Kingdom). The inclusion of Ana Leita Aguiar's chapter is intended to show the links between Africa and its enslaved descendants adopted by local indigenous peoples in the world, and to initiate a wider conversation about the genocide, ecocide and epistemicide of indigenous and other enslaved peoples. What new understandings and insights can we gain from the global precolonial and indigenous hybridities of Africa and its connections to the wider world by asking new questions within the global South?

How do we listen differently in that much unexplored global indigenous archive? Zaayman's (2019) doctoral work on the anarchive invokes that call through questioning the archive and its limitations; in particular the vast available knowledge that is tangibly missing from the official archive. In Chapter 1, 'Writing ourselves back into history: The liberating narrative of who we are', Sylvia Vollenhoven draws on her earlier literary work, *Keeper of the Kumm* (2016), to foreground the understanding that science is diffused with spirit, and that landscape speaks of stories denied. Vollenhoven contends that, 'while archives are not alive, they are charged with those lives'.

Vollenhoven's chapter is followed by Muthien's provocation of the archive in 'Rematriation: Reclaiming indigenous matricentric egalitarianism'. Muthien celebrates an ancient African deity who spread to the Greco-Roman world and at times takes on different names around the world, *Hymn to Isis* (3rd or 4th century CE), to deploy methodologies common to indigenous feminisms. Her chapter draws on at least two decades of her own work with global feminists in decolonising research with matricentric societies. In Chapter 3, *Ukubuyiswa* of maternal legacies of knowledge for balanced social science studies, Babalwa Magoqwana expounds on what it would mean to reclaim our women knowledge holders. *Ukubuyiswa* is a metaphor and a language of ritual. Her essay develops her key contribution made in *Whose History Counts* (2018), in which she argues for *uMakhulu* (grandmother) as the body of knowledge that 'stores, transfers and disseminates knowledge and values'. Magoqwana's work in this field has been highly impactful in scholarship in South Africa and elsewhere as an illustrative argument of Toyin Falola's (2020) 'ritual archive'. Based on decades of scholarship, June Bam's chapter, 'Feminism-cide and epistemicide of Cape herstoriography through the lens of the ecology of indigenous plants', builds on the work of Magoqwana. gertrude fester-wicomb's chapter illustrates the language of indigenous knowledge of mothers and grandmothers that has been hidden. fester's work also builds on Magoqwana's 'repositioning of *uMakhulu*' by 'Repositioning *!uiki Ilnaosa/aia/*'.

Hence reflecting on the work presented in these chapters, when certain scholarship claims that the Khoe and San are extinct at the Cape, and that knowledge of the precolonial only resides further inland as a result, then we are called to engage in Tisani's (2018) provocation to call for *ukuhlambulula* (to cleanse), to affirm, to reclaim. This *ukuhlambulula* process requires rigour and commitment to an intellectual project in foregrounding Mafeje's (1991) advocacy for 'authentic interlocutors' beyond exteriority.

The *ukuhlambulula* process in this book starts with the iconic poem as a tribute to Sarah Baartman by Diana Ferrus, *I've come take you home*. Written shortly after 1994 with the inception of the first democracy in our country, and coinciding also with Mbeki's 'I am an African' tribute

(1996) to the Cape's Khoi and San, there was overwhelming recognition then that an ancestral mother (an *Ausi* or *Ousi*, an *uMakhulu*, a *Taras*), whom South Africans, as a nation, had to fetch (to officially visibilise) in order to look forward. It was a 'Sankofa bird' moment, in the Akan people's metaphor, of looking back in order to look forward. In this book, a number of the authors write metaphorically by 'looking back' at the *Ausidi* (*Ousies*), *Taradi* and *ooMakhulu* in their own lives.

In looking forward, Sarah Malotane Henkeman writes an invocation to deep listening in her 'Ancestral letter to unborn descendants' (Chapter 8). This is where the book concludes its South African conversation and moves into Ana Lígia Leite e Aguiar's provocations for further rethinking in a global South context in '*The Falling Sky*: Some notes about originary peoples in Brazil'.

Ferrus's iconic poem provokes the Sankofa bird 'homecoming': 'I have come to take you home where I will sing for you, for you have brought me peace, for you have brought us peace.' When we, as South African indigenous women, brought Sarah home, we asked ourselves: what have we brought 'home' in terms of knowledge production and decoloniality – then close to 20 years later? Through changing the name of the University of Cape Town's (UCT's) Jameson Memorial Hall to Sarah Baartman Hall during 2019, we acknowledge deeper transformations in higher education that we need to enact as indigenous feminist scholars, so that decoloniality is not just a metaphor. Ferrus begs from us, as fellow writers and thinkers, to find peace beyond the limitations of poetic metaphors in scholarship. This invocation for peace relates to Tisani's call for *ukuhlambulula* and Aboriginal Australian scholar, Miriam Rose Ungunmerr Bauman's *dadirri* (deep listening). Through our writing we hope to learn from these indigenous scholars by reflecting back on deep time, deep pasts, through this catalytic, globally uncertain pandemic-present, towards collectively creating profound futures of benefit to all.

By looking back, we look forward to contributing towards a new African future in which the knowledge of indigenous women is valued in rethinking and re-interpreting our pasts.

All chapters herstoricise the accepted 'histories' and theories of how we came to understand the African past in the way that we do, how to problematise and rethink that discourse, and provide new and different 'herstorical' lenses, philosophies, epistemologies, methodologies and interpretations.

What is it that we need to give, as thinkers and scholars, to create hopeful futures of a world that is more in balance with itself as it explores deep time and deep pasts? The uncertainties created by COVID-19 brought these knowledges and philosophies and their increased relevance to the surface. The capitalist global world now knows that something has to give, has to fundamentally shift. Recognising and valuing indigenous knowledge of women in the rethinking of our pasts, and how they inform our collective dis-eased present, may be a good starting point to restore the ecology and societal balance so sorely needed.

As diverse indigenous women, we do not pretend to hold all the answers. Further, due to the limitations of this inaugural volume, and of any book for that matter, we certainly are not able to cover all the multigenerational knowledge we collectively hold in these few pages. But we hope that this publication catalyses the important research for producing new knowledge and methodologies on the precolonial, and for asking the new and more appropriate questions.

What all the authors of this volume do agree on is that there is a profound ongoing presence of the precolonial past in traces of memory, in multigenerational knowledge and rituals. It exists in its diversity, as captured in the concluding poem by Muthien. Interspersed with creative poetry by indigenous writers, this book hopes to invoke deep listening in you as the reader, inviting you on this journey to listen between the lines, and to listen deeply.

References

Abrahams, Y. 1996. Disempowered to consent: Sara Bartman and Khoisan slavery in the nineteenth-century Cape colony and Britain. *South African Historical Journal*, 35(1): 89–114.

Abrahams, Y. 1997. 'The great long national insult: 'Science', sexuality and the Khoisan in the 18th and early 19th century', *Agenda*, 13(32): 34–48.

African Women's Development Fund. 2016. 'Charter of Feminist Principles for African Feminists'. Online at: https://awdf.org/the-african-feminist-charter/ (Accessed 15 January 2021).

Falola, T. 2020. 'Ritual archives', *The Palgrave Handbook of African Social Ethics*. London: Palgrave Macmillan, pp. 473–497.

Kopenawa, D. and Albert, B. 2013. *The Falling Sky: Words of a Yanomami shaman*. Cambridge, MA: Harvard University Press.

Mafeje, A. 1971. 'The ideology of "tribalism"', *The Journal of Modern African Studies*, 9(2): 253–261.

Mafeje, A. 1991. *The Theory and Ethnography of African Social Formations: The case of the interlacustrine kingdoms*. Dakar: CODESRIA.

Magoqwana, B. 2018. 'Repositioning uMakhulu as an institution of knowledge'. In J. Bam, L. Ntsebeza and A. Zinn (eds). *Whose History Counts: Decolonising African pre-colonial historiography, 3*. Cape Town: African Sun Media.

Mamdani, M. 2020. *Neither Settler nor Native: The making and unmaking of permanent minorities*. Cambridge, MA: Belknap Press.

Mbeki, T.M. 1996. 'Adoption of RSA Constitution Bill'. Online at: www.gov.za/about-government/tm-mbeki-adoption-rsa-constitution-bill# (Accessed 21 February 2021).

Mellet, P.T. 2020. *The Lie of 1652: A decolonialised history of land*. Cape Town: Tafelberg.

Santos, B.D.S. 2016. 'Epistemologies of the South and the future', *From the European South: A Transdisciplinary Journal of Postcolonial Humanities*, (1): 17–29.

Smith, L.T. 1999. *Decolonizing Methodologies: Research and indigenous peoples*. London: Zed Books.

Tisani, N. 2018. 'Of definitions and naming: "I am the earth itself. God made me a chief on the very first day of creation."' In J. Bam, L. Ntsebeza and A. Zinn (eds). *Whose History Counts: Decolonising African pre-colonial historiography, 3*. Cape Town: African Sun Media.

Zaayman, C. 2019. 'Seeing what is not there: Figuring the anarchive'. PhD dissertation, Centre for Curating the Archive, University of Cape Town.

1

Writing ourselves back into history
The liberating narrative of who we are

Sylvia Vollenhoven

> I look into the mirror
> A girl with a gemsbok face stares at me
> She knows when to eat the springbok meat
> Follows the guidance of her Ancestors
> Understands that science is suffused with spirit
> But her landscape speaks of stories denied.
> (Vollenhoven, 2016)

Every artistic process becomes a synthesis of all our experiences. This is a chapter in four acts, a kind of four-part harmony, that synthesises the threads of several artistic processes. The aim is to explore the motivation and origins of creative artistry by going beyond conventional research methods.

In recent times, countless South African artists, across all disciplines, have taken on the responsibility of Re-membering,[1] of discarding a defective narrative of who we are as a people and addressing the damage done by centuries of colonialism and Apartheid. The result has been

---

1 An established concept in theorising around memory, loss and restoration. See for instance, Jay Ruby's *A Crack in the Mirror Reflexive Perspectives in Anthropology* (1982); and Michael White's *Re-authoring Lives: Interviews and Essays* (1995).

art that provides us with new narratives to replace the diseased parts of the factual and fictional body of storytelling we have inherited ... Remembering.

My own storytelling is aimed mainly at addressing neglected or distorted aspects of South African history. Please note that I use the present tense when writing because it feels more accurate and is more reflective of the way physical and non-physical events are ordered outside of neat, manufactured timelines.

In this chapter I examine the four main elements that have driven my artistic approach:
- The context and motivation: Writing ourselves into history
- The instability of separate selves: Red tea and wholeness
- Storytelling processes for wholeness: An invitation to dance
- Conclusion: Journeys across inner and outer landscapes

THE CONTEXT AND MOTIVATION: WRITING OURSELVES INTO HISTORY

Storytelling and mainstream media may be posing the same questions, but often these different disciplines are many worlds apart. My initial foray into the world of telling stories for a living leads me into a media environment that requires you to leave your critical faculties behind.

My career begins on a small newspaper in the 1970s. The *Cape Herald* is owned by the rich, white Argus company but is aimed at the Black working-class people of the Cape Flats. The content is strictly controlled by a British editor appointed by the white, male, middle-class (invariably middle-aged and urban) South African bosses. We hardly ever question why we should straight-jacket our world to fit into the diminished perspective of the management. We are discouraged from taking history or politics too seriously and pushed towards the titillation of crime, sport and frivolity. The confines of being blinkered in this stifling box is a fitting metaphor for where we find ourselves in the 21st century. Our story is still controlled too often by bourgeois economic interests with agendas that mitigate against telling the truth about who we are.

This chapter is written from the perspective of a storyteller who has gone in search of a healthier way of positioning myself and my people in the landscape of our history. When I begin going down this road, I do not understand clearly what I am undertaking and why. The stories lie waiting in the unseen expanses of myself.

This lack of knowing the exact destination, or the means of

getting there, is completely contrary to everything I have been taught as a journalist. But fortunately, the blind trusting that is required is perfectly attuned to my early training (a kind of apprenticeship) with my maternal grandmother, Sophia Petersen. When I ditch almost everything that I have been taught about storytelling at the Argus Company[2] Journalism Cadet School, the chaos is overwhelming, completely destabilising. But to avoid clichéd creativity, we have to embrace a disorderly artistry, a process that involves bypassing the intellect. My whole life has been a preparation for the writing I begin when the stranglehold of journalism weakens.

Embracing a new kind of narrative has required a different way of life that opens up the doors of perception, to allow the unhindered flow of inspiration between the realms of the seen and unseen self.

I have been inspired to address primarily the problems caused by problematic histories and by the fact that Khoe and San characters, my First Nations Ancestors, hardly ever drive mainstream storytelling in South Africa. A turning point in my writing and understanding of myself comes with the discovery of the story of //Kabbo in the Bleek–Lloyd Archive, housed at the University of Cape Town.

In 1870, //Kabbo /Uhi-ddorro Jantjie Tooren, a pipe-smoking, revolutionary Bushman[3] hunter, driven by his need to safeguard his fragile culture, travels hundreds of miles through the Karoo to find city people whom he has heard can write down stories and preserve them in books. The result of this vision quest is an archive recorded over a thousand days and nights. More than a century later, this Bleek–Lloyd Archive is entered into UNESCO's *Memory of the World Register*. It contains over 100 notebooks and more than 12,000 handwritten pages. In this work of Victorian philologist Wilhelm Bleek, his sister-in-law, Lucy Lloyd, and their informants, //Kabbo is the main informant as well as their teacher.

The Bleek–Lloyd duo's account of their meeting with //Kabbo paints him as a passive informant whom they 'discover' in the Breakwater Prison in the 1800s. Many researchers, academics and artists repeat this version of events. When I am working with his story, I often smell the

---

2   The Argus Group that owned the *Cape Herald* newspaper, among other titles, was a precursor of Independent Media.
3   The term Bushman is considered pejorative by some but there are groups of indigenous people, especially in the Kalahari, who have reclaimed this word because they prefer its inherent power to the word San, colonial nomenclature that is considered problematic.

faint odour of pipe tobacco in a seemingly empty room. According to the archive accounts, //Kabbo loves his pipe. It is during one writing session in 2015, when the smell is particularly strong, that the following comes to me:

> When //Kabbo was in his early thirties, the colonial governor extended the boundaries of the Cape Colony, taking away almost all his people's land, and thereby providing a conducive environment for Boer commandos to hunt them down.
>
> //Kabbo had a vision that he could save his people. And so, in 1870, //Kabbo /Uhi-ddoro Jantjie Tooren, a pipe-smoking, revolutionary Bushman hunter, driven by his need to safeguard his fragile culture, travelled hundreds of miles to find city people as he had heard that they could write down stories and preserve them in books.
>
> The result of this vision quest is an archive recorded over a thousand days and nights (Vollenhoven, 2016: 2).

As a hunter and visionary, //Kabbo knows his terrain better than any interloper. In the archives there are many accounts of his prescient dreams and abilities as a rainmaker. It is much more likely that, having lost so much due to colonial incursion and aggression, he realises that their most precious possession – the stories of who they are – should be saved. It is also likely that he has a dream that someone in distant Cape Town could assist with his Vision Quest. In this scenario, he allows himself and some of his fellow crusaders to be captured. Instead of being a passive participant in the grand plans of a Victorian academic and his researcher assistant, he becomes a co-creator of the Bleek–Lloyd Archive to tell the story of our people.

The overarching aim of my writing and storytelling in recent times has been to place this kind of rich legacy squarely in the hands of ordinary people everywhere, especially the descendants of our First Nations – people who remain largely unaware of the existence or significance of visionary ancestors like //Kabbo. It is a continuation of the work //Kabbo, started in the mid-1800s. The result so far has been:

- *A Writer's Last Word* (writer): a theatre play (co-authored with Basil Appollis) about the Cape Town writer Richard Rive. The play is a tribute to his work, especially the novel *Buckingham Palace, District Six*. This play is renamed *My Word! Redesigning Buckingham Palace* for a run at the Jermyn Street Theatre in London's West End.

- *Buckingham Palace, District Six* (SA producer): a feature film in development, which is an adaptation of the Richard Rive novel. The context of the film is that, although Apartheid used race as a determinant to destroy communities in the 1960s and 1970s, the gentrification of inner cities worldwide is no different and continues to this day.
- *The Keeper of the Kumm* (author): a non-fiction novel that engages with //Kabbo by journeying through my internal landscape and the modern world, where traces of him are found everywhere. By going in search of //Kabbo, I explore his global relevance and the opportunity he represents to re-story South Africa.
- *The Keeper of the Kumm* (author): a dance drama and factional theatrical adaptation of the book, which is a conversation across time and space between a modern journalist and //Kabbo, her 19th-century Ancestor.
- *Cold Case: Revisiting Dulcie September* (author): a theatre play that revisits the unsolved assassination in 1988 (possibly by an Apartheid hitman with the collusion of French authorities) of the ANC's representative in France.
- *Krotoa Eva van de Kaap* (author): a theatre play commissioned by the Volksoperahuis of the Netherlands. The play opened in Amsterdam with a subsequent six-week, nationwide run in the Netherlands and a sold out run in South Africa.
- *Rooibos Restitution* (producer): a documentary film that captures the struggle of the Khoe and San people to get recognition as the traditional knowledge holders of the uses of rooibos. An epic battle to acknowledge and protect First Nations' indigenous knowledge, which leads to victory for that recognition after the film is released.
- *Pirates of the Drakensberg* (writer and SA producer): a television series in development. It is the story of KhoeSan resistance against colonial aggression in the 19th century. This six-part drama series will follow the adventures of the Khoe Chief Madoda (his name became the word for manhood), his powerful shaman wife, Hoho, and a band of rebels who built a most unusual settlement in the lower reaches of the Drakensberg.
- A work in progress: the story of *Blanche and Alex La Guma*. Another creative collaboration with Basil Appollis for The District Six Museum and the Artscape Theatre Centre. Alex La Guma, one of our most notable writers of the 20th century, hailed from District

Six. He spent most of his life in exile and died in Cuba in 1985. He was a defendant in the Treason Trial but is not very well known in South Africa. His works helped characterise the movement against Apartheid. La Guma was awarded the inaugural 1969 Lotus Prize for Literature.

Sick and tired

Sick to death of marginalised Bushmen, the dancing tourist cliché, in skins clinging to fragile First Nation connections, I set out to create healthier stories of our common ancestry and heritage.

This is more than mere professional research and writing. It is my belief that a serious illness I suffered in recent times has been part of an 'Ancestral Calling' to undertake this work. I have been fortunate to find creative collaborators, a traditional healer and other professionals, who work outside of the confines of the mainstream, who have assisted me.

Starting with the conventional archives, books, interviews and digital resources, I have conducted meticulous research into the world of the people who have chosen me to tell their stories. I find, sometimes in the most unusual ways, the points where their reality and mine intersect.

The journeys through South Africa, in conversation with a range of experts and ordinary people, mirror internal journeys on a parallel landscape. In this way I build credible realities, based on the experiences gained along the way. These experiences have put modern flesh on the skeletal heritage of conventional history books.

> Globally there is an awakening to a new way of thinking, a new way of seeing ourselves in the landscape of the past. With this awareness, neat time lines give way to a non-linear, interrelated reality (Vollenhoven, 2016: 4).

This reality reflects Einstein's assertion that we invented time only because we could not cope with everything happening at once. But while the world respects Indian mystics or revers Greek mythology, African spiritual traditions of non-linear perceptions of time have much less currency, even in our own hearts.

In her thesis, 'Weaving the past with threads of memory: Narratives and commemorations of the colonial war in southern Namibia', Namibian scholar Memory Biwa (2012) looks at oral history and performances re-enacting colonial history as alternative repertoires of representation, resistance and reinvention. She argues that 'these practices depart from a conventional way in which to view an archive and history, and that these memory practices point to the ways in which the logic and acts of the colonial war and genocide were diametrically opposed through acts of humanisation' (Biwa, 2012: 6). In a chapter about women making quilts and titled 'Stories of the patchwork quilt: Recalling transnational narratives of war', Biwa (2012: 98–99) states:

> These extra-linguistic sensory perceptions of material experience display a double enactment where material objects were sensed and sensed with. These sensory perceptions presented during performances are what I refer to as 'threads' of material experiences embedded in the very fabric of historical re-enactment. In performance they were used along with gestures to confirm, support or silence specific historical narratives. Also, they were used as a means to communicate unconscious and known historical experience. In another sense they were used during performance to open up ways in which to explore unreconciled historical narratives between the bearer and the perceiver. These performances replete with artefacts and gestures were used as self-reflexive instruments to interrogate unreconciled narratives.

My storytelling is redolent of a broader movement that is using the power of creativity to create a new understanding of our traditions and of ourselves. However, these are strongly research-based works. I engage innovatively with text, locations, artefacts and art, excavating literal and figurative signatures of the character's world ... interrogating its relevance in ours.

Along the way I examine the ambiguities of hybridisation. I explore objects, events, records and people's stories, not simply as residues of cross-cultural interaction, but also as active agents in shaping identities and communities. The research approach has been developed with the collaboration of several creative partners, mainly Basil Appollis, whose work as an actor, director, singer and writer is widely known.

Together, Basil and I have a common starting point, that is, that conventional written history is a very narrow prism and prison. It is a view of the past that ignores a range of methods available to us to access where we have been and, therefore, it reduces greatly who and what we are, now and then. Because we acknowledge that we are up against a written history that continues to occupy a supreme perch in this hierarchical understanding of who we are, we deliberately work with themes that will destroy this status quo.

Writing ourselves into history requires a fresh approach that breaks down the barriers between the divine and the secular; tradition and modernity; spiritualism and materialism; us and them.

Breaking down these barriers brings us to a new understanding of who we are. There seems to be an understanding inherent in mainstream storytelling, that is, that we choose the stories we tell and that we shape them intellectually. I have found that this is not the case with stories that matter. My mundane everyday life does not dictate the artistic work I produce. I am chosen by the stories that I tell. My artistry dictates the life that I live, and I am guided by the stories that I tell. The reverse would be akin to the idiomatic tail wagging the dog.

THE INSTABILITY OF SEPARATE SELVES: RED TEA AND WHOLENESS

'We must walk the sky for we are heaven's things.'[4]

A teapot, old and dented but scrubbed to a brilliant silver shine, bubbles on the stove with 'bush tea'. We are allowed only this herbal rooibos brew as children. According to my grandmother's health regime, kids are damaged by drinking 'Engelse (English) tea'. Whenever we move house, my grandmother plants an array of herbs at the new place. Buchu for infections, wormwood or bitter 'als' for every stomach ailment, rosemary to make hair pomades, wild dagga for my mother's asthma ... the list is long.

It becomes embedded in my mind that healing involves caring, personal rituals as well as the plants that grow all around us. Often the contents of the grocery cupboard double up as medicine. Ginger, garlic, olive oil, salt, lemons, honey or vinegar really come into their own when we are ill. It is a world of wholesomeness and wholeness.

I am sitting on my grandmother's lap, swaddled in her hand-made kiddie quilt. She is holding a book of Bible stories for children in one hand and the other arm cradles me. A few times I begin to slip off Mama Sofie's lap because her grip loosens when the story grabs her. I always fall asleep before the story ends but that does not mean Mama stops reading. When

---

[4] //Kabbo, *The Day's Heart Star*. The Digital Bleek and Lloyd Archive (June 2872). University of Cape Town.

I am older, she tells meandering stories about her youth. Late at night she divides the large kitchen table in half. At one end she spreads an old blanket to do the ironing and at the other end I sit with my schoolbooks. The books and the ironing are shamefully neglected. Sometimes there is a sudden interruption. Ma puts down the iron and berates spirits who have wandered uninvited into our cosy kitchen story circle.

I learn that the world of storytelling is intimate and without limitations. We can talk as easily with each other as we do with those whom we cannot see, and everyone has the ability to join us. It is a world of fluid borders. But there is a deep division in our house. We never talk like this when my mother is around. I learn from an early age that good Christians do not engage with unseen worlds.

It is the festive season sometime in the sixties. The high point of the Christmas holidays is our annual visit to my grandmother Sophia Petersen's Ancestral Home, Swellendam. We step off the train and leave behind our city habits. My grandmother comes alive in a way that I never see in Cape Town. I love crossing over into this world of farm animals, wheat fields, vats of home-made ginger beer and woodfired ovens perpetually producing bread. In the city I am shy and withdrawn. Here among my cousins, I enjoy the elite status of the cool kid who dresses in fancy frills and speaks another language. 'Praat Engels vir die kinders' ['Speak English for the children'] urges Ballie, the son of Ma's sister Auntie Rachel Pekeur. I respond with recitations out of my schoolbooks. Everyone's favourite is 'Baa Baa Black Sheep'.

In Swellendam I learn about the feeling of belonging for the first time. But I also learn about hierarchies and stories that have cachet. I don't think about how my cousins relate to my affectations when I speak. My mother has taken elocution lessons with Irish nuns, so when any of us speak in public it's as if we have all been to Sister Bernadette's classes.

As a young adult, my journalism ambitions dictate that I go in search of stories with cachet, told in a style that has been handed down by the powers that run the media organisations and training institutions. Here there is no place for the stories that emanate from a time of wholeness and wonder. To be a successful journalist, you have to accept a dissection of yourself into many compartments. The spirit self stays at home. The intellectual self writes stories. The unseen realms or the rich world of African custom, ritual and tradition only ever make the headlines in 'trashy' or 'down-market' publications. 'Respectable' journalism focuses on a very narrow prism of the dissected self. I become accomplished at this disabled way of being and rise to the top of my profession.

In the mid-eighties the Apartheid beast is being slain. As befits a monster in its death throes, the state unleashes its most brutal aggression on a nation rising up. I meet Ernst Klein, the foreign editor for the largest Swedish daily newspaper. My stories about the impact of Apartheid on the ordinary lives of people have caught his attention. I become the Southern African correspondent for his newspaper, Expressen. *For the first time in my career, I am asked to write about my life as a young Black woman dodging bullets and burning barricades, on the streets of South Africa. The result is a regular column for* Expressen *in far-away Stockholm. 'Get away from rapportage,' Klein urges. 'People in Sweden want to know what life is really like under such a regime.' At the insistence of* Expressen's *chief editor, Bo Strömstedt, I interview my mother and grandmother. The story about us – three generations of women thriving despite Apartheid – is given prominence in the Sunday magazine. It gets the attention of delegates at an international PEN gathering. I disentangle myself from the myth of journalistic objectivity and win Sweden's most prestigious journalism prize.*

I learn that the low value placed on the stories of ordinary Black people by South Africa's mainstream newspapers at the time is not an international reality. It gives me the confidence to write things I have never written before. Many times, I write stories that defy the strict laws and censorship of the States of Emergency in 1980s South Africa. But breaking down barriers within and without takes time.

In the summer of 1991, a young man comes knocking at my door. He is looking for a creative partner to write a play about the Cape Town author Richard Rive. John Slemon, the iconic director of the Baxter Theatre, has commissioned him. Actor Basil Appollis has heard that Rive was my Latin teacher at high school. Ignoring the fact that I have no idea how to write a play, I sign up as co-writer. One night in the midst of the writing process, I dream of the late Richard Rive. He is dancing up and down among the crowd on opening night. The remarkably pale colour of his eyes stand out in the dream. When I tell Basil about this, he says, 'But don't you remember that his eyes were almost grey, very unusual for a Black person.' At about the same time, Basil and I meet a complete stranger who claims to be a 'seer'. She describes Rive and tells us how happy he is about the play we are writing. But the journey to opening night is complex. Along the way Basil and I get married, South Africa becomes a democracy and we move to Johannesburg. Seven years after the collaboration starts, the play opens at the National Arts Festival and has a run in Cape Town to commemorate the 21st anniversary of the Baxter Theatre in 1998.

I cannot separate who I am from the stories that I am chosen to tell. I learn from the process of developing the Rive play – called *A Writer's Last Word* in South Africa and renamed *My Word! Redesigning Buckingham Palace* for the run on London's West End – that the important stories come knocking at my door. I don't have to go out searching for them. To write the Rive play, we explore conventional research methods. But instinctively I am guided to reach beyond the books, interviews and archives.

I begin to approach the writing and research as if it is a direct communication with Richard Rive. One day, Basil remarks on a few lines describing Rive's initial encounter with poet Ingrid Jonker in the play. He says he likes the way Rive writes: 'It was a warm evening. She had a pale blue silk scarf, wrapped around her throat. Like genteel protection against some illness' (Vollenhoven and Appollis, 1998). I tell him that's not Rive's writing, it's mine. I am taken aback at how easy it has become to blend Rive's work with my own writing.

> The '80s is the decade of the worst apartheid excess. This evil we have given the name of 'separateness' knows that it cannot last forever ... Deep inside myself sits a twisted understanding of my place in the world. We have allowed the separateness to seep into every aspect of ourselves. There are apartheid churches, apartheid schools, apartheid social functions and apartheid sports. We live and dream this separateness (Vollenhoven, 2016: 147).

Early in the new millennium, writing my creative non-fiction novel, *The Keeper of the Kumm,* is intensely cathartic. The separateness inside myself has to come to an end and telling this story is the way to get there. All around me people have begun to question a social order that requires so much division within and without.

In an almost hidden valley of the Cederberg mountains lies Wupperthal. In 2017, when the people of this village are about to rise to prominence for staking their claim to the Traditional Knowledge of Rooibos, I get a call from the lawyer who is fighting their case. Lesle Jansen of the NGO, Natural Justice, tells me she has heard me talk on the radio about KhoeSan identity and history. She wants me to make a film about the landmark agreement they are negotiating. It will see KhoeSan communities compensated for the first time in history ... paid for their traditional knowledge of rooibos. The process of making the documentary film takes many months and many trips to the Cederberg belt.

I get to learn the real story of rooibos for the first time. There are constant attempts by a host of foreign countries to patent the uses of rooibos. In one landmark case, Lesle Jansen and the Natural Justice organisation fight alongside the Swiss NGO, the Berne Declaration (now called Public Eye), to stop the multinational Nestlé corporation from patenting uses of rooibos. The battle takes place in the Swiss courts. The global giant loses (Natural Justice, 2010).

During the shooting of my film *Rooibos Restitution*, community leader Barend Salamo tells stories of similar biopiracy attempts. He tells of foreigners who have travelled to the Cederberg to collect rooibos plants. But this member of the fynbos family refuses to grow anywhere else. The micro climactic conditions in the Cederberg belt cannot be replicated. Oom Barend says one group managed to make the plants grow because they took soil from the Cederberg mountains. But their success is short-lived. When the roots grow long and encounter the foreign soil, the plant dies (Vollenhoven, 2017).

During my time in the Cederberg, I learn that indigenous people in remote villages can be global players who change the course of history. As an adult I still drink rooibos tea, almost to the exclusion of all other kinds of tea, and somehow this gives me a closer bond with the people I am filming in the mountains. The fact that their destiny is intertwined with a finicky fynbos bush helps me see my grandmother's approach to healing in a whole new light. The threads of our connections with the natural world are complex and have to be honoured.

In more recent times, I am lying on my bed, somewhere between being awake and asleep. The room starts to buzz as if a whirlwind is on its way. I look around and see nothing, but I feel a swirling movement. The very air is being stirred up. I know instinctively to lie very still, accepting and trusting whatever is happening. I feel a force lifting me up off the bed and I close my eyes, offering no resistance. This happens from time to time. It is always exactly the same process. I am aware of a movement that becomes faster and faster. I have a sense of myself being very still while an unseen force is carrying me and moving at hyper speed. The speed picks up and there is no sound at all. But communication happens. I know what to do and what not to do. Always when the movement stops and I open my eyes, I am in a place that I have never experienced before. As a child my grandmother would clap her hands with joy when I tell her of 'special dreams'. 'There are dreams and there are visions,' she would always say, 'and we have to listen to the visions.'

We are a people who know how to make stones speak, who have always known the importance of setting down an enduring archive. Our rock texts are testament to our understanding of the value of reaching out to our descendants. So, it follows that as a people we have not lost the ability to communicate across physical barriers and across time and space. Colonial aggression, followed by apartheid's near annihilation of the understanding of who we are as the Khoe and San people, has been but a temporary disruption on our journey. We are now busy journeying from the woundedness of recent centuries to wholeness.

Memory Biwa states that although some histories have been silenced, there are ways in which we are alerted to 'other knowledge regimes'. Biwa (2012: 99–100) goes on to say:

> On the other hand, sensory memory, both as conscious and unconscious embodied histories alert us that there were other knowledge regimes by which historical narratives became known and represented that were not necessarily recorded in official histories. Although the colonial war and genocide were silenced in official historiography, there were other forums in which the war was not silenced. During 'moments of rest', 'stillness', such as during communal events in these communities, the resistance of ancestors to colonialism was recalled through various embedded and embodied mediums employed to narrate material and unconscious experiences of the war. These sensory memory regimes, which would be defined by observers as a loss or an absence, were often structured during these memorial events in narratives and re-enactments as an 'absent presence' of the past.

Biwa quotes Tarshia Stanley's (2007) writing on the movie *Eve's Bayou* saying: 'The ways in which these narratives were embodied by these women recalled their histories as significant linkages with their communities concerning their political and spiritual lives expressed through a particular intertextual matrix of historical representation read as the "ancestral presence".'

When we seek to Re-member, to put ourselves back together again and end the instability of separate selves, we have to work with the 'ancestral presence of the past'.

STORYTELLING PROCESSES FOR WHOLENESS: AN INVITATION TO DANCE
For me the most comforting place in my early years as a journalist, in the multi-storey *Argus* building on Cape Town's St George's Street, is the library. It is a time before the possibilities of digital research. I spend hours going through the archives. But the *Argus* hardly ever has prominent stories about Black people. Soon I realise that, as one of the few Black journalists in the newsroom, I am creating a new archive.

In the 1980s I use my status as a senior journalist to depart from the regular news agenda and focus on stories about why the government is attempting to destroy the fishing village of Kalk Bay[5] or what life is like for domestic workers, or the growing power of the student movement. Each prominent placement and byline give me the courage to explore my society even further. But while white owned, conservative newspapers have become slightly more flexible, the confines of journalism at this time still do not allow for serious inquiry into the questions that matter.

Initially when I make the leap from rapportage to creative writing, it is not easy to emerge from the blinkers. The process of being fully proficient in a new style of storytelling is slow on every level. Writing a play about Cape Town author, Richard Rive, feels like fumbling down a long, dark corridor. It is hard to fully trust a new creative direction, with very few precedents to follow.

> *A Writer's Last Word* was commissioned as part of the Baxter Theatre's 21st-anniversary commemorations in 1998. The play, a one-man show, opened to critical acclaim on the main programme at the National Arts Festival in Grahamstown with my co-author, Basil Appollis, playing Rive.
>
> Writer, teacher and academic, Richard Moore Rive (1 March 1931–4 June 1989) was stabbed to death by young men whom he had invited into his home. He was murdered a few days before the adaptation of his novel, *Buckingham Palace, District Six*, opened at the Baxter Theatre. It was the first time that his work, previously banned by the Apartheid government, was produced in his home country (Vollenhoven and Appollis, 1998: Foreword).

After endless research, interviews, creative brainstorming and the occasional inspiring dream, I sit down to write. Sometimes when I read

---

5   An area declared 'white' under Apartheid, with a settlement of 'Coloured' fishermen of Philipino and local origin.

the words that I have written, it feels completely new to me as if I am encountering it for the first time. It is even stranger when I watch Basil rehearse the lines because it feels like watching something written by someone else.

Basil and I develop a method of working that involves him doing much of the research and giving constant guidance on content, structure, mood and direction of the work. There is a synergy in our collaboration, which means we can rely on a delicate synthesis of technical skills and creative intuition. The collaboration is not without a generous amount of creative tension, but we agree on the important aspects of the work we are doing in the post-Apartheid milieu. He says:

> In 1994 we had to liberate ourselves from the tyranny of Apartheid first. But it took a while to free ourselves from cultural tyranny so that we could tell authentic stories in our own voices. Cutting loose from a context in which our stories were mangled to suit foreign tastes or had to pander to the insecurities of white South African audiences, has taken time and it is an ongoing process.[6]

With this freedom to reflect truthfully on who we are as a nation, comes the responsibility to rely on a range of methods to access our stories, especially those narratives that have been neglected or distorted to serve the agenda of a bygone era.

It is not necessary to deal here with the more traditional methods of accessing historic stories and characters. These are well known. But it is essential to reflect on how we use or interpret the information found in books, archives, interviews and digital resources ... How we read artefacts.

In addition to attempting honest reflection, we need to grapple with difficult questions:
- How do we ensure that unconventional methods of doing research have a rightful place in storytelling?
- How do we set down experiences that sometimes defy description?
- How do we pin down ideas, processes and experiences that do not fit easily into the neat boxes of conventional expectations?

One day in the winter of 2013, during a consultation with sangoma Niall Campbell, who has practices in Botswana and South Africa, I ask him

---

6   Personal interview, 23 June 2020. All Appollis quotes in this chapter are from the same interview session.

the same questions. I expect him to say that it is not possible. He looks at me and says very pointedly: 'It's difficult but you have to try.' I regard this as a personal injunction and take a fresh look at my writing.

With a part of me looking back over my shoulder for assurance from my unseen guides, I attempt to combine the seemingly irreconcilable worlds of spiritual communication and research. This is not a definitive exploration of unconventional research methods. It is what I have found, from my creative experience, to be the most effective. It is a way of life, a way of working, aimed at facilitating maximum cohesion between the different aspects of my larger self. It is completely normal:

a. *Dreams and journals:* Since 2006 I have kept detailed journals, mainly aimed at examining dreams more closely. Observing and recording patterns, I have been able to incorporate the guidance from dreams into my creative processes. The journals are a tangible way to track dreams and other intangible processes or occurrences that fuel creativity. On any one day we inhabit several different mood states as artists. A journal assists with keeping track of who we are from one minute to the next and year by year.

b. *Communication processes*
   i. Hypnotherapy and regression: This is not a tool I have used often. But when I have made use of credible, professional hypnotherapists, it has helped me to make huge leaps of progress with a story.
   ii. Trance and meditation: In 2004 I started a regular routine of quiet time. In the beginning nothing much happened. Now, close to two decades later, these sessions have become as essential to the quality of my creative artistry as eating is for my physical wellbeing.
   iii. Ritual: Having been raised in a fundamentalist Calvinistic religion, the absence of important ritual resulted in a kind of cultural starvation for me as a young woman. Consulting with traditional healers and trusting my instincts, I have devised regular rituals. These are aimed mainly at keeping open the lines of communication between my intellect and ego (the aspects of myself that I need to produce stories for consumption in the physical world) and my broader intelligence.

iv. Guidance: Just listening ... I sit myself down and observe what comes to the fore. It differs from meditation or trance because it can happen anywhere. From the bustle of a shopping mall to a busy social gathering or the bucolic ambience of a walk in the forest ... when I really listen, I can hear valuable guidance. Call it Voices (sometimes the gentlest whisper only) or Guidance or Notions or Instinct, it boils down to a clear direction that differs significantly from the rough and tumble of intellectual busyness.

c. *Teamwork:* Creative brainstorming, the most valuable tool in the creative arsenal, is sitting down with collaborative, generous artists who appreciate the linkages between artistry, guidance and intuition. My artistry relies on periods of solitude that work in tandem with these group sessions, to take the work to another level.

d. *Lifestyle changes:* When I am involved in a creative project (and especially in the lead up to a new project) I am unable to drink alcohol or eat red meat. I avoid consuming too much starch, carbohydrates, sugar (even fruit sugar) or dairy and wheat products. A well-functioning physical system means that the lines of communication, between the source of my creativity and the part of myself that has to set it all down, are as wide open as possible. At the start of almost every day, I follow a routine of physical exercise (often dancing) followed by breathwork and, finally, a spell of meditation. The powerful buchu herb still features prominently in my health regime.

Walking backwards along the neat timelines of the processes that have produced (or are producing) the various works mentioned in the context and motivation section, I will illustrate how these research methods have been used effectively. This is by no means an exhaustive list. It serves merely to illustrate how this method of integrating the whole self can work.

Dreams, journals and The Keeper of the Kumm

In a journal entry dated Wednesday, 2 November 2011, there is a rough sketch of a circular structure. The entry below it states: 'Had a dream about this structure last night.' There are three concentric circles. In the middle is a well. The next circle is the 19th-century journey of //Kabbo /Uhi-ddorro Jantjie Tooren, as recorded in the Bleek–Lloyd Archive.[7] The outer circle is an intersecting journey of myself as the Storyteller and //Kabbo. Three transversal columns that cut across all the circles leading to the centre, are simply headed /Kaggen (the Mantis figure that dominates KhoeSan folklore). These three columns have sub-headings that include, 'dance'. I don't know it at the time, but five years later this structure becomes the basis of my play, *The Keeper of the Kumm* (the dance drama adaptation of the non-fiction novel of the same name).

About three weeks later I record a dream, accompanied by a feint and seemingly hesitant sketch of a place I have seen in the dream. I have been battling an illness that I cannot shake and which has been getting worse since I returned from Ghana, where I lived for a few years. The entry above and below the sketch, states (Personal journal entry, August 2011 to June 2012):

> I need help. My physical system feels like it is on the brink of some kind of collapse. Mentally I feel like I'm on the verge of a breakdown. The slightest bit of mental or physical exertion makes me utterly exhausted. The other night I dreamed that I have to consult a healer, sangoma type man. He lives in a place that is very specifically pointed out in the dream.

The simple drawing has an entrance that leads to a kind of square. There are three little blocks with an X. One has a label that states, 'third house'. The street ends in a cul-de-sac that leads to a 'field, garden and cabbages'.

The journal entry further states:

> When I get to the place, I enter from the far entrance of the square, which is off a field of cabbages. Finally, I am inside the house. Bev Mitchell is with me. The Healer and Bev leave me alone in a room. A horrible energy attaches itself to my back and the back of my arms. It is busy immobilising me, getting me down physically. I try to scream for help from Bev and The Man, but they don't hear me. I am left

---

[7] The Digital Bleek-Lloyd Archive is available as a collection at the University of Cape Town's Lucy Lloyd Archive, Resource and Exhibition Centre (Llarec) project. http://lloydbleekcollection.cs.uct.ac.za/.

alone to battle with this horrible evil energy & at times I am writhing on the floor, on my stomach.

I have never consulted a sangoma before nor do I know anyone remotely fitting this description. A few days later, my friend and fellow filmmaker, Bev Mitchell, arrives from Johannesburg to stay for a while. A friend invites Bev and me to a sweat lodge experience in nearby Hout Bay. When we get to the venue, Bev Mitchell realises that the man conducting the ritual is Niall Campbell, a sangoma she knows well. She introduces us.

I make an appointment with Niall. He lives in No 3 but his street is not a cul-de-sac. Shortly after I begin regular consultations with Niall, he moves house ... to a cul-de-sac. I ask him about the field of cabbages, and he explains that in African spiritual traditions, cabbages signify healing.

Sessions with Niall begin a rocky road to healing and the start of writing the *Kumm* novel in earnest. On the day of the winter solstice on Friday, 21 June 2013, which coincides with a super moon, Niall performs a demanding *ukufemba* ritual. The aim of the ritual is to drive out the dark energies that have entered my system. The energy that I dreamed of two years previously is finally exorcised.

Almost exactly three years later, the *Kumm* novel is launched and, at the same time, the dance drama adaptation opens at the National Arts Festival in the winter of 2016. I do not choose to undertake the gruelling task of writing a play and a book at the same time. The writing pours out of me in a stream that is hard to contain. These events are described more fully in *The Keeper of the Kumm* (Vollenhoven, 2016).

Communication processes in //Kabbo's story

On a warm summer's day in 2004, I am listening to Dr Baruch Banai (a medical practitioner who has turned his back on mainstream medicine) at a workshop in Johannesburg, where I am living at the time. He claims that it is possible to access memories from times and places we inhabit beyond this earth and beyond a current lifetime. He mentions a hypnotherapy practitioner called Desiree Coertze, who assists people with accessing these memories.

One part of me thinks this is wild, new age mumbo jumbo, but another part of me is intrigued. The content of that talk stays with me and pops up in my awareness from time to time. About two years later, I track Desiree Coertze down and begin many months of what she calls 'regression therapy'. In the lives I explore under hypnotherapy with

Desiree, I am either a storyteller, a healer or a strategic messenger. It deepens my understanding of my role as a writer.

When I am researching the *Kumm* book in Cape Town years later, I come across a similar hypnotherapist named Claudia Klein. A session with her (filmed for the feature documentary based on the *Kumm* book) reveals under hypnosis that I was related to //Kabbo in another life.

> In search of a rational explanation for my obsession with the photographs and stories of //Kabbo, I find a hypnotherapist who does past life regression.
>
> German expat Claudia Klein is hesitant when we begin the session to see if I can recall any useful information about why I've begun to tell //Kabbo's story. I don't know what to expect but I tell her all about my research and beginning to write a story. She says:
>
> 'The term past life is incorrect. Is there such a thing as time? The other life – it could be parallel or it could be future – is probably a better term. You feel a calling and if you don't act on it, typically it will manifest in the body to give you a wakeup call.'
>
> In a short while, or so it seems, I am in a deep state of hypnosis but sharply aware. The presence of //Kabbo, until now ethereal and finding expression mainly through my writing, becomes tangible (Vollenhoven, 2016: 274).

My communication with //Kabbo as I write the book becomes clearer and more frequent. Trusting this new way of accessing a character, I write down everything I hear or dream. My house is a colourful mess of flipcharts and sticky notes, as well as piles of notebooks and journals. I wake up at odd hours with disconnected phrases and sections that need to be written down. There are no neat, chronological chapters coming out of this process. Just as I begin to doubt that this chaotic collection of writing will ever amount to anything, a dream structure for the book arrives to rescue me from nagging thoughts of insanity.

I follow the structure of the dream, collate all the seemingly chaotic bits of writing, and a book emerges. When Tafelberg sends two senior editors, Erika Oosthuysen and Kristin Paremoer, to personally deliver the first copies of *The Keeper of the Kumm* to my house in 2016, I feel like a bit of a fraud. The names of many 'people' should be on the cover.

Communication processes, guidance and the Krotoa play

The writing of the theatre play, *Krotoa Eva van de Kaap*, happens at a time when Basil and I are sharing a small flat in Cape Town. The synergy is perfect. I am able to lock myself in a room for many days, just listening and writing. Emerging from the 'writing room', I can consult Basil as I go along about structure and direction.

When I go through the archives, especially the letters and journals of Dutch East India Company (VOC) Commander Jan van Riebeeck and his replacement, Zacharias Wagenaer, sections leap out at me with a vigour that drives the work. The *Krotoa* researcher is taken by surprise when I tell him that one section in the archives speaks to me. The researcher has been working with this story for years and has not noticed it until now. It is not there in the archive that her husband, the Danish surgeon Pieter van Meerhoff, beat her up when they are posted to Robben Island, but my attention is drawn to this entry in the Wagenaer journal, and I feel Krotoa's pain:

> April 11th – A boat arrives from Robben Island with a letter from the Superintendent (Meerhoff), requesting immediate surgical assistance for his wife (Eva), who had, whilst sitting on a bench, fallen over, and coming in contact with the side of the staircase, received a terrible wound above her left eye. As she was continually fainting away, some serious apprehensions regarding her were entertained. The boat was therefore immediately sent back with the surgeon (See 14 April.).
>
> April 14th – The surgeon returns from Robben Island and reports that the Superintendent's wife (Eva), had received such a wound above her left eye in consequence of her fall, that she is lying insensible (dat sy in een spadius leyt), he therefore believed that she had a fracture in the cranium. However, he hoped for the best. Thirty more sheep received from the Island, as well as lime (Leibbrandt, 1896).

The matter-of-fact tone of the entries, as well as the details about 'sheep' and 'lime' make it even more chilling. Consulting constantly with Krotoa or !Goa/gõas (her name among the Goringhaicona), I write a scene where there is a fight with her and her husband Pieter van Meerhoff. It leads me to write the following as an ending for the play. This is an extract of the text in this section:

> She runs away and Van Meerhoff chases after her. Off stage we hear

crashing and screams. He comes back carrying her. Lays her down on the table, sits by her for a while and then leaves. Krotoa gets up slowly.

> KROTOA (to the audience)
> He wrote to ask the Commander Wagenaer for surgical assistance.
> (quoting the letter)
> 'Krotoa was sitting on a bench. Falling over she came into contact with the side of the staircase. I believe she has a fracture in the cranium. She is lying insensible.'

Krotoa starts as a child slave for the Dutch but as a teenager becomes the chief translator and negotiator for Jan van Riebeeck. In the final moments of the play, she is in prison on Robben Island. Her husband has been killed while hunting for slaves in Madagascar and her children, Pieternella, Jakobus and Salomon, have been taken away from her. A Dutch writer, Willem Ten Rhijne, is visiting her with a view to writing about her remarkable life:

KROTOA
I know many languages but I am no longer allowed to speak.
(comes closer, speaking conspiratorially)
Ek het by die grote tafel van Kommandant Wagenaer gesit en my mond het bietjie oorgeloop.
[I sat at the large table of Commander Wagenaer and I said too much.]

Gedoopt in de naam van God de Vader, de Zoon en de Heilige Geest. Eva, kind van het Verbond verzegeld door de Heilige Geest en voor euwig gemarkeerd als Christen 'eigen. Amen.
[Baptised in the name of God the Father, the Son and the Holy Ghost. Eva, child of the Covenant sealed by the Holy Spirit and marked as Christ's own forever.]

I have tried to remember them
All ... but there's only one face.
I don't know whose face it is I see.
[*Probeer so hard om hulle almal te onthou.*
Net een gesig nou voor my.

Weet nie aan wie dit behoort nie.]

My people believe that we die when
our thinking strings are cut ... our hearts fall down.
My heart fell down when my children were taken away.
The wound in my head never healed.
On the island they stopped worrying about me 'fainting away'.
On a rainy Sunday in July 1674 my thinking strings were cut.
They were all here ... Pieternella, Jakobus and Salomon.
Nobody else came.

Krotoa dies in prison on Robben Island.[8] Willem Ten Rhijne is one of the last people to talk with her. *Krotoa Eva van de Kaap* is written in English, Afrikaans, Dutch and Khoekhoegowab.

Communication processes and teamwork

My collaboration with Basil Appollis works well for many reasons. His processes when rehearsing or performing the plays we are working on are very similar to my own. Believing in the work and trusting the process that gets you to the final product is not always easy.

Basil is in rehearsal for the stage adaptation of Richard Rive's novel, *Buckingham Palace: District Six*, at Cape Town's Baxter Theatre in June 1989, when the author is murdered in his home.

> That changed my life. Up to that point I saw Richard almost every day. He was so excited about having his play performed in his own country in his hometown.[9] I also happened to lose my father in the same month Richard was murdered. I remember thinking that my father, who had been ill in hospital and couldn't come to the theatre, could now finally come and see me perform.
>
> When Richard died, as an actor ... it's almost as if you can take on the character without fear because he's not sitting there watching you. He can rather be part of the performance. Many times, while I was performing Richard in a one-man show and I felt a little bit tired I would just say: 'Hey, Richard you better come and help me

---

8   Some feminist activists in the Revivalist Movement contest this.
9   The Apartheid government banned most of Richard Rive's work in the years leading up to the Baxter Theatre adaptation in 1989 of *Buckingham Palace, District Six*.

here because tonight I don't think I can do this alone.' And he is always around. That's always my best performances despite how I feel. I would say: 'Come, come, this is after all your show as well.'

Basil explains further how he goes about accessing a character for his performances:

> There's a lot of advantages in just observation. I had the privilege of doing that. But it is becoming Richard that is a whole other ball game. I have to employ my skills first of all but secondly, it's about access. I practise meditation because whenever I have a moment of stillness, I feel that I can have access to him. Sometimes he talks, sometimes he doesn't talk. Sometimes he is very happy, at other times he shows his disapproval. Then I just have to listen. I have to trust my instincts because playing a character is also focusing on the essential human values and emotions. I have to trust myself as the vessel through which I can access those emotions. I also have to open myself to the messages. It's reaching a sense of emptiness where you open yourself to receiving the messages. When I communicate, I almost don't see any difference between when he was alive and when he was departed. I have to reach a moment of stillness and I have to access him, feel him. If I have a question he will answer and it's quite normal, for me anyway. I do this sometimes with my actors in rehearsals. I say: 'Go fetch your character at the station and I'm sure he'll be here tonight for the performance.' My instinct is basically about opening myself up to receive answers, to have the communication.
>
> There is a day during the production when the character arrives. With Richard it was actually after his death, on the opening night of *Buckingham Palace* at The Baxter. That is when he arrived for me. I knew he was there. It was an atmosphere and a feeling. A little bit later in the same run, Richard became a much more intimate part of me. It was a feeling as if I had swallowed him. And then there's no more tension because the character's just there and is so relaxed and fine and happy. A lot of people who wrote about that performance still felt it was Richard on stage, it wasn't me. They felt he was there, he was there and he was spooking or something. That also happened for me with my father who died shortly after Richard. You feel as if you swallowed them.

As the director of the solo play, *Cold Case: Revisiting Dulcie September,*

Basil Appollis recalls a moving moment while rehearsing for a performance in Paris, with actress Denise Newman. Dulcie September is jailed as an ANC activist before going into exile in the 1970s. When she is assassinated in Paris in March 1988, she is the ANC representative in France (for other perspectives, see Mabuza, 1989; Busby, 1992). Basil says:

> There is a moment in the play where Dulcie receives a letter in prison in South Africa, telling her that her mother has died. Denise is a mature actress with consummate technical skills, but she was struggling with that particular moment.

In Act 2 of the play, Dulcie is in jail in Kroonstad, 1 215 kilometres from her home in Cape Town. The Apartheid authorities deliberately move people as far away as possible from support systems and relatives. It is the coldest winter Dulcie September has ever experienced and she says in the play:

> DULCIE
> We were far from family and loved ones.
> We were allowed one letter in, one letter out and one visitor a month.
> I eagerly await my letter from home.

Dulcie takes a letter out of a box, opens it excitedly and then reads silently. She becomes visibly shaken. She attempts to sit down but misses her seat, then collapses onto the floor and cries. Sitting on the floor she recovers herself and addresses the audience.

> Mummy had died.
> It was in Kroonstad that I first saw snow.

Surrounded by the crew of the French festival production fussing with technical details, the actor and director realise they need to do something special to find the power of this moment in the cold Free State prison. Basil says:

> I stopped everything. We were in this theatre in Paris. There were translators and technical people and phones going. I told everyone to take a break so that I could work on that moment with Denise Newman. The scene had become so technical that the moment didn't have weight or emotion any more. That's when I felt that Dulcie was

present. I recall that the translator didn't go for a break. It was a sudden realisation that Dulcie is there with Denise. I was talking, taking Denise through the scene step by step ... receiving the letter, reading the words. I told Denise: 'Then it dawns on you that you are not going to ever hear her voice again. You want to sit down, and you can't find your seat. Then it hits you.' As I looked around, the translator was in tears. In that moment Denise understood and said, 'Thank you Basil, this is why you are here.' I thought, 'OK Denise, Dulcie is also here. Everyone's present.'

Dulcie was present when we did the play in South Africa but in France, we felt her so much more strongly. We were now in a country where she was killed after all. I would dream about her. I would talk to her. I told her I wanted to do something credible. It wasn't easy rehearsing in a darkened theatre in the middle of Paris where no one could understand my English and I didn't understand their French. We had to work with translators. I just called on Dulcie and said: 'We better do a good job here. We can't let our side down.' I was also thinking about her family coming from London to the performance in Paris. Eventually we had a tremendous response to the play at that festival.

Presenting a challenging South African work to a foreign audience is daunting. I am commissioned to write *Krotoa Eva van de Kaap* by the Volksoperahuis of Amsterdam. It is the story of the young niece of the Goringhaicona Chief Autshumao who works as a slave in the household of the Dutch commander at the Cape, Johan van Riebeeck, in the mid-1600s. The story is told from Krotoa's perspective and employs the device of a modern film set to explore Krotoa's relevance in the 21st century. The Dutch colonial responsibility for modern social problems (for instance, poverty and alcoholism among the indigenous people) is a strong thread running through the work. After the opening night in Amsterdam, the play tours the Netherlands for six weeks. There is a standing ovation at the premiere and on most nights in the Netherlands and South Africa, where the run is sold out.

At the start of the collaboration in Cape Town, we meet Jeff Hofmeister, the head of the Volksoperahuis. I am intimidated by having to delve into not only Krotoa's painful story, but also having to work with Van Riebeeck, a character who epitomises for me, 17th-century Dutch colonial brutality. Krotoa is treated so badly by Van Riebeeck and his compatriots that she becomes an alcoholic and dies in jail on

Robben Island, after her children are taken away from her by the Dutch Reformed Church.

Before the meeting with Jeff, I am guided to request a meeting room at the Castle of Good Hope in Cape Town, the site of the fort and the household where Krotoa lived. Not only do the authorities at the Castle agree, but they also give us the room that once served as the VOC's office.

When telling ancestral stories, there are certain protocols to be observed. I have to ask permission from my spiritual family to work with visitor spirits, much in the same way that you do not invite strangers into your family home without first consulting with your relatives.

Jeff Hofmeister, an urbane man who is proud of his Indonesian/ Dutch heritage, is a bit taken aback when I arrive at the Castle with a clay pot, the African sage we call *kooigoed* (literally bedding) or *mphepu*, a set of kudu horns and an array of traditional cloths. Before we can go inside and begin the creative brainstorming session, we have to acknowledge our Ancestors and call on their guidance. We spend some time outside in the Castle's forecourt, burning the *kooigoed* or sage inside the horns and calling on our Ancestors. With the ritual done, we continue burning the herbs in the clay pot and carry it smoking into the meeting room.

The stage is set for telling a story from Krotoa's perspective. International creative collaborations can be difficult and fraught with tension, especially when tackling stories that have been so distorted in the colonial archives. But not once in the production process do the Dutch owners of the project disagree with the direction we are taking. Some days I would wonder mischievously about the value of carrying smoking kudu horns (borrowed from a Khoe chief and traditional healer friend) into other meetings as a way of avoiding conflict. *Krotoa* is so well received that after the Dutch ambassador to South Africa sees the play, he recommends that his government provide even more support for future runs.

One night after a performance in a small town in the Netherlands, Basil is sitting in the audience doing his usual checks for giving notes to the cast. When the lights go down at the end of the play, a most unusual thing happens. There is no applause, only silence. This has never happened before. He says:

> In that moment I thought, I wonder if they know the play is finished, that we are done. But I actually just went with the silence. The story

was quite hard; it was hitting home that night, so much so that I didn't take a lot of notes any more. The audience just sat in silence and it was a powerful feeling. I didn't want to be the first to get up, so I just sat there. Then after quite a long time – the actors had left the stage already – people started talking to each other very softly. Mories, a Dutch producer friend, came that night to see the production. Mories Römkens was one of the founders of Holland's famous Winternachten Festival. He came over to me and he said, 'God that was powerful!' And, it was definitely a feeling of, 'What the f... just happened here?' I could sense that it was the first time they learnt the real story of Krotoa, of Van Riebeeck, and it hit them hard.

Having done Rive in London, Dulcie in France and Krotoa in Holland, I've seen first-hand that there is a curiosity now for a different kind of South African story, a new kind of narrative. There's a lot that is great about theatre in Europe ... the technical skill of actors and the sets are beautiful, but it is oh so tired. Our stories are authentic and when we tell them unapologetically, we stand out.

As African storytellers, we have something unique to offer the world when we turn away from the separation inside ourselves; when we create art using all our abilities and calling on the assistance of those who have gone before. When I turn my attention to employing all my abilities, working deliberately to understand more fully the connection between my limited individual intellect and a larger collective intelligence, I produce the best creative work of my professional career.

Niall Campbell says things change significantly when we recognise and work with ancestral spirits. He says many people have consulted him in recent times because they need help with a Bushman Ancestral Calling:

> The Khoe and the San people ... went through terrible, terrible trauma. The history in the last 200 to 300 years is very bitter. Their experiences are coming through their descendants and we try to cleanse ourselves in this way. I am very much in agreement that it has to do with a traumatic past that these Ancestors are now rising up in people. One of the greatest things is just simple acknowledgement. As South Africans, when we start to do that, already a lot of healing takes place. That acknowledgement is the most healing thing. With that we can start to say we are related.[10]

---

10   Niall, Campbell. Personal video interview, 20 August 2013.

It is not my intention to play down the importance of conventional research. The more routine methods of enquiry are essential, and historic storytellers have a heightened responsibility to be conscientious and accurate in the methods they embrace. Exploring storytelling processes for wholeness – quite literally in *The Keeper of the Kumm* play, taking up the ancestral invitation to dance – requires an added layer of diligence if we are to redress the injustice of the past.

Conclusion: Journeys across inner and outer landscapes

A journey to criss-cross an inner landscape would not be complete without traversing the vast expanses of South Africa. An essential part of my research journey has been trips to places of significance for the stories we have told.

For example, a week-long brainstorming session in the historic enclave of Genadendal, helps to shape the play *Krotoa Eva van de Kaap*. I am joined by Basil, who is directing *Krotoa*, and Tim Knight, the script advisor. We walk around the village and visit the museum. We write the quality of things past and still alive, into the work. In the Cederberg I walk the Sevilla Rock Art Trail and find that I am able to read the rock text so much better than I could when looking at images in books.

At another time, we visit //Kabbo's birthplace in the Northern Cape. These journeys help us see and feel intricate patterns that trace the connectedness between the physical world and the forces that combine when important stories have to be told. The challenge is to weave the valuable finds in the archive with intuitive practices. The whole process is strengthened by paying homage to the importance of physical spaces.

While archives are not alive, they are charged with those lives. Working with the archive is like standing on a diving board. It projects you into the deep waters that flow between the then and now.

//Kabbo's ancestral water well, Bitterputs (mentioned prominently in the Bleek–Lloyd Archives), is now on the farm Arbeidsvreugd near Kenhardt. North of Kenhardt is the vast expanse of the Kalahari. Nestled in the red dunes of this desert landscape is the home of Oom Petrus Vaalbooi, whose standard introduction to himself is a slap with his flat hand on his chest and a proclamation: '*Ek is a Boesman van die Kalahari, nie a San of 'n KhoeSan nie. Wat se ding is dit?*' ['I am a Bushman of the Kalahari, not a San or a KhoeSan. What is that?']

I do not have to tell Oom Petrus the story of //Kabbo as we sit on a stationary donkey cart outside his homestead, in the shade of a thorn tree. Here oral history survives and the 19th-century visionary cum rainmaker, whose story is immortalised in a university archive, is legendary. Oom Petrus has his own ideas of why //Kabbo has returned to talk with people. Why he has come calling on his descendants for his story to be told once more. Oom Petrus says our people are in chaos, we carry the tragedies of the past with us. The trauma of dispossession and the massacres of previous centuries lie in our hearts waiting to be acknowledged. Across the Kalahari, he says, communities are struggling to make progress because of their problems with alcohol addiction, unemployment and joblessness. At the root of these pathologies is our struggle with identity. We don't know who we are, and we don't know where we come from. We are equally disconnected from our African spiritual identity.[11]

In front of us the large Vaalbooi homestead is an echo in face brick of Oom Petrus' concerns. The once luxurious farmhouse – built for a white family in the Apartheid era and now owned by a family who cannot maintain the mansion with its giant thatch roof – is a metaphor for the rundown state of things in general. We have to delve into our past to understand the present, Oom Petrus tells us.

Suddenly, in the middle of the interview we are capturing on camera, Oom Petrus takes me completely by surprise. He says:

Kyk, ek het 'n Oom gehad, Oom Jan was sy naam. Hy was 'n profeet. Hy was 'n Petersen, net soos jy. Hy het altyd gesê, as die Petersens op 'n dag hier kom met 'n groot storie, moet ek luister. [I had an uncle, Oom Jan was his name. He was a prophet. He was a Petersen just like you. He always said that when the Petersens come here with a very important story one day, I should listen.]

I met Oom Petrus for the first time the previous day. I have not told him, and few people know, that my birth name is Petersen. Vollenhoven is the adopted name of my stepfather's family. I let him finish the story of his uncle the prophet and then I ask him how he knows my maternal family name, the one on my birth certificate. He says:

Hierdie ding pla my al vandat jy eers hier aangekom het gister. Toe jy hier kom sien ek my orlede Oom Jan Die Profeet so voor my. Jy het hier

---

[11] Petrus Vaalbooi, Personal interview, 24 March 2013. All quotes from Vaalbooi in this chapter are from the same interview session.

gekom omdat ons mense in die moeilikheid is. Kyk hoe lê die kinders rond sonder werk. En die drank vat ons kinders weg van ons af. //Kabbo is nou hier onder ons omdat ons sy hulp nodig het. Ons moet iets doen om ons kinders weg te kry van die drank af, om ons kinders to red. [This is a thing that has been bothering me since you arrived here yesterday. When you came I saw my late Uncle Jan, the prophet, here in front of me. You have come here because our people are in trouble. Look how our children are lying around here without work. And alcohol is taking our children away from us. //Kabbo has come into our midst because we need his help. We must do something to get our children away from the bottle, to rescue our young people.]

Oom Petrus tells stories of growing up with powerful women who could become lions at night, of leaders who identified gifted children at an early age so that they could be schooled in traditional healing practices and of his own powers to see past the physical nature of things.

The matter-of-fact tone of his narrative style is an indication that he does not see these events as extraordinary. For Oom Petrus, this is all very normal.

In a paper titled 'Transforming the legacy of land dispossession: Archive, orality and healing in the context of San story-telling', Marlene Winberg (2015) writes about healing 'the fractured identities of generations of dispossessed families'. She also writes about 'intergenerational and ancestral story-telling as an oral tradition that transcends time and space, requiring from us to re-figure our notions of archive as a closed corpus that holds exclusive access to knowledge of the past' (Winberg, 2015: 52). She says further that 'our material records [should] be opened up, re-assembled and re-patterned to honour the legacy of centuries of dispossessed human beings and [should] address the healing of those whose stories are embedded in the landscape' (Winberg, 2015: 52).

By focusing on a handful of specific story-tellers from the 19th, 20th and 21st centuries whose names and places of origin we can identify, this article has presented a view to the tension and fluidity between archival documents and living orality, how one informs the other and collapse previously closed boundaries. It cited examples of how this process lends itself to creating digital content for our youth, opening up the possibility of digital literacy in an age where historical information is no longer a series of facts in the closed books of the past.

In this context, our ideas about becoming good ancestors may be further informed by the concept of transformation that is so luminously transmitted through the practice of story-telling; that we are simultaneously the past, present and future; ourselves and the other – and in this paradigm of multiple possibilities, have the power for transforming the traumatic legacy of dispossession through the healing art of story (Winberg, 2015: 53).

To travel further down this road of a 'paradigm of multiple possibilities' we need to pay attention to the processes that will get us there. Each day, especially when I am writing or working on a film, I pay careful attention to the requirements of my whole system: first some physical exercise, and then a few rounds of powerful breathwork. This is preparation for more subtle meditation practices. At least once a week I burn *kooigoed* or *mphephu* and call upon my Ancestors so that I can share what I am doing, thank them and acknowledge their role. Only after these practices and rituals are complete, do I engage in writing and the business of the day. The buchu herb dominates an array of natural supplements on my breakfast table.

It is now exactly seven years since the sangoma Niall Campbell performs a demanding *ukufemba* cleansing ritual and my *Kumm* book is completed. It has been a time of learning and relearning that there is no such thing as magic. Synchronicity of people, events and resources coming together at just the right times and in just the right quantities to produce the work I need to do, used to take my breath away. It is not that I have become blasé, on the contrary... When you work with all your abilities and ensure alignment with your physical as well as unseen world, synchronicity is just a normal everyday occurrence.

It is a way of life that unleashes a creative energy that is limitless. In the past eight years, since I turned 60, I have produced (or executive produced) and directed 26 half-hour films, 17 short films, as well as eight longer documentary films (about an hour or more each). I've written a creative non-fiction novel, as well as three more plays for the theatre, and launched an online resource for journalists.[12] Several other projects are in development and in recent times I have taken up a full-time position at the University of Johannesburg as the institution's first ever

---

12 Founding editor of *The Journalist*, www.thejournalist.org.za .

professor of practice. It is a workload that would not have been possible for me when I was much younger and still captive of the notion that my professional life is separate from my spiritual existence.

I have survived and thrived after the narrow confines of 20th-century journalism only because my life has been book-ended by stories that matter... Because I was introduced to real storytelling and the real nature of things by a rooibos-loving grandmother.

A POSTSCRIPT

After submitting the first draft I awake suddenly in the middle of the night. Before I open my eyes, I am afraid because I sense there are people in my room and they are busy with some silent activity very close to my bed. Although my eyes are still closed, I can sense that the room is not quite dark. I wonder if it is morning already. I feel the people moving away from my bedside. Instinctively I keep my eyes closed. The 'people' leave, the fear subsides, the room becomes completely dark again and I go back to sleep. The next morning, I awake with a realisation that there are essential pieces missing in this chapter. I revisit my writing and submit another draft with added sections on my mother, my father, //Kabbo and Krotoa. That night I sleep peacefully.

There is only one serious drawback that I have encountered when working closely with spiritual guidance. Sometimes there are the strangest glitches with my cell phone, my laptop or my desktop computer. Friends doing similar work, talk about similar experiences. My understanding is that there are times when the combined energy of my own system and the spirit guides around me just does not gel with the more low-level energy that drives electronics.

Sometimes my devices freeze because I need to rest. An earlier version of this chapter disappears from the inbox of the person to whom I send it. I go over it again and find small but important things that need changing. Teamwork and collaboration have taken on a whole new meaning.

This chapter is dedicated to my father Ebrahim 'Braima' Hendricks whom I got to know only after he died, my mother Eileen Petersen Vollenhoven who has passed on some of her many creative talents and all my relations who have helped me Re-member.

REFERENCES

Biwa, M. 2012. 'Weaving the past with threads of memory: Narratives and commemorations of the colonial war in southern Namibia'. PhD dissertation, University of the Western Cape.

Busby, M. 1992. *Daughters of Africa: An international anthology of words and writings by women of African descent from the ancient Egyptian to the present*. New York: Pantheon Books.

Leibbrandt, H.C.V. 1896. *Precis of the Archives of the Cape of Good Hope* (Vol. 1): Jan van Riebeeck, 1619–1677. Cape Town: WA Richards and Sons.

Mabuza, L. 1989. *One Never Knows: An anthology of black South African women writers in exile*. Johannesburg: Skotaville Publishers.

Natural Justice. 2010. *Rooibos Robbery: Nestlé accused of biopirating South African genetic resources*. Online at: https://naturaljustice.org/rooibos-robbery-nestle-accused-of-biopirating-south-african-genetic-resources/ (Accessed 22 June 2020).

Stanley, T.L. 2007. 'The three faces in *Eve's Bayou*: Recalling the conjure woman in contemporary Black cinema', in S.R. Sherman and M.J. Koven (eds). *Folklore/Cinema: Popular film as vernacular culture*. Logan, UT: University Press of Colorado and Utah State University Press, pp. 149–165.

Vollenhoven, S. 2016. *The Keeper of the Kumm*. Cape Town: Tafelberg.

Vollenhoven, S. 2017. *Rooibos Restitution*. Vision in Africa, Natural Justice and Heinrich Böll Foundation. Documentary film.

Vollenhoven, S and Appollis, B. 1998. *A Writer's Last Word*. Theatre play.

Winberg, M. 2015. 'Transforming the legacy of land dispossession: Archive, orality and healing in the context of San story-telling', *Oral History Journal of South Africa*, 3(2): 44–54.

2
Rematriation
Reclaiming indigenous matricentric egalitarianism

Bernedette Muthien

> HYMN TO ISIS[1]
> For I am the first and the last
> I am the venerated and the despised
> I am the prostitute and the saint
> I am the wife and the virgin
> I am the mother and the daughter
> I am the arms of my mother
> I am barren and my children are many
> I am the married woman and the spinster
> I am the woman who gives birth
> and she who never procreated
> I am the consolation for the pain of birth
> I am the wife and the husband
> And it was my man who created me
> I am the mother of my father
> I am the sister of my husband
> And he is my rejected son
> Always respect me
> For I am the shameful and the magnificent one.
> *3rd or 4th century CE, 'discovered' in Nag Hammadi, Egypt, 1947.*

---

1 Ancient African deity who spread to the Greco-Roman world and at times takes different names around the world; Coelho (2012) and Schmitz (1844).

Not a fairy tale

All tales ostensibly have a beginning and an end. Some sagas continue in the endless cycles of narration, like waves in the ocean, drawing energies from the infinite collective. This chapter is one such story, drawing on the wisdoms[2] of the past and present, and hoping to offer at least one spring daisy to the future.

The many herstories of anti-patriarchal struggles must highlight the endurance of matricentrism before and during patriarchy, the plethora of diverse societies across the continent, and fractals of indigenous matricentric societies around the world.

As discussed in this chapter, in my earlier work and the work of others (see Further Reading at the end of this chapter), matricentric and matricentrism, with or without the hyphen, simply means societies in which women are at the centre. I did not invent the idea of matricentrism – it is an ancient indigenous practice the world over. Canadian feminist Andrea O'Reilly[3] is credited as having originated the concept of 'matricentric' as meaning *mothers* at the centre, a quite different notion to *women* at the centre. This sort of attribution, and even inadvertently 'staking a claim' (as recently as this century) on an *ancient* practice, is akin to Columbus 'discovering' the Americas, which had for millennia already been populated by advanced civilisations. So I use matricentric, as I will explain later, as a woman descendant of indigenous matricentric peoples from southern Africa, referring to societies with *women* at their centre, which, as this chapter will show, have particular characteristics.[4]

African feminisms have historically largely opposed, ignored or skirted the reality of matricentric societies, with all their contradictions and other survival mechanisms. As recently as 20 years ago, renowned African feminist academics, fearful of being written off by patriarchy,

---

2   The plural 'wisdoms', like 'feminisms' or other polyvocal and polymorphous words, imply heterogeneity, plurality and diversity.

3   O'Reilly is also credited with being one of the progenitors of the 'Motherhood Movement' and 'Motherhood Studies', birthing journals (*Journal of the Motherhood Initiative for Research and Community Involvement*) and other publications; see O'Reilly (2016).

4   This is not to deny the significance of O'Reilly's work and the important *MIRCI* Reclaiming Motherhood movement. It is merely to show how different and more inclusive an indigenous understanding is, as this chapter will show. I have also presented my indigenous matricentric work at international *MIRCI* conferences over the years, and I have respect for O'Reilly and the movement's important work, including its support of indigenous feminisms.

asserted that then-nascent studies into indigenous matricentric societies were illusory, that the matricentric was a myth. Yet the ancient family stories and realities lived not only in indigenous heads but also in our very bones. These diverse stories and realities are now increasingly finding their ways into publications by diverse African feminists[5] all narrating their own matrilineal societies.

Indigenous wisdom is not only plural and diverse, but also appears infinite, with its origins perpetually unknown, like the Irish leprechaun's[6] pot o' gold at the end of the rainbow, or the infinitely expanding universe or multiverses.

When I speak of 'bones', I refer to this endless stream of knowledge, which Babalwa Magoqwana discusses in Chapter 3 in this volume, knowledge passed on to and through us through aeons. For Magoqwana knowledge comes via and from 'ancestors'. For others, that knowledge exists in our collective unconscious and we can tap into and deploy it at any time, whether embodied via guides or dreams or just flowing free like unbranded air. As methodology, this may appear foreign to conventional academics, to colonisers and goldminers who 'stake claims'. To many indigenous scholars, and many indigenous feminists in particular, we do not claim to have invented or discovered anything. We are merely transmitting ancient knowledge.

Medical scientists like Kate Ruth Linton have written about cellular memory, which has been reported for decades. For instance, following heart transplants, a recipient may acquire some of the personality characteristics of their donor via the donor organ (heart) (Linton, 2003).

The idea of cells outside the brain storing memories and, indeed, energies, is not new to indigenous peoples, who routinely 'clear' negative or traumatic energies or experiences of the past, ceremonially or spiritually, popularly called 'smudging', by the burning of incense and/or cleansing herbs such as sage, also known as *mphepho* in Nguni languages or *khoegoed/kooigoed* by the Khoe.

The fields of especially psychology and psychiatry have grappled with notions of cellular memory for more than a century, from Carl Jung's 'collective unconscious' to Bert Hellinger's 'family constellations', to the critical trauma recovery work of Vamik Volkan and others. Jung's

---

5 For example, from Zambia in the works of Yaliwe Clarke and Chaze Matakala, Namibia's Elizabeth Xhaxhas, and Mozambican Paula Assubuji.

6 South Africa has *tokoloshe*, a possible equivalent of the Irish leprechaun, variously laughed at and/or feared, as people often fear the less visible or less known.

collective unconscious refers to the 'soul' or consciousness shared by all humankind. A German Catholic missionary named Hellinger, who was in South Africa during the 1970s, extracted the shamanic practices of Zulu sangomas, during which the sangoma calls in the spirits of the Ancestors to heal the patient. Hellinger turned these 'family constellations' into a global mega-industry (Hellinger, 2003a; 2003b),[7] with no financial or other rewards to the people who inspired the work and still humbly practise it today – shamanic practices, which Magoqwana also discusses in Chapter 3.

The work of the Turkish-Cypriot academic psychiatrist, Vamik Volkan, is widely employed in peace and reconciliation studies, and trauma recovery (Volkan et al., 2002). Volkan's work on 'chosen trauma', post-traumatic stress disorder (PTSD), and transgenerational transmission of trauma is particularly useful in indigenous studies, in contexts of genocides of peoples, knowledge and practices, notions drawn on by, among others, Iroquois scholar Barbara Alice Mann (2003; 2004; 2019; also see Muthien, 2008a). The idea of carrying trauma from generation to generation, and the imperative to heal or interrupt such trauma, is not new to indigenous peoples, in knowledge and practice.

Indigenous scholars have written about the past being embodied in the present, 'embodiment', from artefacts to other experiences, positive or negative or neutral. In the words of Moreton-Robinson (2013: 12):

> The ontological relationship occurs through the inter-substantiation of ancestral creator beings, humans and country; it is a form of embodiment based on blood line to country. As such Indigenous women's bodies signify our sovereignty. As the descendants of these ancestral creator beings Indigenous people derive our sense of belonging to country through and from them.

Hodgetts and Kelvin (2020:109) discuss

> the importance of artefacts as embodiments of the traditional knowledge and skills of ancestors. [Indigenous people] view them as touchstones that link the past with their own personal histories. These deep emotional connections make them things of the heart ... Most community members feel that artefacts connect them to their

---

7   https://www.hellinger.com/en/family-constellation/ (Accessed 11 December 2020).

ancestors or that the artefacts embody the spirits of their ancestors. Traditional Inuvialuit teachings therefore require that people avoid disturbing artefacts, particularly those associated with graves.

In the indigenous feminist collection, *Archaeologies of the Heart* (Hodgetts and Kelvin, 2020), contributors call for general and feminist knowledge production to be more heart-centred. Hodgetts and Kelvin (2020:97) draw on Hilary Rose (1983), who

> suggested that feminists should ground their epistemology in 'hand, brain, and heart', by which she meant that it should not only be about the abstraction of thought (the brain) but also about activism (doing – the hand) and what she called 'caring labour' (the heart). Caring labour is nurturing work, the intimate, emotionally demanding labour ...

Thus this chapter acknowledges consciousness, and past–present–future as continuous, like waves in the endless ocean. It also seeks to transcend the traditional academic focus on the intellect, and to speak more with compassion, from the heart, drawing on ancient wisdom, to which I definitely do not 'stake a claim' or, indeed, can even footnote, but instead, acknowledge indigenous wisdom as endless, as matter in an ever-expanding space.

Hence, this chapter will reflect on some of the many African societies that are matricentric today, on some of the central tenets of these practised egalitarianisms, and how we can mainstream these learnings into our thinking and in our practices of co-creating alternatives to the dominant capitalist heteropatriarchy.

This chapter deploys methodologies common to indigenous feminisms, including that of elders like Ifi Amadiume (Ibo, Nigeria/United States of America), Linda Tuhiwai Smith (Maori, Aotearoa/New Zealand) and Barbara Alice Mann (Iroquois, United States), as indigenous African feminists continue to develop their own matricentric publishing opportunities. Twenty years of my decolonising research into matricentric societies is condensed here (see Further reading at the end of this chapter), but additional resources, including support, are readily available in our matricentric bodies, lives and stories.[8]

---

8   Not entirely unlike 'cellular memory' and 'embodiment' as briefly discussed here.

O-VOID

Most mammalian life stems from a womb, from the maternal. The English word 'mammal' is derived from the Latin 'mamma' or 'breast'. And so human life springs from the womb, from the mother, mitochondrial DNA, a genetic gift from mother to daughter ad infinitum.

Based on this very mitochondrial DNA (matrilineal genes), geneticists, archaeologists and other scientists assert that all human life stems not only from the vast continent of Africa (such as East African 'Lucy') (Slezak, 2014; Garvin Institute of Medical Research, 2019; Smillie, 2019), but also from the semi-arid Kalahari or Kgalagadi, a desert that straddles six southern African countries: Angola, Botswana, Namibia, South Africa, Zambia and Zimbabwe. This area is said to have been an oasis – literally and metaphorically – some 200,000 years ago. Since the onset of depredations and genocides of European colonialisms[9] in the region, the Kalahari has been the habitat of the San people, pejoratively known as Bushmen, or people who live in the Bush. San, however, merely means human, people, *Homo sapien*.

Among others, Hahn (1881) has pointed out that San denotes low status (also see Hahn cited in Goodwin, 1952). The Nguni word 'bantu' merely means humankind, (not-gendered) person, *Homo sapien*. However, under colonialism and Apartheid, the term 'bantu' became pejorative, and the people called 'Bantu' were stigmatised, oppressed and abused. Likewise, the term San merely means people. However, under the yokes of colonialisms, this term and the people, like so many other indigenous peoples, became derided, abused and oppressed. While some San prefer the term Bushman, especially in post-Apartheid South Africa, others are reclaiming the term San, in particular in countries neighbouring South Africa, like Botswana. Far be it for anyone to tell another what to call themselves. Hence I show unwavering respect to indigenous peoples, irrespective of what they choose to call themselves, whether in the past, the present or the future.

Quentin Atkinson, a biologist and linguist from New Zealand who analyses parts of words or sounds called phonemes, postulates that human language stemmed from the Kalahari San based on the proliferation of click sounds (Atkinson 2011). Barbara Alice Mann

---

9   Colonialisms are used in the plural here to show the different kinds and varied manifestations of colonialisms, including Belgian, British, French, German, Italian, Portuguese and Spanish, over different eras.

notes[10] that she remembers 'being told that human language derived from the "click languages" in [her] freshman Anthropology course in 1970 or 1971!' Thus our indigenous elders constantly remind us that what we might think is revolutionary and new is actually ancient and even collective knowledge. This constant re-membering keeps us grounded and humble.

Tracing the first human, the first woman and language to the Kalahari San is important for a number of critical reasons. The San are known to be matrilineal and matrifocal; matricentric societies are centred on the feminine. Lineage is traced from mother to daughter. This is distinct from a patriarchal society where lineage is traced from father to son – a hierarchical society in which the feminine is reviled in favour of the phallic.[11] By contrast, being matricentric the San practise social and gender egalitarianism, with elected rather than hereditary leaders of any gender (Muthien, 2008a).

CHICKEN OR EGG: MATER PATER ARCHE

The word 'patriarchy' is derived from its Greek roots, *pater* and *arche*, which can be translated as *father rule*, and interpreted as men ruling over other men, women and children. Men ruling land, seas and skies.

One might argue that this dominating attitude is encouraged and codified in the three Abrahamic monotheisms that strongly influenced the constitution of the colonial mind, when reading their religious texts (the Torah, the Bible and the Koran). Indeed, how can one not foresee this hierarchical devaluating pattern when the Bible in Genesis 1:28, explicitly states men's responsibility is to *dominate* the Earth, women, children, slaves, animals and other possessions? Seventeenth-century British philosopher John Locke's foundational human rights philosophy. is based on this very patriarchal consciousness, especially in justifying colonial expropriation of native lands.[12]

Since women are the sources of all human life, the German political

---

10 Email communication, 23 December 2020.

11 In patriarchy, people are taught to worship the phallus and to denigrate the feminine. Think 'dick' vs 'cunt'. Eve Ensler's *Vagina Monologues* play is one of too many examples.

12 For a further reading on Locke's philosophy on rights in a European context, see Rogers (1996). It is no small irony that Locke is credited with inspiring not only European Enlightenment, but also the Constitution of the United States. In reality, the US Constitution is derived from the Great Peace of the Haudenosanee, the matricentric indigenous peoples who still exist across the Americas, with modern scholars including Barbara Alice Mann (2003; 2004; 2006) at the University of Toledo.

philosopher Heide Goettner-Abendroth (2009) argues that women do not need to rule over others, as the men who generate patriarchy feel the need to. For Goettner-Abendroth, the meaning of matriarchy is not to be understood as *Mother Rule*, but as *Mother in the Beginning*. Also derived from Greek roots, *mater* and *arche*, but *arche* is interpreted in the alternative definition of 'in the beginning', 'in the principle' or even 'at the origin'.

We might further reflect on the different living postures that these two interpretations of patriarchy and matriarchy imply with what Goettner-Abendroth (2007:100) controversially suggests:

> In the case of the term 'Matriarchy', we are not obliged to follow the current, male-biased interpretation of this word as signifying 'domination by the mothers'. [...] the Greek word *arche* has a double meaning. It means 'beginning' as well as 'domination'. Therefore, we can translate 'Matriarchy' accurately as 'the mothers from the beginning', while 'Patriarchy', on the other hand, translates correctly as 'domination by the fathers'. // The word 'Patriarchy' could also be translated as 'the fathers from the beginning'. This nevertheless leads to its meaning as 'domination by the fathers', because not having any natural right to 'beginning' (creation of life through birth), they have to enforce it through domination! By the same token, since the mothers clearly *are* the beginning by their capacity to bring forth life, they have no need to enforce it by domination.

In other words, this womb from where we all root. There is a popular poster in public protests around the world that says: 'I did not come from your rib. You came from my womb.' Alluding to the Biblical Eve being fashioned by God from Adam's rib in the Garden of Eden, the poster deploys wit to speak truth, to describe science rather than myth: all human life stems from a womb.

Given the potential for misconception, and the dichotomising with patriarchy, I intentionally avoid the term 'matriarchy', preferring the more descriptive 'matricentric' for these societies that exist around the world to this day, despite patriarchal onslaughts.

INDIGENOUS IS NOT ONE VILLAGE,[13] AFRICA IS NOT A COUNTRY[14]

Decolonisation and restoration of our ancient and existing indigenous knowledge is significant given that matricentric societies still exist across every continent, and notably in Africa, including Algeria, Angola, Botswana, Burkina Faso, Eritrea, Ethiopia, Ghana, Ivory Coast, Malawi, Mali, Morocco, Mozambique, Namibia, Nigeria, South Africa, Zambia and Zimbabwe – a literal A to Z of matricentricity still survives today.

The second-largest and second-most populous continent after Asia, Africa covers 6 per cent of Earth's total surface area and 20 per cent of its land area. Our over 1.3 billion people account for almost 17 per cent of the world's total population.[15] Comprising between 54 and 56 countries, with up to 3,000 different languages still spoken, Africa is an embodiment of diversities. Having faced patriarchal colonisations from different parts of the world over various time periods, Africa has shifting herstories and political-economic geographies. This rainbow of matricentricity is visible in the blue-eyed desert Kabyle or Berber people[16] of North Africa (not unlike the grey-eyed Seneca Bear clan of Barbara Alice Mann [2007] in Ohio), the tall Dagara or Dagaaba of West Africa, and my own matrilineal San of the Kalahari.

The Algerian Kabyle Malika Grasshoff (2007) demonstrates that women's magic was expressed in every domain of their daily lives, that their traditional society was incapable of functioning without women who ensured its material and spiritual unity. Malidoma Some (1994; 1998) and Sobonfu Some (1997; 1999) of the Dagara variously discuss their matrilineal and gender-fluid culture, as does Nigerian Ifi Amadiume (1997; 1998; 2000; 2002; 2003; 2005; 2015), and increasingly more people across this immense birth-continent of humankind.

Given the vastness of diversities and herstories, patriarchal colonisations, slaveries and dispossession, the United Nations

---

13 The expression 'indigenous is not one village' is my own, derived from local and global activisms and scholarship that challenge the ignorance of imposed homogeneity on diverse peoples and contexts.

14 The phrase 'Africa is not a country' was popularised over decades by diverse African activists and scholars who wished to dispel the global North's ignorance about Africa and reflect this vast continent's extraordinary diversity. See also the satiric essay by late Kenyan writer Binyavanga Wainaina (2005).

15 Online at: https://www.worldometers.info/world-population/africa-population (Accessed 14 September 2020).

16 Online at: http://www.makilam.com/ (Accessed 14 September 2020).

Declaration on the Rights of of Indigenous Peoples Article 31, iterates that

- Indigenous peoples have the right to *determine their own identity or membership* in accordance with their customs and traditions. This does not impair the right of indigenous individuals to obtain citizenship of the States in which they live.
- Indigenous peoples have the right to determine the structures and to select the membership of their institutions in accordance with their own procedures.[17]

Thus, when I speak of my mother's healing herbs and her people's matricentricity, it is my chosen identity or membership, in a moment, in all its heterogeneous, polymorphous polyvocality. Ironically,[18] supported by the United Nations and UNDRIP since at least 2007, we indigenous speak for and define ourselves.

Rematriation

For some 20 years we indigenous matricentric women around the world have explored the concept of Rematriation:

> Rematriation of ancestral remains, spirituality, culture, knowledge and natural and other resources, instead of the more Patriarchally associated Repatriation. In simpler terms, merely meaning back to Mother Earth, a return to our origins, a return to life and co-creation, rather than Patriarchal destruction and colonisation, a reclamation of germination instead of semination. As a restorative imperative, it is most relevant to feminists in general, since we, like Native peoples, need to reclaim our Feminist ancestry, our feminist spirituality, our feminist culture/s, knowledge and control over natural and other resources. We need to chart paths, strategic

---

17 United Nations Department of Economic and Social Affairs: Indigenous Peoples, United Nations Declaration on the Rights of Indigenous Peoples, Adopted by the General Assembly, 13 September 2007. Online at: https://www.un.org/development/desa/indigenouspeoples/declaration-on-the-rights-of-indigenous-peoples.html (Accessed 11 December 2020).

18 Ironic because, aside from the idealisms of peace after brutal genocidal wars, the very foundation of the United Nations and its precursor, the League of Nations, was in favour of victorious post-war colonial powers carving up the world and its peoples, often arbitrarily, as evinced by the San who inhabit the Kalahari which straddles six southern African countries.

interventions, dreams and realities that are not mere alternatives to HeteroPatriarchalCapitalisms, but entirely reconfigure our cosmos, Rematriate our societies (Muthien, 2011).[19]

Iroquois scholar Barbara Alice Mann has credited the Mohawk poet and writer Susan Deer Cloud[20] with first popularising the concept of Rematriation:[21]

> The first step toward sanity is the Rematriation of the Truth. A term coined by the Mohawk poet, Susan Deer Cloud, 'Rematriation' retools culture in terms of matriarchal giving. Regarding speech, it means that the Gift of Breath replicates reality; it does not invent some myth convenient to bullies. Rematriation of the Truth means that everyone has access to all the facts, all the time, to facilitate the One Good Mind of Consensus.
>
> However, Euro-Christians have a fraught relationship with truth and lies. The distinction between Native and settler civilization could not be more broad or more obvious. Natives see The Lie as the animating feature of all Western discourse, but Europeans wink at lying, coddle it as cute or maybe annoying, but do not regard it as anything too important (Mann, 2011).

Several other indigenous feminist scholars have similarly sought to rematriate indigenous spirituality, knowledge and practice, including the Sto:Loh (Salish) Lee Maracle in Canada, who writes of 'rematriation of our [indigenous matriarchal] governing structures' (2006: 30), and 'rematriation as the alternative to Western legal invasion' (2006: 32):

---

19 At the Women's Worlds Conference in Toronto, Iroquois Barbara Alice Mann from the United States and Pnar Valentina Pakyntein from India were part of our path-breaking special panel on Rematriation, attended by some of the leading feminists of the world.

20 Online at: http://www.gift-economy.com/articlesAndEssays/rematriationtruth.html (Accessed 2 December 2020).

21 Much of our knowledge sharing as indigenous scholars and activists is through conversations, in person during visits and conferences, via email, telephone and messaging. This anecdotal sharing cannot necessarily be translated into a neat, scholarly footnote or bibliographic reference. We are just aware that at some point in the past, some elder or indigenous sibling had shared wisdom, and hence we must honour and acknowledge them thus, even if only verbally, aware that knowledge is not individually owned but collective and infinite. It is in this beautiful way that Mann pays tribute to Deer Cloud, as I honour Mann and others.

> I need to retrace my own steps, the steps of my mother, my grandmother, my great-grandmother, right back to our original selves. I need to re-view their journey and reclaim the cultural base upon which we organized ourselves and our communities (Maracle, 2006: 30).

It may be useful to note that some scholars, including myself, deliberately use 'rematriation', rather than the patriarchally derived and more commonly known 'repatriation', which several other renowned indigenous feminist scholars still use, in a positive, rematriated sense. The distinguished scholar Sonya Atalay speaks of 'repatriation' as contributing 'to healing through embodied practice and storywork' (Atalay, 2019). I profoundly respect Atalay and others for using common, patriarchally derived terms such as 'repatriation'. It is precisely to rematriate the indigenous matricentric that I seek the *mater* over the *pater*, that I deliberately and meticulously use 'rematriation' rather than 'repatriation'.

I thus always pay tribute to my indigenous elders: Deer Cloud, Mann, Maracle, Atalay, Amadiume, Bam and others, as we continue to recreate and co-create for ourselves our indigenous languages, meaning and lifestyles.

In 2020, delightfully, there are now entire websites[22] and other publications devoted to Rematriation as an indigenous imperative.

The key principles of Modern Matriarchal Studies, according to German philosopher Heide Goettner Abendroth (2009) are:
- it is concrete rather than abstract in the world;
- it is not mother rule but non-hierarchical;
- it is based on consensus through systems of councils that are grassroots, consultative, participatory and democratic;
- distribution (sharing) versus accumulation (hoarding);
- meeting needs versus power over;
- compassionate rather than selfish;
- radically oriented towards life rather than the patriarchal war industries;
- with political action always spiritual rather than the patriarchal detachment of the Enlightenment;
- science, politics and spirituality are all connected.

---

22 For example, https://rematriation.com/ and https://rematriatingboriken.com/rematriation/ (Accessed 14 September 2020).

Nigerian Ifi Amadiume speaks of matriarchitarianism and 'the matriarchal umbrella', which she sees as less of a totalitarian patriarchal Eurocentric equivalent or opposite, and more as an alternative social structure, deeply rooted in indigenous and African kinship (Amadiume, 2002; 2005a), a 'paradigmatic pluralism in thought systems and social formations' (Amadiume, 1997; 2002).

Amadiume's 'matriarchal umbrella' refers to inclusive 'traditional societies' of 'protective women's culture' 'headed by matriarchs', 'women generated socio-cultural institutions, that historically have empowered and benefited all women in specific societies and cultures in Africa through women's solidarity (Amadiume, 1987; 1997).

Amadiume speaks of the necessity for feminist indigenous scholarship to be interdisciplinary and intersectional, including spirituality, and even prophecy. She rematriates 'the concept of the traditional in Africa to mean precolonial African cultures' that are *not* static or delineated by rigid time breaks. This rematriated traditional is dynamic: past, present and perhaps even future. For Amadiume, 'the matricentric unit is the smallest kinship unit. Its material basis is concrete and empirical, while the material and ideological basis of patriarchy embodies a contradiction. Patriarchy is disputable since fatherhood is a social construct.' Amadiume advocates for matriarchitarianism as an indigenous movement, rematriating activisms back to our centre, our core, our (African) calabash.[23]

Motherer

There is often confusion about patriarchal hierarchisation of genders and sexualities, which has always been considered fluid, dynamic and variegated in indigenous societies. Similarly with the notions of parenting, motherhood, fatherhood, kinship. None of the roles are rigid or exclusive.

To transcend the myriad issues around any biological essentialism of 'mother', Genevieve Vaughan (2015: 41) proposed 'motherer',[24] so that anyone, irrespective of gender identities, can choose or be elected to 'mother', to be a 'motherer', to raise children. This is in line with many indigenous societies, especially across Africa and elsewhere, where the

---

23 Riane Eisler's European chalice is an equivalent, *cf. The Chalice and the Blade.*

24 For more information about Genevieve Vaughan and the gift economy, please see http://www.genevievevaughan.org/ and http://gift-economy.com/ (Accessed 2 December 2020).

mother's brother, the uncle, raises the boy children or male-identified children, at times called a 'male mother'. Indeed, Amadiume uses the gender neutral Ibo term *ya*, arguing in her groundbreaking 1987 book, *Male Daughters, Female Husbands*, that gender constructions, as used by Western scholars and Western feminists, were not known in Africa until the colonial enforcement of binaried, hierarchical, patriarchal genders. Thus the European and colonial imposition of gendered concepts such as a male human being for humanity (for instance, Thomas Paine [1791] *Rights of Man*) and even male gods (in monotheistic patriarchal religions such as Judaism, Christianity, Islam, and even Buddhism).

Unlike the European 'he' or 'she', Amadiume contends that the Ibo *ya* means anyone, without any gender. Its neutrality is another reminder of the fact that there are other ways to perceive the binary gendered concepts that Europeans imposed, where the male pole is super-valued and the female under-valued (starting with the European and patriarchal highest representation of divinity as a male god). Amadiume, who hails from a matriarchal society and has written extensively on matriarchy in Africa, speaks to the decolonising imperative of rematriation:

> When we look at women's contributions and approaches to development in Africa, we see that generally women are guided by teachings deriving from what I would call a 'relational matriarchal principle' that sees us all as human beings and children of one mother, *umunne*. I believe this to be a general and basic African ethic of kinship. It can further be a non-racist and non-patriarchal basis for an alternative global citizenship in the struggle for human rights, social justice and an inclusive development (Amadiume, 2005a).

Goettner-Abendroth has spoken about 'motherly or matriarchal men', and Evo Morales from Bolivia refers to himself as a 'matriarchal man' from an indigenous 'matriarchal' peoples.[25] In fact, in 2009 the Morales government in Bolivia established the Ministry of Cultures, Decolonization and Depatriarchalization,[26] whose mission is to 'decolonize and de-patriarchalize [and to] reverse this inequality

---

25 'Traditionally, there is no division of tasks or rights between men and women.' See 'Aymara People: Language, Culture and Religion. Online at: https://study.com/academy/lesson/aymara-people-language-culture-religion.html (Accessed 12 December 2020).

26 Online at: https://en.wikipedia.org/wiki/Ministry_of_Cultures,_Decolonization_and_Depatriarchalization; and https://comunicacion.gob.bo/?q=20201120/31286 (Accessed 4 December 2020).

between nationalities, as well as between men and women'. This Ministry still exists. Progressive South African male Khoe leaders, such as Khoekhoegowab teacher at the University of Cape Town, Bradley van Sitters, among others, similarly rematriate the matricentric.

Indeed, Van Sitters, in a note titled 'On the subject of Taras', asserts that

> In Khoehoegowab the words for depicting female/woman are khoes and taras... One finds a very good explanation of the epistemology of the word taras in Hahn's (1881: 19) description expressing the notion that 'taras is the woman, as ruler of the house. Taras is also a woman of rank, a lady.' Closer investigation into the word indicated that the root ta- or da- means to 'conquer, to rule, to master, and the suffix -ra expresses a custom or an intrinsic peculiarity'... From my own personal oral history research in Kuboes, die *'om-draai'* dorpie in the Richtersveldt, community leader, Danab Gert Links expressed the traditional view that women had more say in the household than men. This is documented in Hahn's (1881: 19) account that 'in every Khoikhoi's house the woman, or taras, is the supreme ruler; the husband has nothing at all to say'. Within the matriarchal community of the Khoekhoe where women had an elevated status above men to be honoured and respected, men took a prominent role in public but at home the wife's consent in all matters was the norm. In the case the man acted out uncustomary, he would be penalised and his nearest female relations would put a fine on him, consisting of cows and sheep, which would be added to the stock of the wife. Interestingly, Hahn noted that in the house the wife always occupied the right side of the husband and the right side of the house.[27]

Notwithstanding Hahn's colonial gaze mis-interpreting the notion of 'power' as 'over' (patriarchal rule), rather than a shared resource (matricentric egalitarianism), Van Sitters refers to his Khoe people as 'matriarchal', with the meaning akin to my own sense of matricentric, with women at the centre of society.

Zambia (see Clarke, 2017; 2021) and Malawi are two other countries with matrilineal peoples, and arguably matricentric peoples, where a person is described through their relatives. For example, if I am related to the male in the family, I am called by masculine terms, irrespective

---

27 Personal communication, 22 February 2021.

of my biological sex – I become an uncle, and so on. Thus, gender and, indeed, sexualities are fluid in these indigenous societies.

Some European anthropologists have written of up to 13 genders in Native American societies. Clearly, this is nonsense. The varieties of expressions of gender and sexualities are dynamic, fluid, infinite and beyond colonial abacuses (see Amadiume, 1997–2015; Muthien, 2003a; 2003b; 2007).

THE MATRICENTRIC

Matricentric[28] social structure and social values are inextricably interdependent. Egalitarianism and fluidities of all things are at its core: social, gender, generational, sexualities, all ad infinitum.

Patriarchal colonisation imposed ideological gendered hierarchies and biased beyond-heteronormative sexualities. So, too, the notion of a male human being or humanity (for example, *Rights of Man*) as the centre of the cosmos, and even a male god in monotheistic patriarchal religions – such as Judaism, Christianity and Islam, and patriarchalised ancient religions like Hinduism and Buddhism, which are either multi-gendered or beyond gender at the root. Like the Dagara and many other indigenous peoples, the Kalahari San have female deities or dual-gender deities (Muthien, 2008a). The language of divinity and deities here simplifies complex and ancient spiritual practices, which are not patriarchal, dominating, hierarchical, vengeful and oppressive, as they can be in European or 'Western' religions. Other indigenous scholars, such as Iroquois Barbara Alice Mann, prefer 'spirits' to 'deities' and Jung refers to 'universal consciousness': 'Have you seen the light?'

One Kalahari healer, Ma Meneputo,[29] describes her carefree childhood, hunting small animals like rabbits and young buck with a bow and arrow, and making and playing with dolls – no Euro-formed, binaried, colour-coded games for her. When she does healing circles, it is her lifelong male partner who holds a space for her, gently offering her water as she emerges from the trance state, a form of care that patriarchy inverts to have the domesticated, enslaved wife care for her conqueror hero, Prince Patriarch.

---

28 Each of the elements of matricentric societies are entire fields of study on their own, and hence in-depth explication in this introductory chapter is not possible. However, there are many resources; see the Reading list at the end of this chapter.

29 Manunga, Ma-Meneputo. n.d. 'Healing hands: Interview with Kalahari San Healer', South African San Institute, Kimberley.

The Khoe and San have had renowned women leaders, as noted in the meticulous records of colonial administrators, referring to indigenous leaders as 'captains' ('*kapteins*'), a rather lowly rank when compared with a more accurate analogy of 'general'. Two communities of the Hessequa, who lived near Swellendam, were led, respectively, by a female leader, Lang Elsie, and encamped nearby, a male leader, Nouga Saree. The Bontebok National Park, where the Hessequa originally lived, named its rest camp after Lang Elsie (Van Rensburg, 1975; Skinner, 1980; Van Hemert and Meffert, 1991),[30] referring to her as:

> a remarkable female captain ... Between 1734 and 1800 she lived with her followers at the southern part of the Park, grazing their stock all the way to the Buffeljags River. Visitors to the park can still see the open werf area where Lang Elsie's kraal of woven reed huts was situated. Next to this open space are the ruins of a small stone house where Captain Lang Elsie lived, according to the author of *Geskiedkundige Swellendam* (Tomlinson, 1943).

Today there are still solid stone wall remnants, not only of Lang Elsie's home, but also of the walls surrounding the community. The views of the water and surrounding mountains are spectacular, the sun striking the mountain peaks during the day were used as a sundial to tell the time, and were thus named after the colonial and enslavement-era clock hours (for instance, 'one o'clock peak', etc). Not only did the Hessequa live surrounded by abundant wildlife, including the bontebok after which the park is named, but they also had large kraals of sheep and cattle, the walls of which still stand today. When the nature reserve was first established by European colonisers during the 1800s, Hessequa graves were found covered with 'blue mountain stones'.

TODAY THE KHOE AND SAN still elect their leaders for fixed terms, and the current leader of the Kalahari is Katrina Esau, also popularly known as Ouma Geelmeid. The South African government bestowed national orders on Ouma Geelmeid and posthumously on her predecessor, Dawid Kruiper, in 2014.[31]

---

30 Online at: https://www.sanparks.org/parks/bontebok/tourism/history.php (Accessed 13 December 2020).

31 Online at: https://www.brandsouthafrica.com/people-culture/south-africa-honours-its-heroes-with-2014-national-orders (Accessed 13 December 2020).

In several African countries, especially older childless women enter into traditional marriages with younger women, procreate and raise children; an arrangement that transcends heteronormative patriarchy, extensively written about by Amadiume (1987) and others.

Many Euro-formed social scientists studiously count up to 13 genders in some indigenous societies, always trying to label and classify, box, imprison, strangle (see, for example, Amadiume, 1987; Muthien, 2003a; 2003b; 2007). In Michel Foucault's *The Order of Things* (1966), he critically engages with the epistemic assumptions, discourses and notions of 'truth' of historic eras, even considering the creation and definition of the notion of 'man' as a historic, ideological invention and construct. Thus the hegemony of LGBTQQIA++ in human rights advocacy and research is also dysconsonant with indigenous fluidities – a human who can potentially love other humans at any moment in time and circumstance, trying to act freely within a rigid and oppressive patriarchy, which restricts our choices to Greek letters, when in reality life is a continuous series of moments, breaths and being, like the indistinct colours of a rainbow that flow into one another like drops in liquid. For the indigenous matricentric, fluidity is preferred to hierarchies and domination.

Nonviolence or peace, carefully codified through centuries of complex conflict resolution methodologies, are intrinsic to matricentric societies, as evinced from the plethora of colonial texts referring, for instance, to 'the peaceful Bushman'; cooperation and collectivity over competition and rampant individualisms; creativities over the rigidities of Roman-Dutch law, rules and roles.

The Gift Paradigm[32] in which needs are met through unilateral gifting, without patriarchal reciprocity or bartering, is a critical element of matricentric societies. Here generosity is practised over patriarchal selfishness and greed.

Connected to all the above is love or compassion – com-passion, feeling with, feeling for, akin to the African notion of ubuntu: I am because I belong, I am because I care. To be compassionate, to love, one needs trust and respect. Love of self and all can be contrasted with patriarchal self-loathing and systemic distrust and hatred of all, seen, for example, in the proliferation of firearms and mass shootings, especially in the United States, mostly perpetrated by white men.

---

32 For example, www.ifge.net and www.gift-economy.com (Accessed 2 December 2020).

One needs women, and motherers of all varieties, at the centre of societies, co-creating social values and practices that are humane and nonviolent, that nurture and foster individual and collective growth, that heal and care, that do no harm and definitely do not exploit.

Interconnectedness and interdependence can be juxtaposed with psychotic patriarchal cleavages, separations, discombobulations, head from heart, top from bottom, the European Cartesian notion, 'I think therefore I am', expressed in the work of Rene Descartes (1644), versus an indigenous 'I care and belong therefore I am'.

Indigenous societies have compassionate spiritualities at their core, with feminine or dual-gender deities, rather than a vengeful, raging, patriarchal deity that inspires fear rather than love.

There is a distinct contrast between the patriarchal 'power over', and the matricentric, egalitarian 'power as a resource', to be shared in abundance and with respect, like every other resource. In indigenous societies, there have been epic processes of societal evolution, with complex ways of reinforcing egalitarianism, including laughter – literally laughing a foolish egocentric person back into the collective and humility.

Indigenous people are often called naïve for being trusting, honest, transparent. This indigenous behaviour is very different from, for example, Viennese artifice, which is reliant on masks and layers of obfuscation. The 'naïve' (indigenous/indigene) relates to other indigenous people as kin, unlike the extractive gazes and practices of the colonial. These are some of the basic elements of the indigenous matricentric, which our burning planet needs desperately.

TRUST ME, I'M TELLING YOU STORIES: MAKING AN EXAMPLE OF SHOSTAK ON NISA

Marjorie Shostak[33] became an anthropologist without a doctorate in the United States; a woman who made her name, fame and fortune off the Kalahari San, and at least one Kalahari woman, whom she called Nisa. During the 'Gold Rush' of anthropology in the 1970s, and with only a Bachelor's (basic) degree, Shostak accompanied her medical anthropologist husband, Melvin Konner,[34] on an expedition

---

33 Shostak has her own Wikipedia page, among other claims to fame: https://en.wikipedia.org/wiki/Marjorie_Shostak (Accessed 3 December 2020).

34 Online at: https://en.wikipedia.org/wiki/Melvin_Konner (Accessed 3 December 2020).

to the Kalahari. Konner's Wikipedia page says: 'He spent two years doing fieldwork among the Kalahari San or Bushmen, studying infant development and the hormonal mechanism of lactational infertility.' Sharon Groenmeyer also refers to 'lactational infertility' in Chapter 5 in this volume, from an indigenous woman's perspective. Shostak accompanied her husband on his professional research field trip, as spouses often do. While Konner was conducting his research, Shostak found company among the welcoming, generous Kalahari women, and Nisa in particular, from whom she extracted immense knowledge but no wisdom. Shostak and Konner, without irony, also made a fortune off *their* 'Paleolithic Diet' (Eaton, Shostak and Konner, 1988), drawing on the lifestyle and nutrition of the Kalahari San.

Shostak wrote a groundbreaking book *about* Nisa (Shostak, 1981), rather than *with* Nisa, and in thanks gave her a couple[35] of cows. Shostak then developed breast cancer, and wanted Nisa to cure her. She obtained generous sponsorship from a US pharmaceutical company, which funded her off-road vehicles, expensive equipment and other research expenses. When it comes to global North pharmaceutical companies, one can safely assume that they will extract indigenous plants and plant knowledge for their own profit rather than for the benefit of indigenous communities from which the ancient knowledge is derived. I am thinking here of foreign companies repeatedly trying to patent our indigenous rooibos tea, all the way to a court judgment protecting indigenous knowledge and assets (see Amusan, 2014). Likewise, there is the literal exploitation of the indigenous cactus, hoodia, which is used by foreigners to lose weight, but originally used by indigenous hunters to curb their hunger while on epic big game hunting expeditions on foot. Small wonder then that one struggles to find altruism in modern Western pharmaceutics.

Shostak's gifts for Nisa were some tea and beads, all meticulously recorded in her bestselling second book (Shostak, 2000). She reminds one of the colonisers at the Cape, trading beads and mirror shards for cattle and other valuable indigenous assets, meticulously (and unconsciously perhaps) recording their exploitation of the indigenous. A disappointed Shostak interrogates Nisa about the whereabouts of the two cattle previously gifted, which the starving Kalahari community had

---

[35] 'Couple' here means precisely two, rather than the abundant indigenous 'couple' that can count up to 20 or more.

slaughtered in the absence of other food.

Nisa, meanwhile, has reached menopause and has become a powerful shaman or healer. Her healing is always in the context and service of her community. There are no pop star healers in the Kalahari, who charge mega-bucks for services, workshops or yoga – merely humble people going about their days, doing the best they can for each other.

On her second major trip to the Kalahari, generously funded by her pharmaceutical company sponsor, and in search of a cure for her breast cancer, Shostak complains about having to pay a nominal amount (especially in US dollars) to Nisa's relatives to drum for the spiritual celebration and healing ceremony, which Eurocentric anthropologists call a 'trance dance'.

Shostak operates on assumptions firmly located in the exchange paradigm from which she hails: what is the maximum profit I can get for the least investment, just like extractive capitalism. She gets books, funds, fame and fortune, all in exchange for a couple of cows, some tea and condensed milk, and a few beads. She even wants a cure for her own cancer, but she is too stingy, too mean-spirited, to gift the healing ceremony drummers for their hard, spiritual work.

Shostak eventually leaves the Kalahari, miserable and sick. She tragically dies of breast cancer at the age of 51 in 1996. Her husband and friends posthumously complete her second book on Nisa (Shostak, 2000), and she is hailed as an 'anthropological deity', an 'expert' on the Kalahari San. A heartrending story. In life, Shostak fails to receive or understand the message. One wonders how many people who read her two books on Nisa, especially the second one, get the message.

Meanwhile, Nisa has also been ill, and she eventually dies a simple death, without fanfare, without posthumous publications, without material fortune. Date and cause of Nisa's death: unknown. One can simply contrast Nisa's relative happiness in a world of poverty (as defined by the World Bank), with the spiritual poverty that Shostak and her followers so poignantly, mindlessly represent.

African-American feminist poet and spiritual warrior Audre Lorde also died of breast cancer. One of her more famous teachings is that one cannot use the master's tools to dismantle the master's house (Lorde, 1983). Patriarchy (and capitalism) will not be dismantled if we use patriarchal or capitalist tools.

One cannot stone Shostak for her mindless exploitation, or her entourage, including her husband and their collaborators and supporters. Instead one feels devastated by their shameless behaviour, and inability to learn and heal, in spirit and in body. One has compassion for Shostak, locating her in her milieu: New York City and Atlanta, US academia, capitalism, patriarchy and exploitation, although she was a (Baby) Boomer, born during the 1940s, and ostensibly committed to equal rights for women. Shostak simply knew no better. She could not learn. Or change.

Indigenous compassion stems from complex technologies developed over centuries by indigenous peoples the world over – indigenous knowledge written about and profitably exploited by scholars and charlatans around the world.

In a groundbreaking essay on indigenous diplomacy, Leanne Simpson (2013) writes that indigenous diplomacy is based on *relationships*, and she emphasises the word 'relationships'. Her paper is beautifully titled 'Politics based on justice, diplomacy based on love: What indigenous diplomatic traditions can teach us'. Simpson asserts that 'political and philosophical traditions emphasize good relationships – with the natural world and with neighbouring nations – as the basis of good governance and a good life.' She affirms that:

> Treaties, from this perspective, are alliances with a commitment to continual renewal. Our politics are embedded within our spirituality, making treaties a shared, sacred bond between peoples. They are a commitment to stand with each other, a responsibility to take care of shared lands, and an appreciation of each other's well-being. They are based on a profound mutual respect, and they are meant to be transformative. They transform conflict into peace by holding parties accountable for past injustices. They transform hardship into sustenance. They transform abuse of power into balanced relations. Treaties and other Indigenous diplomatic traditions transform differing perspectives into, as the Haudenosaunee say, 'one mind'.

Unlike the Euro-formed[36] United Nations and Euro-formed politics, which is talk-talk-talk and less accomplishment, Simpson confirms that 'indigenous diplomacy is not so much about dialogue, but about action and embodiment'. In the most poignant ways, indigenous poets like Ifi Amadiume communicate, Simpson speaks of peacemaking as 'diplomacy based on love – the love of land and the love of our people – and this alone has the power to transform Indigenous-state relations into a relationship based on justice, respect, and responsibility.' Thus, instead of hating Shostak and others, I firmly locate her exploitative, stubbornly ignorant[37] and mean-spirited behaviour in the Euro-formed society in which she was socialised. She knew no better. My compassion is uncomplex, indigenous, ancient, apt.

Inconclusion

For decades, indigenous scholars and activists have wrestled with, among others, resistant mainstream feminists, including in Africa, elite feminists deeply immersed in patriarchal institutions of the academy and donor funding, fearful of upsetting their careful positionalities and hard-won privileges within the patriarchy. We must continue to challenge the ways in which even the African feminist mainstream centres the normative, for example, in the patriarchal abhorrence of the matricentric, and gender and sexualities fluidities, as well as the ways in which other intersectionalities (including socio-economic class and education) are privileged and advanced.

Not only should we rematriate our historically derided indigenous siblings, but we should also critically review our relationship with the majority of women everywhere – the majority of women dispossessed by patriarchy and at times exploited for knowledge and experience by the academy, NGOs and activists.

The hitherto (even unintentionally) elitist African and other

---

36 Here 'Euro-formed' refers to what Iroquois scholar Barbara Alice Mann writes of as an imperialist, colonising, annihilating narrative and practices. The 'Orientalist' 'Western' gaze is similar in its imperialist lens of indigenous cultures. Narratives of 'the global North' are similar.

37 June Bam refers to 'ignorant ignorance' in Chapter 4 in this volume, citing De Sousa Santos (2009).

feminisms should recentre the majority of women who were historically marginalised by intersectional oppressions. Liberation, rather than transformation, can be attained only through concerted actions by and for the majority. Thus, even privileged African and/or indigenous feminists, including myself, should relinquish power to, and work in solidarity with, the majority of 'ordinary' women hitherto ignored, exploited and abused – quotidian women who must and will lead the struggles towards post-patriarchal egalitarianisms; all women, including indigenous women.

In the words of Ma-Meneputo, a Kalahari San healer (South African San Institute, *c.* 2004):[38]

> The San people found power in the light of the moon. The ancients made a queen and hoisted her up into the sky where she became the moon. The people danced in the light of the moon. This is where we found [find] our healing power.

May our Moon inspire us to continue Rematriation, a return to the Mater, the Mother/er, the Uterus, where beginning and end are all one: a return to Indigenous Compassion.

REFERENCES AND FURTHER READING

Abrahams, Y. 1994. 'Resistance, pacification and consciousness: A discussion of the historiography of Khoisan resistance from 1972 to 1993 and Khoisan resistance from 1652 to 1853.' Master's thesis, Queen's University, Kingston, Canada. Unpublished.

Abrahams, Y. 2000. 'Colonialism, dysfunction and dysjuncture: The historiography of Sarah Bartmann.' PhD dissertation, History Department, University of Cape Town. Unpublished.

Abrahams, Y. 2001. 'Colonialism, dysjuncture and dysfunction: Sarah Bartmann's resistance'. Paper presented at a seminar of the African Gender Institute, University of Cape Town, 6 November.

Abrahams, Y. 2004. 'Writing history without hatred, for healing: Sarah Bartman in the context of colonial slave women in the Cape, *c.* 1788–1810'. Paper presented at the conference 'Ten Years of Democracy

---

38 Manunga, Ma-Meneputo, n.d. *Healing hands: Interview with Kalahari San healer*, South African San Institute, Kimberley.

in Southern Africa: Historical Achievement, Present State, Future Prospects', Centre for Southern African Studies, Queens University at Kingston, and the Department of History, University of South Africa, Pretoria, 22–25 August.

Abrahams, Y. 2007. 'The sounds of silence; Or; The head in the sand approach to historical research: A non-review of Rachel Holmes's *African Queen: The real life of the Hottentot Venus*'. In *Kronos*.

Allen, P.G. 1992 (1986). *The Sacred Hoop: Recovering the feminine in American Indian traditions*. Boston, MA: Beacon Press.

Amadiume, I. 1987. *Male Daughters, Female Husbands: Gender and sex in an African society*. London: Zed Books.

Amadiume, I. 1997. 'Gender, political systems and social movements: A West African experience'. In *Reinventing Africa: Matriarchy, religion and culture*. London, New York: Zed Books, pp. 109–143.

Amadiume, I. 1998. 'Religion, sexuality and women's empowerment in Nwapa's *The Lake Goddess*'. In M. Umeh (ed.). *Emerging Perspectives on Flora Nwapa: Critical and theoretical essays*. Trenton, NJ: Africa World Press, pp. 515–529.

Amadiume, I. 2000a. *Daughters of the Goddess, Daughters of Imperialism: African women, culture, power and democracy*. London: Zed Books.

Amadiume, I. 2000b. 'Blood solidarity, bodies of power: Framing sexuality and agency in African matriarchal cultures', Keynote lecture Bremen, International Women's University, IFU, Hannover, Germany.

Amadiume, Ifi. 2002. 'Bodies, choices, globalizing neocolonial enchantments: African matriarchs and Mammy Water', *Meridians*, 2(2): 41–66.

Amadiume, I. 2003. 'Prophecy, authenticity, oppositional models: Writers and politics in Africa', *The New Centennial Review*, 3(3): 5–25.

Amadiume, I. 2005a. 'Women and development in Africa', *SGI Quarterly*. January. http://www.sgiquarterly.org/feature2005Jan-3.html (Accessed 31 July 2011).

Amadiume, I. 2005b. 'Theorizing matriarchy in Africa: Kinship ideologies and systems in Africa and Europe'. In O. Oyěwùmí (ed.). *African Gender Studies: A reader*. New York: Palgrave Macmillan, pp. 83–98.

Amadiume, I. 2005c [1987]. *Afrikan Matriarchal Foundations: The Igbo case*. New Jersey: Red Sea Press.

Amadiume, I. 2015. 'Let my work not be in vain: Doing matriarchy, thinking "matriarchitarian" with Africa in the twenty-first century'. In E. Sall (ed.). *Africa and the Challenges of the Twenty-first Century: Keynote addresses delivered at the 13th General Assembly of CODESRIA, 2015*. DAKAR: CODESRIA.

Amusan, L. 2014. 'The plights of African resources patenting through the lenses of the World Trade Organisation: An assessment of South Africa's rooibos tea's labyrith journey', *African Journal of Traditional, Complementary and Alternative Medicines (AJTCAM)*, 11(5): 41–47.

Atalay, S. 2019. 'Braiding strands of wellness: How repatriation contributes to healing through embodied practice and storywork', *The Public Historian*, 41(1): 78–89.

Becker, H. 2003. 'The least sexist society? Perspectives on gender, change and violence among southern African San', *Journal of Southern African Studies*, 29(1): 5–23.

Besten, M.P. 2005. 'Transformation and reconstitution of Khoe-San identities: AAS Le Fleur I, Griqua identitites and post-apartheid Khoe-San revivalism (1894–2004).' PhD dissertation in History, University of Leiden.

Chondoka, Y.A. 1988. *Traditional Marriages in Zambia: A study in cultural history*. Ndola: Mission Press.

Clarke, Y. 2017. 'Re-imagining fluidity: Gender and Africanity', Colloquium Celebrating 30 years of Ifi Amadiume's award-wining text: *Male Daughters, Female Husbands: Gender and sex in an African society*, Rhodes University, South Africa, September 2017. Online at: https://www.grocotts.co.za/2017/09/22/politics-department-hosts-colloquium/ (Accessed 20 September 2020).

Clarke, Y. 2021. 'Considering "gender fluidity" in Zambia and Uganda: Femininities, marriage and social influence', *Journal of Contemporary African Studies (JCAS)*, 39(1): 56–69.

Coelho, P. 2012. Hymn to Isis (3rd or 4th century AD), https://paulocoelhoblog.com/2012/05/30/hymn-to-isis-3rd-or-4th-century-bc/ (Accessed 30 March 2021).

Colson, E. 1975 [1958, 1967]. *Marriage and the Family among the Plateau Tonga of Northern Rhodesia*. Manchester: Manchester University Press.

Davies-Vengoechea, X. 2004. 'A positive concept of peace'. In G. Kemp and D.P. Fry (eds). *Keeping the Peace: Conflict resolution and peaceful societies around the world*. London: Routledge.

De Wet, P. 2007. 'Restoring humanity: First Nation indigenous Khoe-San peoples in South Africa', paper presented at the World Social Forum, Nairobi, Kenya, January.

Descartes, R. 1644. *Principles of Philosophy*.

Diop, C.A. 1955. *Nations, Negres et Culture*. Paris: Editions Africaines.

Diop, C.A. 2003 [1981; 1990]. 'Origin of the ancient Egyptians'. In G Mokhtar (ed.). *General History of Africa, Vol. II: Ancient Civilizations in Africa,*

Abridged edition. Cape Town: New Africa Books. A UNESCO publication.

Donkoh, W.J. 2000. *Baffour Osei Akoto: A biographical sketch*, Kumasi.

Donkoh, W.J. 2000. *Osei Tutu Kwame Asibe Bonsu (The Just King)*. Accra: Woeli Publishers.

Eaton, S.B., Shostak, M. and Konner, M. 1988. *The Paleolithic Prescription: A program of diet & exercise and a design for living.* New York: Harper & Row.

Eaton, S.B., Shostak, M. and Konner, M. 1989. *The Stone-Age Health Programme: Diet and exercise as nature intended.* San Franscisco, CA: Harper Collins.

Eisler, R. 1988. *The Chalice and the Blade: Our history, our future.* San Francisco, CA: Harper One.

Felton, S. and Becker, H. 2001. 'A gender perspective on the status of the San in Southern Africa'. Regional Assessment of the Status of the San in Southern Africa, Report Series, Report No. 5. Windhoek: Legal Assistance Centre.

Foucault, M. 2005 [1970, 1966]. *The Order of Things: An archaeology of the human sciences.* London: Routledge.

Fry, D.P. 2004. 'Conclusion: Learning from peaceful societies'. In G. Kemp and D.P. Fry (eds). *Keeping the Peace: Conflict resolution and peaceful societies around the world.* New York and London: Routledge.

Fry, D.P. 2006. *The Human Potential for Peace.* Oxford: Oxford University Press.

Garvan Institute of Medical Research. 2019. 'The Homeland of Modern Humans'. Online at: https://phys.org/news/2019-10-homeland-modern-humans.html (Accessed 9 April 2021).

Gimbutas, M. 1963. *The Balts.* London: Thames and Hudson.

Gimbutas, M. 1982. *Goddesses and Gods of Old Europe.* London: Thames and Hudson.

Gimbutas, M. 1989. *The Language of the Goddess.* London: Thames and Hudson.

Gimbutas, M. 1991. *The Civilization of the Goddess: The world of Old Europe.* New York: Harper Collins.

Gluckman, M. and Colson, E. (eds). 1959. *Seven Tribes of British Central Africa.* Manchester: Manchester University Press.

Goettner-Abendroth, H. 2007. 'Matriarchal society and the gift paradigm: Motherliness as an ethical principle'. In G. Vaughan (ed.). *Women and the Gift Economy: A radically different worldview is possible.* Toronto: Inanna Publications.

Goodwin, A.J.H. 1952. Commentary on 'Jan van Riebeeck and the

Hottentots', *The South African Archaeological Bulletin*, 7(26): 86–91.

Goettner-Abendroth, H. (ed.). 2009. *Societies of Peace: Matriarchies past present and future*. Toronto: Inanna Publications.

Grasshoff, M., aka Makilam. 2007. *The Magical Life of Berber Women in Kabylia*. (Trans. E. Corp.) New York: Peter Lang.

Green, J. (ed.). 2007. *Making Space for Indigenous Feminism*. London: Zed Books.

Hahn, T. 1881. *Tsuni-llGoam: The Supreme Being of the Khoi-Khoi*. London: London: Trübner & Co. Reprinted in 2019 by Facsimile Publisher.

Hellinger, B. 2003a. *Farewell Family Constellations with Descendants of Victims and Perpetrators* (Trans. C. Beaumont). Heidelberg, Germany: Carl-Auer-Systeme Verlag.

Hellinger, B. 2003b. *Peace Begins in the Soul: Family constellations in the service of reconciliation* (Trans. C. Beaumont). Heidelberg, Germany: Carl-Auer-Systeme Verlag.

Hodgetts, L. and Kelvin, L. 2020. 'At the heart of the Ikaahuk Archaeology Project'. In K. Supernant, J.E., Baxter, N., Lyons and S. Atalay (eds). *Archaeologies of the Heart*. New York: Springer International.

Holmes, R. 2007. *African Queen: The real life of the Hottentot Venus*. New York: Random House.

Johansen, B.E. 1982. *Forgotten Founders: Benjamin Franklin, the Iroquois and the rationale for the American Revolution*. Opifswich, MA: Gambit Incorporated.

Kaberry, P. 1952. *Women of the Grassfields: A study of the economic position of women in Bamenda, British Cameroon*. London: Colonial Research Publication No 14. Online at: http://www.era.anthropology.ac.uk/Kaberry/Kaberry_text/ (Accessed 18 January 2021).

Kemp, G. 2004. 'The concept of peaceful societies'. In G. Kemp and D.P. Fry (eds). *Keeping the Peace: Conflict resolution and peaceful societies around the world*. New York and London: Routledge.

Kemp, G. and Fry, D.P. (eds). 2004. *Keeping the Peace: Conflict resolution and peaceful societies around the world*. New York and London: Routledge.

Kuokkanen, R. 2007. *Reshaping the University: Responsibility, indigenous epistemes, and the logic of the gift*. Vancouver: University of British Columbia Press.

Lee, R.B. 1979. *The !Kung San: Men, women, and work in a foraging society*. Cambridge: Cambridge University Press.

Lee, R.B. and DeVore, I. (eds). 1976. *Kalahari Hunter-Gatherers: Studies of the !Kung San and their neighbors*. Cambridge, MA: Harvard University Press.

Levell-Harvard, D.M. and Corbiere Lavell, J. (eds). 2006. *'Until our Hearts are on the Ground': Aboriginal mothering, oppression, resistance and rebirth*.

Toronto: Demeter Press.

Linton, K.R. 2003. 'Knowing by heart: Cellular memory in heart transplants'. *Montgomery College Student Journal of Science & Mathematics*, 2 September. Online at http://citeseerx.ist.psu.edu/viewdoc/summary?doi=10.1.1.535.2414 (Accessed 11 December 2020).

Lorde, A. 1983 [1981]. 'The master's tools will never dismantle the master's house'. In C. Moraga and G. Anzaldua (eds). *This Bridge Called my Back: Writings by radical women of color*. New York: Kitchen Table Women of Color Press.

Mair, L.P. 1953. 'African marriage and social change'. In A. Phillips (ed.). *Survey of African Marriage and Family Life*. London: Oxford University Press.

Makilam (M. Grasshoff). 2007a. *Symbols and Magic in the Arts of Kabyle Women*. New York: Peter Lang.

Makilam (M. Grasshoff). 2007b. *The Magical Life of Berber Women in Kabylia*. New York: Peter Lang.

Mann, B. 2003. *Native Americans, Archaeologists and the Mounds*. New York: Peter Lang.

Mann, B. 2004. *Iroquoian Women: The Gantowisas*. New York: Peter Lang.

Mann, B. 2006. *Daughters of Mother Earth: The wisdom of Native American women*. Westport, CT: Praeger Publishers.

Mann, B. 2007. *The Grey-Eyes: A lineage memoir*. Toledo, OH: Foreword Publishing.

Mann, B.A. 2011. 'Rematriation of truth'. Indigenous panel on Rematriation, Women's Worlds Conference, Toronto. Online at: http://www.gift-economy.com/articlesAndEssays/rematriationtruth.html (Accessed 2 December 2020).

Mann, B.A. 2019: *President by Massacre: Indian killing for political gain*. Santa Barbara, CA: Praeger, an imprint of ABC-CLIO.

Manunga, M-M. n.d. 'Healing hands: Interview with Kalahari San healer', edited by M.S. Winberg, South African San Institute, Kimberley.

Maracle, L. 2006. 'Decolonizing native women'. In B. Mann (ed.). *Daughters of Mother Earth: The wisdom of Native American women*. Westport, CT: Praeger.

Mitchell, J.C. 1956, 1966, 1971. *The Yao Village: A study in the structure of a Malawian tribe*. Manchester: Manchester University Press.

Moloi, V. 2008. 'The organic roots of the African matrilineal society'. http://africaunbound.com/index.php?option=com_content&task=view&id=98 (Accessed 2 December 2020).

Moraga, C. and Anzaldua, G. (eds). 1983 [1981]. *This Bridge Called my Back: Writings by radical women of color*. New York: Kitchen Table Women of

Color Press.

Moreton-Robinson, A. 2013. 'Towards an Australian indigenous women's standpoint theory: A methodological tool', *Australian Feminist Studies*, 28(78): 331–347.

Muthien, B. 2002. Book Review: *Peace and Conflict Studies: An Introduction*, Ho-Won Jeong, Ashgate, 2000. *Journal of Peace Research*, 39(3): 373–379.

Muthien, B. 2003a. 'Why are you not married yet? Heteronormativity in the African women's movement'. In *Fito*, feminist e-zine edited by Desiree Lewis.

Muthien, B. 2003b. 'Heteronormativity in the African Women's Movement'. In *Women's Global Network for Reproductive Rights Newsletter*, 79, 2003, #2.

Muthien, B. 2005. 'Beyond victims: Power and agency for African and other women'. Presented at Writing African Women, Poetics and Politics of African Gender Research Conference, University of the Western Cape, South Africa, January.

Muthien, B. 2006. 'Cite, site, and sight of the women's movements', *Development, Women's Rights and Development*, 49(1): 99–101.

Muthien, B. 2007. 'Queerying borders: An Afrikan activist perspective'. In N. Giffney and K. O'Donnell (eds). *Twenty-First Century Lesbian Studies*. Abingdon: Routledge.

Muthien, B. 2008a. 'The KhoeSan and partnership: Beyond patriarchy and violence'. Master's thesis, Stellenbosch University, South Africa.

Muthien, B. 2008b. 'Be/Coming homegirls: Beyond victims: Power and agency for African and other women'. In M. Meyer and E. Ndura-Ouédraogo (eds). *Seeds of New Hope: Pan-African Peace Studies for the 21st Century*. Trenton NJ: Africa World Press.

Muthien, B. 2008c. 'Playing on the pavements of identities', In M. Van Zyl and M. Steyn (eds). *Performing Queer: Shaping sexualities*. Cape Town: Kwela.

Muthien, B. 2009a. 'Beyond patriarchy and violence: The KhoeSan and partnership'. In H. Goettner-Abendroth. *Societies of Peace: Matriarchies past present and future*. Toronto: Inanna Publications.

Muthien, B. 2009b. 'B/coming home girls: Beyond victims: Power and agency for African and other women'. In M. Meyer and E. Ndura-Ouedraogo (eds). *Seeds of New Hope: Pan-African Peace Studies for the 21st century*. Trenton NJ: Africa World Press, pp. 249–268.

Muthien, B. 2010a. 'People of people: Egalitarianism and Ubuntu as gifts in context of the KhoeSan'. Seminar by International Feminists for a Gift Economy and the International Women's House, Rome, Italy.

Muthien, B. 2010b. 'Human security and layers of oppression: Women in South Africa'. In B. Reardon and A. Hans (eds). *The Gender Imperative: Human security vs state security.* London: Routledge.

Muthien, B. 2011. 'Rematriation of women-centred (feminist) indigenous knowledge'. Women's Worlds Conference, Toronto, http://www.gift-economy.com/articlesAndEssays/rematriation.pdf (Accessed 14 September 2020).

Oevernes, S. 2004. 'Surviving the cold: Khoe San identity management among street-people in Cape Town'. PhD dissertation, Anthropology Department, University of Tromso. Unpublished.

O'Reilley, A. 2016. *Matricentric Feminism: Theory, activism, and practice.* Toronto: Demeter Press.

Pakyntein, V. 2011. 'The matri-centred Pnar family', Women's Worlds Conference, Toronto.

Parkington, J. 2007. '//Kabbo's sentence'. In P. Skotnes (ed.). *Claim to the Country: The archive of Wilhelm Bleek and Lucy Lloyd.* Johannesburg: Jacana Media.

Powers, J. 2004. 'Review of *Male Daughters, Female Husbands*', *African History*. Online at: http://www.suite101.com/article.cfm/african_history/110213 (Accessed 10 January 2021).

Radford Ruether, R. (ed.). *Women Healing Earth: Third World women on ecology, feminism, and religion.* Mary Knoll, NY: Orbis.

Richards, A.I. 1969. 'Bemba marriage and present economic conditions', *The Rhodes-Livingston Papers*. Manchester: Manchester University Press, pp. 28–39.

Riemvasmaak. 2005. *Riemvasmaak: Place of many sorrows – place of many hopes.* Kakamas: Riemvasmaak Development Community Trust.

Rogers, G.A.J. (ed.). 1996. *Locke's Philosophy: Content and context.* Oxford: Oxford University Press.

Sanday, P.R. 1981. *Female Power and Male Dominance: On the origins of sexual inequality.* Cambridge: Cambridge University Press.

Sanday, P.R. and Ruth Gallagher Goodenough (eds) 1990. *Beyond the Second Sex: New directions in the anthropology of gender.* Philadelphia, PA: University of Pennsylvania Press.

Schmitz, L. 1844. 'Hym to Isis'. *The Classical Museum: A Journal of Philology, and of Ancient History and Literature*, 1, 34-40.

Selolwane, O.D. 2004. *Ethnic Structure, Inequality and Governance of the Public Sector in Botswana.* Part of UNRISD Project on Ethnic Structure, Inequality and Governance of the Public Sector. United Nations Research Institute for Social Development.

Shostak, M. 1981. *Nisa: The life and words of a !Kung woman*. Cambridge, MA: Harvard University Press.

Shostak, M. 2000. *Return to Nisa*. Cambridge, MA: Harvard University Press.

Simpson, L.B. 2013. 'Politics based on justice, diplomacy based on love: What Indigenous diplomatic traditions can teach us', *Briarpatch*. https://briarpatchmagazine.com/articles/view/politics-based-on-justice-diplomacy-based-on-love (Accessed 3 December 2020).

Skinner, J.D. 2005 [1980]. *The Mammals of the South African Sub-region*. Cambridge: Cambridge University Press.

Skotnes, P. 1996. *Miscast: Negotiating the presence of the Bushmen*. Cape Town: University of Cape Town Press.

Skotnes, P. 1999. *Heaven's Things: A story of the /Xam*. LLAREC Series in Visual History. Cape Town: University of Cape Town Press.

Skotnes, P. 2007. *Claim to the Country: The archive of Wilhelm Bleek and Lucy Lloyd*. Johannesburg: Jacana Media.

Slezak, M. 2014. "Found: closest link to Eve, our universal ancestor". In *New Scientist*. 8 October 2014. URL: https://www.newscientist.com/article/mg22429904-500-found-closest-link-to-eve-our-universal-ancestor/ (Accessed 9 April 2021).

Smillie, S. 2019. 'Origins of modern man revealed — Africa is in us all'. In *Daily Maverick,* 29 October. Online at: https://www.dailymaverick.co.za/article/2019-10-29-origins-of-modern-man-revealed-africa-is-in-us-all/ (Accessed 9 April 2021).

Smith, L.T. 1999. *Decolonizing Methodologies: Research and indigenous peoples*. London: Zed Books.

Some, M.P. 1994. *Of Water and the Spirit: Ritual, magic and initiation in the life of an African shaman*. London: Penguin Books.

Some, M.P. 1998. *The Healing Wisdom of Africa: Finding life purpose through nature, ritual and community*. New York: Putnam.

Some, S. 1999. *Welcoming Spirit Home: Ancient African teachings to celebrate children and community*. Novato, CA: New World Library.

Some, S. 1999, 1997. *The Spirit of Intimacy: Ancient African teachings in the ways of relationships*. New York: Quill – Harper Collins.

South African Human Rights Commission. 2004. *Report on Inquiry into Human Rights Violations in the Khomani San Community*.

South African Human Rights Commission. 2005. 'Media release: *Report on Inquiry into Human Rights Violations in the Khomani San Community*.'

Stone, M. 1976. *When God was a Woman*. New York and London: Harvest and Harcourt Brace & Company.

Supernant, K., Baxter, J.E., Lyons, N. and Atalay, S. (eds). 2020. *Archaeologies of the Heart*. New York: Springer International.

Swanger, J. 2007. 'Book Review: *Women and the Gift Economy: A radically different worldview is possible*', *Canadian Women's Studies*.

Thomas, E.M. 1959. *The Harmless People*. London: Penguin.

Tomlinson, L.L. 1943. *Geskiedkundige Swellendam*. Cape Town: Nationale Pers.

Van Hemert, M. and Meffert, P. 1991. *Die Khoisan van die Overberg*. Drostdy Museum, Swellendam.

Van Rensburg, A.P.J. 1975. 'Die geskiedenis van die Bontebok Park', *Koedoe: African Protected Area Conservation and Science*, 18(1): 165–190.

Vaughan, G. 1997. *For-Giving: A feminist criticism of exchange*. Austin, TX: Anomaly Press.

Vaughan, G. (ed.) 2004a. *The Gift: A feminist analysis*. Roma: Meltemi.

Vaughan, G. 2004b. 'A brief introduction: The gift economy'. In G. Vaughan (ed.). *The Gift: A feminist analysis*. Roma: Meltemi.

Vaughan, G. 2007. *Women and the Gift Economy: A radically different worldview is possible*. Toronto: Inanna Publications.

Vaughan, G. 2015. *The Gift in the Heart of Language: The maternal source of meaning*. Milano: Mimesis.

Volkan, V. 2000. 'Large group identity and chosen trauma', *Psyche*, 54(9): 931–953.

Volkan, V. 2001. 'Transgenerational transmissions and chosen traumas: An aspect of large-group identity', *Group Analysis*, 34(1): 79–97. http://gaq.sagepub.com/cgi/content/abstract/34/1/79 (Accessed 8 December 2020).

Volkan, V. 2006. *Killing in the Name of Identity: A study of bloody conflicts*. Chicago, IL: Pitchstone Publishing.

Volkan, V.D., Ast, G. and Greer, W. 2002. *The Third Reich in the Unconscious: Transgenerational transmission and its consequences*. New York: Bruenner-Routledge.

Wade, N. 2011. 'Phonetic clues hint language is Africa-born', *The New York Times*. Online at: https://www.nytimes.com/2011/04/15/science/15language.html (accessed 5 April 2021).

Wainaina, B. 2005. 'How to write about Africa', *Granta*, No 92. Online at: https://granta.com/how-to-write-about-africa/ (Accessed 11 December 2020).

Wildtschut, M-J. (ed.). *c.* 2004. 'Healing hands: Interviews with !Xun San Healer Meneputo Manunga'. Kimberley: Southern African San Institute Oral History Project.

green kalahari
Bernedette Muthien

here
        in this vast
                ageful
                kalahari
        my pores
                expand
        all eyes – bloom
        with knowing
                expansive
        as blue open-armed heavens

        mineral-soaked soil
        burning bright ochre
        colour of life
        colour of creativity

        soft streaky clouds
        mirrored in deep brown irises
        quotation mark wrinkles
echo
        landscapes pleated
                thru so much time
                there is no
                        string

divine recipe reads
fold this
into that
> slowly
> carefully
> over time
> until you see
> soft peaks

> my heart
> holy mother
> is this
> forever
> sacred
> ratio

'my god is in die natuur' (my god is in nature) – Una Rooi

3

Gendering social science
Ukubuyiswa of maternal legacies of knowledge for balanced social science studies in South Africa[1]

Babalwa Magoqwana

INTRODUCTION

If the agenda of the humanities and social sciences in South Africa was always linked to the racialising project of the Apartheid state to resolve the 'native question' (see Lalu, 2011), what should be their agenda since the advent of the democratic dispensation in 1994? Bernard Magubane (1968) once challenged social anthropologists to imagine a future in which 'strange societies' and 'primitive' people disappear. The disappearing of the 'primitive', he argued, would challenge the very existence of the discipline of anthropology, and this was proven true as the discipline later encountered existential crises, with some departments even closing globally. While the very nature of anthropology was part of the defined colonial project, we need to pause and consider similar questions for the rest of the humanities/social

---

[1] Some of the extracts in this chapter form part of the paper titled 'Reconnecting African sociology to the mother' in *African Sociological Review*, 24(2). This work is made possible by the support of the National Research Foundation (NRF) and the National Institute of the Humanities and Social Sciences (NIHSS).

sciences, especially during the COVID-19 pandemic, when medical sciences have become the main perspective from which solutions are sourced, with little attention being paid to, for example, psychosocial and socio-economic aspects of the pandemic. The idea of crisis within social science disciplines is not new or limited to South Africa. Keet (2014) historicised this crisis as global and notes that, as early as 1922, Joseph Stryzgowski, an Austrian historian, pronounced a 'crisis in humanities', while British historian J. Plumb, as early as 1964, 'also wrote on this crisis' (Keet, 2014: 100). Decade after decade, the 'crisis' seems to persist.

It is my suspicion that what Keet (2014) refers to as the 'intellectual stagnation' of the humanities[2] might be the result of the gender knowledge imbalance that has undermined the totality of women's contributions throughout the patriarchal and colonial period. The masculine capitalist model of thinking – in developing and organising society – seems to propel the current crisis in social reproduction throughout Africa. We need new alternatives, and sometimes this means revisiting the old wisdoms and tapping into the maternal legacies of knowledge in Africa. Magoqwana (2018) has argued for *uMakhulu* (grandmother) as the body of knowledge that 'stores, transfers and disseminates knowledge and values'. This chapter is building on this notion of the access to knowledge from the grandmothers in African households as they continue to feed the unemployed and children in rural South Africa today.

Women's legacies in knowledge creation have been *invisibilised*, misread and deliberately forgotten due to focusing on what Paul Zeleza (1996) calls 'the history and lives of great men'. In rereading some of the great historical texts of the 20th century, Zeleza noted that women were 'invisible' and portrayed only in their 'reproductive roles' as mothers, wives, carers, etc. This deliberate exclusion of women from historical accounts was influenced by the European narration of the history of the region, with very few ordinary women's stories, which has influenced how women were written about and inserted into history. Oyèwùmí (2005: 170) gives an example of Yoruba histories, in which female actors were wiped out of history because of the language restrictions of those who were recording the oral histories. 'Since the

---

2   We must also acknowledge the significant changes since the establishment of the National Institute for the Humanities and Social Sciences (NIHSS), which has begun to stimulate the academic project of the humanities, producing more than 200 PhD graduates since its inception five years ago. See the NIHSS annual report. Online at: https://www.nihss.ac.za/sites/default/files/Annual%20Reports/NIHSS_Annual_Report_1920.pdf (Accessed 18 January 2021).

colonial period, the way in which Yoruba history is being reconstituted has been a process of inventing gendered traditions.' Nzegwu (2020: 12) notes that 'legacies of African women exist today and constitute models of power offices'. She further quotes a Nigerian historian, Bolanle Awe, who argues that 'colonialism helped obliterate whatever records of women's achievements there were by giving little recognition to the repositories (and networks) of such information'. This attempt to obliterate and silence women's repositories can be countered by accessing 'living heritage' (Ishmael et al., 2020), which is central to how communities make sense of their daily realities.

Central to our ontological foundations are the wisdoms and knowledges transferred by our grandmothers (*ooMakhulu*), aunts (*rakgadi/makazi*), mothers (*oomama*) and sisters (*oosisi*). Many African leaders have detailed the influence of their maternal heritage in their leadership tactics and histories, including but not limited to anti-Apartheid struggle veterans.[3] Hassim (2019) details the grandmother's influence on the character and leadership values of one of the most influential women leaders in the South African liberation struggle, Winnie Madikizela Mandela.

> While the lineage that mattered in Winnie's heroic narrative was that of her father, Columbus, the authoritative figure was Winnie's grandmother, called Makhulu by her grandchildren ('an extraordinary woman who exercised a great influence on us all'). She was a role model ('tough, robust [...] with the physique of a fighter [...] she taught me the power and strength of a woman'). *Makhulu* rejected the modern, Christian and Westernised aspirations of the *amakholwa*, a group that included Gertrude's[4] family. Instead she emphasised stories of anti-colonial resistance. From her grandmother, Winnie derived a sensibility of race. In part this was by way of a rumour about Gertrude's white ancestry (Hassim, 2019: 1155).

This maternal heritage of knowing was the source of the herstorical excavation process by Thozama April (2012) when she used the autobiography of Katie Makhanya, sister of Charlotte Maxeke. April (2012) confirmed that through the information shared by Maxeke's

---

3   See also Tisani (2020) on the intellectual histories of the Eastern Cape through Nosuthu Jotela.

4   Winnie Madikizela Mandela's mother.

sister, Katie, she was able to confirm Charlotte Maxeke's date of birth.

It is through a focus on the maternal ancestors, who are missing in our different disciplines, that we begin the process of '*ukubuyisa*' of our maternal intellectual ancestors, and going back to our ways of knowing. As Mndende (2002: 142) has argued, 'the ritual of *ukubuyisa* is characterised by speeches that are partly prescribed to maintain order between the deceased and the clan members'. In thinking about the 'welfare of the living' (Mndende, 2002: 142), we need to restore the order that has mostly created a one-dimensional masculine understanding of the Southern African intellectual histories. Tisani (2020) has started unearthing the richly layered herstories of royal women of the Eastern Cape and *ooMakhulu* (grandmothers) of the intellectuals, like Tiyo Soga. Tisani's scholarly pursuit is to disrupt the linear and imposed patriarchal order in rereading the Eastern Cape intellectual histories. For instance, Tisani (2020) has traced the intellectual heritage of this province through Nosuthu Jotela, who was Tiyo Soga's grandmother, concluding that 'Nosuthu was a conduit through which both formal learning and Christianity were conferred to the Soga children and their children's children, and the rest of South Africa'. These histories can be traced only through the combination of archival and oral histories from the living vernacular sources present in different parts of the province.

It is through our grandmothers (*ooMakhulu*), aunts (*rakgadi*), mothers (*ooMama*) that our intellectual foundations of knowledge are shaped. These well-established knowledge foundations are sometimes neglected, 'invisibilised' and disregarded by patriarchal societies and, by extension, academies that seek to create a sense of shame and non-belonging for the younger generation today. It is fitting to acknowledge these maternal contributions from our elders, a status (seniority) that was common to many African societies in accessing power, knowledge, and later sacredness (afterlife) beyond gender categories (Oyèwùmí, 1997). This status cannot be separated from the zeal for change that saw young South Africans (from 1976 to 2015) calling for change and education curricula that reflect the realities of African households and their indigenous mother tongues. It is the combination of the elders (*abadala*) and young people's zeal for inclusive education that motivated this project to focus on the 'legacies', also known as traditions of women's knowledge systems, that inform our ontological voices, but which have been absent in our different disciplines.

Using elders to access knowledge in humanities subjects is not new as the disciplines of history, anthropology and sociology have always tended to rely on these sources in their research methods (for example, drawing on oral history and oral tradition). *Abadala* (elders) are referred to as living ancestors in Nguni cultures. In isiXhosa and isiZulu, ancestors are also known as *abaphantsi* (those who are down below), *amathongo* or *ithongo* (departed spirits), and *amadlozi* (the departed) (Ngubane, 1977: 51). Ancestors are typically concerned with the health and wellbeing of their people. After the process of *ukubuyisa* (or integration back into the family as the spirit through a ritual ceremony – a direct translation meaning 'to return'), ancestors dwell as invisible bodies in our societies (see Ngubane, 1977: 56). The most stubborn ancestors for the process of *ukuthwasa* (preparatory tutelage and mentoring of traditional healing) are the maternal ancestors. Also, the 'old woman is usually persistent in the context of an overdue *buyisa* ceremony. As a parent, she can afford to be harsher to her children and even to her husband' (Ngubane, 1977: 55). The spirits of our maternal grandmothers long for integration (*ukubuyiswa*) in how we know what we know. These maternal histories, and how they connect to the contemporary women's struggles for recognition, have yet to be systematically connected to the curricula, which would then reflect the history that shaped students' ontological and epistemological foundations and to which could relate.

UKUBUYISWA OF MATERNAL INTELLECTUAL ANCESTORS IN SOCIAL SCIENCES

In rehabilitating the social sciences and humanities today, we will need to reintegrate the maternal intellectual ancestors back into the foundations of our disciplines to increase cultural diversity at the same time as challenging the 'fathers of the disciplines' narratives that defines our histories. The absence of the maternal ancestors as archives of knowledge means that we are unable to connect African students to their 'collective memory' and, therefore, we are disabling African students. Reading Fatima Meer's (1976) classic, *Race and Suicide*, would expand the canon in sociology beyond Émile Durkheim's (1897) study of suicide. Centralising the work of Ellen Khuzwayo (1985), with its historical account of violence, as part of the introductory critical gender courses in our universities in Africa, instead of just Frantz Fanon (political theory), we would balance our intellectual foundations to include the power of maternal ancestors. One of the prominent Black feminist writers, Gloria Watkins, was influenced by her great grandmother to write the most acknowledged Black feminist texts under her great grandmother's name – bell hooks. Both hooks and her work –over 30 books on race, class, gender, culture and the arts (including children's books) – have become the canon and have influenced many Black women thinkers. Her maternal great grandmother and her positionality as a Black woman in the United States inspired most of hook's books. The late Toni Morrison, one of the great literary figures of this century, has also shared the impact and influence of her grandmother in her writings (Morrison and McKay, 1983). Morrison's works, with the theme of Black experience and mother–daughter relations, have given many Black writers the space to centre Black experiences in their novels. Both hooks and Morrison have joined a lineage of African women writers who wrote through the ontology of *uMakhulu*. Placing our maternal ancestry in our sociology of knowledge could help us return (*ukubuyisa*), and heal and cleanse our knowledge foundations from the colonial, exclusionary and elitist clutches of knowledge production in Africa. When Tisani (2018) calls for *ukuhlambulula* – cleansing – it means we need to resuscitate and reinstate the spirit and memory of our *ooMakhulu* as the foundation for our sociological imagination. In positioning elder African women as a source of sociological knowledge, we tackle the 'bio-logic' (Oyèwùmí, 1997) that has created a hierarchy in knowledge production. The centralising of *ooMakhulu* (grandmothers), *makazi* (aunts), *ooDabawo* (father's sister), et al. will assist our sociological enterprise to reshape its body of knowledge and provide an inclusive understanding of society beyond the binary thinking that has defined this motherless sociology of our time (Magoqwana and Adesina, 2020).

If our ancestors are interceding on behalf of the majority of Africans *(uluntu)* in correcting and improving sickness, purpose seeking and employment, and socio-economic status, then how is it possible that we have negated such a powerful vessel of sociological explanations about African society? If the ancestor is our archive (Tisani, 2017) to which we must pay attention to heal factors 'troubling' (*inkathazo*) our communities, then why has their knowledge been neglected and categorised as irrational, primitive and even 'barbaric', and not as 'science'? This kind of knowledge has always been used to heal and locate misfortune and suffering in different African societies. It is through *ukubuyisa* of *ooMakhulu* that we de-centre the secular nature of the father's disciplines in how they seek to negate the 'African elders' as the source of knowledge. This is why Mndende (2002: 174) argues that, 'as part of the ritual of *ukunqula* [to invoke the ancestors], the ancestors – both on the paternal and maternal side – need to be acknowledged as *intwaso* [traditional healing process] and cannot be complete if rituals are not done from the father's and mother's side'. This balance in African cosmologies is well established in how knowledge is stored and communicated by the elders. Elders form a significant part of the knowledge-making, irrespective of their gender, as one of the famous proverbs in isiXhosa says, *inyathi ibuzwa kwabaphambili*, directly translated as 'knowledge is sought from those who have experience and wisdom'. This idea of conflating age and knowledge is based on the idea of 'time' being the biggest teacher, without gendering knowledge. This is the main reason why many elderly people in our communities become '*inyathi*' (direct translation: a buffalo), as guides imbued with wisdom, based on this experience.

This chapter therefore hopes to contribute to the broader project of building the vernacular archive through the lives of the elderly informed by the Eastern Cape deep sociology of knowledge. Falola (2017: 703) terms this contribution a 'ritual archive' where

> words as well as texts, ideas, symbols, shrines, images, performances, and indeed objects that document as well as speak to those religious experiences and practices that allow us to understand the African world through various bodies of philosophies, literatures, languages, histories and much more. By implication, ritual archives are huge, unbounded in scale and scope, storing tremendous amounts of data on both natural and supernatural agents, ancestors, gods, good and bad witches, life, death, festivals, and the interactions between the spiritual realms and earth-based human beings.

Falola's theorisation on the 'ritual archive' is viewed with Ngũgĩ wa Thiong'o's (1993) assertion that 'language is the memory bank of the people's collective struggles over a period of time'. What I am arguing is that current feminist struggles can learn something from the language of our grandmothers on how to negotiate power and sometimes use it. In many ways, my work seeks to answer a call by Ifi Amadiume's (2015) preface to *Male Daughters and Female Husbands*, where she challenges African feminists to centre 'Africa's matriarchal heritage' in understanding women's relationship to power in post-colonial society. In a way, I am hoping to contribute to what Tisani (2018) has called *ukuhlambulula* (intellectual cleansing) of herstory. Despite long historical evidence, from both oral sources and written documents on how African women were treated as part of the occult (with supernatural powers) and sometimes treated as equal to men, we have a 'neo-traditionalist'[5] culture (concealed as 'African culture') that seems to distort this history and disregard ancient women's contributions to building African societies.

These rich matriarchal contributions from many parts of the African continent date way before the colonial encounter and speak of how power was organised and shared equally by both men and women. We know of the stories about the rich and powerful African women who ruled kingdoms and controlled markets. These tales and stories of origin (*amabali emvelo*) tend to feature powerful women, such as Sogolon Kedjou of Ghana, whom writers described as with 'deformities and unattractive', but who contributed to the formation of the kingdom of Mali in 1325. We also know of Queen Nzinga of Angola, who practised polyandry and who was one of the richest beneficiaries of the slave trade during the 17th century. She used to 'cross dress' and at times insisted that her husbands dressed as women. She was not an isolated case. Dahomey in western Africa, now southern Benin, is also well known for its women who were soldiers, state-sponsored prostitutes, part of army regiments, ministers and state record-keepers (Romero, 2015). These are complex, richly layered herstories that afford us a fuller interpretation of the past in Africa in its full diversity. In southern Africa, these complex pasts become very clear in the case of the Zulu monarchy in the 18th and 19th centuries. Shamase (2014) details the 'power and strong character' of Mkabayi ka Jama (and her twin sister, Mmama) who 'headed the military harems (*izigodlo*)' and became a regent when Senzangakhona died in 1781. Obviously, this rich powerful history, as claimed by Cheikh Ante Diop (1989), was later eroded by colonisation and religion. It is the invisible and unacknowledged histories of these African women that have reduced them into an ugly 'face of poverty' and underdevelopment in the world today (Aidoo, 1992). Looking at this history for me is about 'recovery of the traditions of knowledge' and memory from *what we know* (and, here I deliberately emphasise this point), which can help us understand the pertinent contemporary problems in our societies and help us to find appropriate solutions.

---

5 See Mkhize and Ntsekhe in their upcoming publication titled 'When *Amalungelo* are not enough: An auto-ethnographic search for African feminist idiom in the postcolony' in *Journal of Contemporary African Studies*.

Sesanti (2009: 213) has argued for the role of senior women in African cultures as the most important role in mitigating patriarchal order. Among Venda, Tsonga and Xhosa people,[6] senior women play a major role in the sacred rituals of these communities, as they have to communicate directly with the ancestors. This was also noticed by Amadiume (1987) in *Male Daughters and Female Husbands*. Amadiume used an ethnographic method to study gender systems of her own community, the Nnobi people in West Africa, where she used her 'kinship ties' and 'local language' to access local histories on family, motherhood, marriage, religion, sex and gender, political organisation of women and many other topics. Writing as the first-born daughter, (*umafungwashe*) she argues that her 'kinship ties' and multiple identities, underscored by motherhood, were used to understand her lineage and woman's political status in Nnobi histories. As *umafungwashe*, she was given the 'wooden bowl' by her father to make her a 'male daughter' (Amadiume, 2017: 133). This meant her position was that of '*inkulu*' (first-born male), which gave her the same rights as the first-born male, despite being female. This role of *inkulu* has been misinterpreted in the postcolonial patriarchal order to oppress and misinterpret African culture. Quoting Nokuzolo Mndende, Sesanti (2009: 214) argues that '(the position of *inkulu*) is one of the areas that amaXhosa (plural of Xhosa) males have now suppressed and women need to fight for it to be brought back to its original status'. This status gave women access to land and lineage rights, as Amadiume (1987) detailed from the Nnobi society. The role of senior women in African societies seems to be that of neutralising male dominance and providing a balance in how we conduct and behave in our societies.

This sense of 'liberated' African traditionalism seems to have allowed the 'unmarried women', or what Lamla (1985) calls 'liberated women' (*amadikazi*), to leave *umzi* (homestead), as they lived their lives without husbands. Using the Mpondo experiences, Lamla (1985: 22) explains that the word '*idikazi*' is derived from the word '*ukudikwa ngumzi*' meaning (in colloquial language) 'to be disgusted by homestead'. This concept, he continues, is based on the meanings of '*idikwamzi*', which is directly translated as women who are 'fed up' with married life. He goes further to narrate the benefits of these women as being artists, dancers, singers and free agents. This notion of 'liberated women' was prevalent even during pre-colonial times, as Delius and Glaser (2004) note, the 'numerical

---

6   The senior woman in Xhosa is called *umafungwashe* (first-born daughter), *Makhadzi* in Venda) and *rakgadi* in Sesotho/Pedi/Setswana cultures.

significant class of women [who] lived in their father's homestead as widows, divorcees, unmarried mothers – who essentially controlled their own sexuality ...'. Lamla (1984) notes that in colonial Mpondoland, most *amadikazi* were later shunned by the society as they were deemed 'immoral' and 'loose'. These sexist and derogatory descriptions tend to continue today when the more traditional public see younger urban women wearing miniskirts, deemed inappropriate dress in African culture. Makoni (2011) argues against the use of 'traditionalism' in suppressing the self-expressions of young women in taxi ranks and other public spaces.

On sexuality, desirability and beauty

Deep historicisation of contemporary challenges requires that social sciences engage the gendered archive. For example, one of the historical texts on African women, written recently in Africa by Patricia Romero (2015), details how African women were sexualised as 'the other', and thus deemed 'not rape-able'. This, of course, is also key in linking rape and race in Pumla Dineo Gqola's (2015) book on the subject of rape in South Africa.

The colonial encounter during the 18th century, between travellers and later missionaries in the Cape, tends to focus on women's sexualised bodies. 'Their women have long breasts', 'long labia', 'thick lips', 'curly hair', all become part of a consistent manner in which Khoe women are described at the Cape in travellers' diaries in the 1600s and 1700s (Magubane, 2004). Gqola (2015: 42) argues that 'the rape of slaves was an integral part of the architecture of slave-ordered Cape society'. She traces the history of rape and slavery to the Dutch East India Company (VOC), captained by Jan van Riebeek in the late 1600s, and the 'Slave Lodge' brothel in Cape Town where rape was institutionalised for both slave women and their children. This history of hypersexualisation of young African women's bodies affected how older travellers viewed a young enslaved African girl, Krotoa, and later *uMakhulu* Sarah Baartman.[7] The 10-year-old African girl, Krotoa, was tasked with caring

---

7   I consider Sarah Baartman as the foundational knowledge from the maternal ancestors who gave us the real meaning of 'intersectionality' (race, class and gender), before the global North began to theorise about it. Being *uMakhulu* for me also means exactly what Yvette Abrahams (2009) said about her being 'aunt Sara', where the mentioning and dissecting of elderly genitals (textually) is considered disgraceful. She also mentions that in her vernacular language it is impossible to mention descriptions, hence she needed to address *Makhulu* Sara as the 'aunt', more as a sign of respect

for the Van Riebeeck family in the mid-1600s. She is often described as lacking 'agency', unable to refuse to act as 'nanny and translator' for the Van Riebeeck family. Krotoa was later described as the 'prostitute' who used her access to the Dutch family for her own survival (Jansen, 2019). This is linked to why many African-American activists today question why young Black girls are always treated as adults without innocence, when innocence is ostensibly granted to young white girls. It seems that Black children in colonial and white supremacist societies are never given the possibilities of being children or being innocent. *When they See Us*, written and directed by Ava DuVernay in 2019, produced similar reactions, when the four-episode series investigated the case of wrongful arrest of five teenage Black boys accused of a brutal rape in Harlem during the 1990s.[8] These historical narratives are linked directly to the contemporary language against Black women and their experiences of violence.

A critical appraisal of these historical accounts of how the body and image of the African woman transitioned into a sexualised accessory is necessary if we are to deal with contemporary struggles against patriarchy, gender-based violence and everyday sexism. The sexualisation of the body of an African woman is clear in Mbulelo Goniwe's sexual harassment case in 2006,[9] where he is recorded to have said (to the young administrator, Njongo Nomawele), 'I thought you were a real Xhosa girl... How can you refuse a Chief Whip as if I am an ordinary man?' (Sesanti, 2009: 218). Of course, this was evident in 2006 during the Zuma's rape trial, of the scrutiny of how the victim 'behaved', which meant 'invitation to be raped'. She was tried and judged using her childhood sexual behaviour to paint her as promiscuous and, therefore, an 'unrape-able' victim (Gqola, 2015). Again, we see a similar narrative in the case of Cheryl Zondi when she was cross-examined during the ongoing trial of Timothy Omotoso[10] in the Port Elizabeth High Court

---

rather than hierarchy.

8 Kenny Herzog, 2019. *When They See Us* is a four-part TV drama. Online at: https://www.vulture.com/article/when-they-see-us-central-park-five-now-explainer.html, and the series' official website https://www.avaduvernay.com/when-they-see-us/ (Accessed 7 December 2020)

9 Goniwe was the Parliamentary Chief Whip of the ruling African National Congress (ANC) at the time.

10 Andrew Harding, 2018. 'South Africa shocked by live rape trial of Timothy Omotoso'. Online at: https://www.bbc.com/news/world-africa-45940338 (Accessed 7 December 2020).

from 2018. There is a strong link between the sexualisation of Black women in history and how they are described and positioned in the archives and the challenges of structural violence and gender-based violence in our societies today. The language of violence by missionaries, and now in contemporary times by African patriarchs, disguised as the custodians of 'African culture', makes it impossible to deal with gender-based violence without prioritising how women are depicted in our knowledge systems and in everyday language. Makoni (2011: 341) has argued against this use of supposed 'tradition' in everyday discourse, to label women as being 'unacceptable' because they dress 'in a miniskirt'. It is through language that unequal gender relations are maintained without proper interrogations of the histories that have created this, and the postcolonial conditions that have accepted it.

Maternal legacies of knowledge need to be resuscitated as part of what Nzegwu (2019) terms the 'sankofaring' approach in theorising. In attempting to decolonise the African historiography and recentre African woman's voices, it is necessary to return and 'take back'[11] old wisdoms to deal with contemporary postcolonial gender-related challenges. In theorising in social sciences today, it is necessary to look back, but also to move forward as we seek to reconceptualise gender power dynamics that tend to be explained using flawed cultural explanations.

ON LANGUAGE, HUMANITIES AND A WOMAN-CENTERED HUMANITIES PROJECT

So how do we allow this rich herstory about African women and their contributions to define our humanities and social science knowledge systems? How do we use the understanding of being *umafungwashe* (the first-born female *kwaXhosa* – as the position of seniority and its responsibilities) regardless of the male counterpart taken as *inkulu* (first-born male)? We know in VhaVenda culture, *Makhadzi* (the brother's sister) is the ear of the community and a spiritual leader who guides and advises the chief. 'The Makhadzi, an aunt is a non-political figure, [she] enhances the voice of the people while serving as the king's eyes, ears and conscience' (Gqubule, 2017: 79). We know the role of *rakgadi* in Setswana, Sepedi and Sesotho and her importance in shaping and

---

11 'Sankofa is literally translated as 'Go back and take it', and connects closely with the Akan proverb: '*se wo were fi a, wo san ko fa a yenkyi*', [meaning] 'it is not wrong to return to take something if you forget it' (Opoku-Agyemang, 2017).

negotiating family dynamics in rituals and social organising in the institution of the family in Africa.

The centring of women in our humanities and social science crisis means that we are investing in rigorous empirical work that centres indigenous languages with a deep herstoricisation of knowledge to understand the indigenous community's ways of being and theorise them in their own terms. For example, Archie Mafeje understood that language represents a specific worldview (Ntuli, 2002) and an ontological foundation. Hence his classic paper on 'Ideology of tribalism' (1971) was based on this deep connection between language and history. The use of indigenous language, and excavation of deep herstories, could help us deal with the growing misrepresentation and appropriation of 'African culture and tradition' by the growing 'neo-traditionalists' (see Mkhize and Ntsekhe, forthcoming) who seem to choose 'our culture' when it suits their heteronormative and patriarchal language. To use indigenous languages as the source of knowledge rather than translation is to rescue and engage the growing misrepresentation of African 'culture' as a justification for misogyny and hatred of 'sexual minorities' in African societies.

There has never been a more urgent need to resuscitate the intellectual herstories of African women, who were and are much more than wives, widows or domestic workers. These can provide an alternative perspective to what we know as knowledge today. The women who were and are the backbone of *what we know* and *how we know it* today, form the ontological foundations of who we are – these are our maternal intellectual ancestors. Most postcolonial states have been struggling with gender and sexuality questions in general, which is why it is essential that we should define the citizenship questions of the future. In as much as we have experienced the links and benefits of Black feminist thought from the global North and its intervention through 'intersectionality- race, class and gender', we have to put more effort into understanding postcolonial gender relations today. It seems that African societies tend to use indigenous languages to articulate and conceptualise issues differently from those in the global North. Therefore, we need to reconceptualise power relations to include gender relations that are mitigated by language and knowledge seniority in our humanities project of the future.

REFERENCES

Abrahams, Y. 2009. 'Ambiguity is my middle name: A research diary'. In N. Gasa. *Women in South African History: They remove boulders and cross rivers*. Cape Town: HSRC Press.

Adesina, J.O. 2006. 'Sociology beyond despair: Recovery of nerve, endogeneity, and epistemic intervention', *South African Review of Sociology*, 37(2): 241–249.

Aidoo, A. 1992. 'The African Women Today'. *Dissent*, 319–325.

Amadiume, I. 1987. *Male Daughters, Female Husbands: Gender and sex in an African society*. London: Zed Books.

Amadiume, I. 1997. *Re-inventing Africa: Matriarchy, religion and culture*. London: Zed Books.

Amadiume, I. 2017. 'Gender field experience, method and theory'. *Journal of West African History*, 3(2): 131–138.

April, T. 2012. 'Theorising women: The intellectual contributions of Charlotte Maxeke to the struggle for liberation in South Africa'. PhD dissertation, University of the Western Cape. Unpublished.

Delius, P. and Glaser, C. 2004. 'The myths of polygamy: A history of extra-marital and multi-partnership sex in South Africa', *South African Historical Journal*, 50: 84–114.

Durkheim, É. 1952 [1897]. *Suicide: A study in sociology*. London: Routledge.

Falola, T. 2017. 'Ritual archive'. In A. Afolayan and T. Falola. *The Palgrave Handbook of African Philosophy*. London: Palgrave Macmillan.

Gqola, P.D. 2015. *Rape: A South African nightmare*. Johannesburg: MF Books, an imprint of Jacana Media.

Gqubule, T. 2017. *No Longer Whispering to Power: The story of Thuli Madonsela*. Johannesburg and Cape Town. Jonathan Ball Publishers.

Hassim, S. 2019. 'The impossible contract: The political and private marriage of Nelson and Winnie Mandela', *Journal of Southern African Studies*, 45(6): 1151–1171.

Ishmael, H., Sowinski, E.A., Forster, K., Joseph, E. and Richards, N. 2020. 'Locating the black archive'. In S. Popple, A. Prescott and D. Mutibwa (eds). *Communities, Archives and New Collaborative Practices (Connected Communities)*, 1st edition. Cambridge: Policy Press.

Jansen, E. 2019. *Like Family: Domestic workers in South African history and literature.* Johannesburg: Wits University Press.

Keet, A. 2014. 'Plastic knowledges: transformations and stagnations in the humanities'. *Alternation*, 21(2): 99–121.

Kuzwayo. E. 1985. *Call me Woman*. Johannesburg: Ravan Press.

Lalu, P. 2011. 'Restless natives, native questions'. Online at: https://mg.co.

za/article/2011-08-26-restless-natives-native-questions/ (Accessed 29 November 2020.

Lamla, M. 1985. 'Liberated women: An explanation and exposition of a local Mpondo problem', *South African Journal of Ethnology*, 8(1): 20–24.

Mafeje, A. 1991. *The Theory and Ethnography of African Social Formations: The cases of the interlacustrine kingdoms*. Dakar, Senegal: CODESRIA Books.

Magoqwana, B. 2018. 'Repositioning uMakhulu as an institution of knowledge: Beyond "biologism" towards uMakhulu as the body of indigenous knowledge'. In J. Bam, L. Ntsebeza and A. Zinn (eds*). Whose History Counts: Decolonising African pre-colonial historiography*. Stellenbosch: African Sun Media.

Magoqwana, B. and Adesina, J. 2020. 'Reconnecting African sociology to the mother: Towards a woman-centred endogenous sociology in South Africa'. *African Sociological Review*, 24(2) 1–24.

Magubane, B.M 2000 [1968]. 'Crisis in African sociology'. In B.M. Magubane. *African Sociology – Towards a critical perspective: The collected essays of Bernard Makhosezwe Magubane*. Trenton, NJ: Africa World Press.

Makoni, B. 2011. 'Multilingual miniskirt discourses in motion: The discursive construction of the female body in public space', *International Journal of Applied Linguistics*, 21(3): 340–359.

Mkhize, N. and Ntsekhe, M. (Forthcoming) 'When Amalungelo are not enough: An auto-ethnographic search for African feminist idiom in the postcolony'.

Mndende, N. 2002. 'Signifying practices: AmaXhosa ritual speech'. PhD dissertation, University of Cape Town. Unpublished.

Morrison, T and McKay, N. 1983. 'An interview with Toni Morrison', *Contemporary Literature*, 24(4): 413–429.

Ngubane, H. 1977. *Body and Mind. An ethnography of health and disease in Nyuswa-Zulu thought and practice*. London: Academic Press.

Ntuli, P. 2002. 'African knowledge systems and African Renaissance'. In C.A. Hoppers (ed.). *Indigenous Knowledge and Integration of Knowledge Systems: Towards a philosophy of articulation*. Cape Town: New Africa Books.

Nzegwu, N. 2019. 'Proper African women': Omumu, disabling subordination and reasserting endogenous powers.' Public Lecture, University of South Africa. Pretoria, 28 May.

Nzegwu, N. 2020. 'Omumu: Disassembling subordination, reasserting endogenous powers', *International Journal of African Renaissance Studies: Multi, Inter- and Transdisciplinarity*, 15(1): 41–58.

Opoku-Agyemang, K. 2017. 'Looking back while moving forward: The case of concrete poetry and *Sankofa*', *Hyperrhiz: New Media Cultures,* 16. doi:10.20415/hyp/016.e07.

Oyèwùmí, O. 1997. *The Invention of Women: Making African senses of Western gender discourses.* Minneapolis, MN: University of Minnesota Press.

Oyèwùmí, O. 2005. 'Making history, creating gender: Some methodo-logical and interpretive questions in the writing of Oyo oral traditions'. In O. Oyèwùmí (ed.). *African Gender Studies: A reader.* London: Palgrave MacMillan.

Romero, P. 2015. *African Women: A historical panorama.* Princeton, NJ: Markus Wiener Publishers.

Sesanti, S. 2009. 'Reclaiming space: African women's use of the media as a platform to contest patriarchal representations of African culture: Womanists' perspectives', *Critical Arts: A Journal of South–North Cultural Studies,* 23(2): 209–223.

Shamase, M. 2014. 'The royal women of the Zulu monarchy through the key role of oral history: Princess Mkabayi kaJama', *Inkanyiso. Journal of Humanities and Social Sciences,* 6(1): 15–22.

Tisani, N. 2000. 'Continuity and change in Xhosa historiography during the nineteenth century: An exploration through textual analysis'. PhD dissertation, Rhodes University, Grahamstown. Unpublished.

Tisani, N. 2017. 'Revisiting and celebrating our literary elders to build a multiversal tomorrow'. Paper presented at Rhodes University Colloquium: Rethinking South African Canonical Writing: Centring the isiXhosa Writings of the 19th and Early 20th Centuries, 21–22 June 2017.

Tisani, N. 2018. 'Of definitions and naming: "I am the earth itself. God made me a chief on the very first day of creation"'. In J. Bam, L. Ntsebeza and A. Zinn (eds). *Whose History Counts: Decolonising African pre-colonial historiography.* Stellenbosch: African Sun Media.

Tisani, N. 2020. 'A fortuitous appearance in history of the enigmatic Nosuthu MaMtshawe Jotelo, a nineteenth-century isiXhosa-speaking woman'. Paper presented at a Nelson Mandela University Colloquium, 28–29 August 2020.

Vilakazi, H. 2002. 'The problem of African universities'. In M.W. Makgoba (ed.). *African Renaissance: The new struggle.* Cape Town: Tafelberg/Mafube Publishers.

Zeleza, T. 1996. 'Gender biases in African historiography'. In A. Imam, A. Mama and F. Sow (eds). *Engendering African Social Sciences.* Dakar, Senegal: CODESRIA Books, pp. 81–115.

MANIER VAN KOPPEN EN ADERLAATEN.

4

Feminism-cide[1] and epistemicide of Cape herstoriography through the lens of the ecology of indigenous plants

June Bam

I contend that the misrepresentation of the San[2] and Khoena-descendant women took place in several powerful ways: linguicide (erasure of language),[3] culturicide (attempted erasure of culture), feminism-cide (attempted erasure of feminist knowledge through total reliance on the masculine colonial archive) and epistemicide (loss of knowledge). The colonial erasure and extraction of botanical and pharmaceutical knowledge and practice, eco-cide, is a critical part of broader epistemicide. Feminism-cide further extends to *Taras*-cide or *Ausi*-cide (attempted erasure of the knowledge and role of indigenous Khoi elder women).

---

1 Denoting the attempted erasure of indigenous feminist knowledge, a term I propose as different to 'femicide' (murder of women).
2 Noting that for the San, there was the devastating and overarching factor of genocide.
3 Thanks Bradley van Sitters and Pedro Dausab, for support on the Khoekhoegowab (Nama) language usage.

Indigenous knowledge of plants has traditionally been assigned to the interdisciplinary ethnobotany (botany, history and ethnography), with studies exploring the difficulties in placing it in 'historiography'. Knowledge of plants has never been validated as mainstream epistemologies of indigenous women, which could contribute to more profound and fuller understandings of our pasts, presents and probable imaginable futures. Termed 'post modernization of landscapes as historiography' (Harris, 1999) to be appraised, such approaches to knowledge have limited us to 'disciplinary' understandings of epistemologies, disavowing a fuller epistemological ecology, which is so central for producing and centring African feminist philosophies on how we know. Many studies on indigenous plants present women as uneducated, and lacking in understanding of biodiversity and conservation. Such studies globally are usually large-scale quantitative audits commissioned by government agencies to control and manage biodiversity, and for the economic benefit of pharmaceuticals and 'sustainability' (see Mahwasane, Middleton and Boaduo, 2013: 69–75). Others advocate for the central role of women in healing and indigenous knowledge (see Alam et al., 2011). Yet global studies show that indigenous women play central roles in conservation, preserving biodiversity and food security (Pidatala and Rahman Khan, 2003). Gender-based patterns of knowledge of plants and their uses by indigenous women are also found elsewhere (Pidatala and Rahman Khan, 2003: 360), consistent with precolonial patterns at the Cape (see Bam, 2021). At the Cape since precolonial times, women have shown far greater knowledge of medicinal plants and their uses than men (Joshi and Joshi, 2000: 182). This is also the case in Namibia where the majority of healers were found to be women (Cheikhyoussef, et al., 2011: 10).

This all being said, using indigenous feminist knowledge of plants as a 'herstoriographical' lens is not an established field in scholarship. Related to this is an interesting recent study by Prigioniero et al. (2020: 60), which uses interdisciplinary methodologies to ascertain the 'historiography' of plants and their connections to interpretations of cultural symbolisms in understanding the past. The study focused on the lotus plant and its interpretive value in 'historiography'. The lotus eaten by the Lotophages – North African people who nourished themselves with the mysterious sweet African plant – is found in Homer's *Odyssey* and is referred to by Herodotus (Prigioniero et al., 2020: 61). Knowledge of ancient Egypt includes knowledge of the plants and their medicinal uses. Today, the blue water lily has almost disappeared from the Nile, yet it was ubiquitously described during the time of the dynasties (Prigioniero et al., 2020: 64). The description of the edible roots, fauna and flora gave us insights into understanding these ancient African histories. While the knowledge of plants has been used historiographically to understand and interpret ancient North African societies, somehow this method has been eschewed to a large extent in southern Africa. Moreover, feminist indigenous knowledge of plants in the region has been subjected largely to quantitative studies to promote an awareness of biodiversity and/or imperatives for economic development (the beneficiaries not always clarified). Yet, feminist indigenous knowledge of plants can assist us in accessing and reimagining pasts in the absence of Western-understood 'written records', through an innovative triangulation method with oral tradition.

How can we reimagine pasts in non-conventional feminist ways? Indigenous matrilineal knowledge sharing starts with what you can see, smell and hear in the landscape. As a self-identified Cape indigenous-descendant scholar, I argue for self-narrativised ('the narratability of self' as discussed in O'Flynn, 2009: 77) feminist *Tara-* and *Ausi*-epistemologies of landscape as a decoloniality imperative. I argue for this, given the large, male-interpreted archive of the woman as subject, the representation of a vacuous body disavowed of knowledge of self and landscape.

This erasure that denied knowledge started with toponymicide (erasure of indigenous names of the landscape as part of that larger ecology) through, among others, the female indigenous Khoekhoegowab form in the Cape landscape region. As illustration, the feminine *doas* means a mountain pass or path – an opening up. *Aus* denotes fountain or flow. *Ousie* used in Afrikaans (with similar pronunciation also of '*ausi*' in Khoekhoegowab) therefore is the well-known, first-born girl and the knowledge keeper and power holder in indigenous-descendant families and communities. There are many feminine Khoekhoegowab names for places, for example, *Cardouw* and *Krakadouw. Tradouw* Pass is derived from *taras*, meaning a woman. Sir Lowry's Pass had a feminine indigenous name *Gantouw* – 'path of the eland'. Feminine Khoekhoegowab place names were corrupted by Afrikaans names and they lost their original meanings through the corrupted recordings by travellers. One such example is the name of a river in George district, which had 14 forms, its original indigenous meaning having been the 'Maiden's Ford'. The derivatives are *Traka de Tkou, Vroue Weg, Krakaou, Radadakouw, Traka da Touw*, the first part referring to the Khoekhoegowab *taras* (woman), and the second part, *daob*, a way or path (Botha, 1926). Similarly, *Touws* River is Khoekhoegowab, not Dutch (Botha, 1926: 33), and has nothing to do with Afrikaans *toue* or ropes. *Aus* means fountain, while '*Tirri*' meaning river. *Gammi-isa* (place of water), is found in present-day spellings of '*Kama*' or '*Kamma*'. *Taras* is found in the naming of the *Tarka* River, meaning 'Maiden River' and *Tarkastad* (Botha, 1926: 166).

The colonial-interpreted terms Khoi and KhoiKhoi are in themselves patriarchal, feminism-cidal, *Taras*-cidal, *Ausi*-cidal and, therefore, profoundly epistemicidal – denoting 'men' and 'men of men'. Historian Yvette Abrahams (1994; 2000) argues that this distortion in meaning came with colonial patriarchy, as 'Khoikhoi' means 'persons belonging to other persons'. 'Khoe' means 'person' (see Fauvelle-Aymar, 2005). I therefore prefer the term Khoena as the gender neutral term (see Van der Spuy, 1997: 258, quoting historian Julia Wells). Indeed, Wells (1998) argued that it was the preferred name that the indigenous people nearest to the Cape of Good Hope called themselves (referring to Moodie, 1838). Patric Mellet (2020) chooses 'Camissa Africans' when speaking about the Cape people (as inclusive of indigeneity in its diversity). In the VOC journal entry of 31 October 1656, the name 'Soanquas' is found, meaning murderers and robbers, (the latter description as denoted in the journal entry of 31 October 1657) (see Botha, 1926). Raper (2010: 170), drawing on the work of Nienaber (1989), states that the Cape governor, Simon Van der Stel, referred in his diary of 31 October 1685 to 'de sonquaas'.

The original indigenous meaning of 'San' is, therefore, similarly devoid of feminism, denoting the absent agency of the *Ausi*. San women are profoundly muted in the colonial historical archive, except where their violent demise is described through their hysterical responses in the male-told histories of the genocide of these women and their children. We are told very little about these women and their agency in the deep southern African past and its landscape.

The Dutch archives (historically predominantly created by white males), as in the nature of colonial archives, have been indifferent to correct original indigenous language spellings and have been inconsistent also in their own renaming of spelling conventions, and often inconsistently and interchangeably used terms within the landscape context, leading to loss of meaning.[4] This process of colonial erasure of knowledge and its ecology in the landscape has been more profound for indigenous women and their descendants, and particularly for females disavowed of the traditional cultural passing on of this knowledge.

Mendez (2015: 44) asserts that

> unlike all others in the colonial/modern gender system, 'Man' is understood to be the sole possessor of subjectivity and knowledge as pre-determined by his 'natural evolution' as a 'rational' being. 'Woman', namely his 'light side' counterpart, is reduced to his negation within the colonial/modern gender system. Thus, if he is of the 'mind', she is of the 'body'.

Related to this is the interesting narrative in which the sexual agency of 'Hottentot' women in the Swellendam region is described vividly after 'socialising' with European travellers, including with the 18th-century European traveller, Sparrman. 'At length the elder of them while she was running, not only fell down, but even seemed to wait for us in that position ... till she drew a large knife, and threatened to plunge it into our hearts, if we dared to approach any nearer' (Sparrman in Forbes, 1975: 208–209); 'these Hottentot women are no more true hottentots and all whores' (Forbes, 1975: 209; fn. 107). Sparrman described their feminism and resistance agency to sexual activity with the travellers as suggesting them to be lazy, cold Hottentot women; dull and inactive; listless; sloth (1975: 209); and he continues with patriarchal proprietorial arrogance, '...with respect to my Hottentots, I was much afraid of the temptations of the women' (Forbes, 1975: 268) 'nor had there been any instance known, that a young woman should be delivered up into the arms of a Christian, or white man, on any consideration whatever' (Sparrman in Forbes, 1977: 34).

It is interesting to note that Cape 'coloured' women were not only de-indigenised and dehumanised through both femicidal and epistemicidal processes involving the body, but they were also de-Africanised through

---

4   Today, we are more familiar with the small traces of knowledge of the landscape that have survived, such as place names like Karoo, which denotes 'dry, sparsely covered, hard' as in Khoekhoegowab's '*kuru*'. Translations into Dutch, English and Afrikaans have erased original meanings in the landscape in many cases, although some have remained in which the San (Bosjemans Kloof, Bushman's River, Sonquas Drift) and Khoekhoegowab origins and meanings are still recognisable.

historically consequent contemporary *poes*[5]-cursing everyday utterances. In this regard, the term 'Africanders' denoting African indigeneity (however defined) used in the mid-1800s for 'coloured' women, was evidently long lost. Through colonial de-Africanisation from the mid-1600s, the indigenous Khoena woman became the vacuous '*Hotnot jintu*' and '*Hotnot meid*', the subject of negative interpretation and for negative exhibit. It is within this context that the recent Stellenbosch University study on the cognitive ability of 'coloured' women justifiably raised eyebrows (see Le Grange, 2019; Nieuwoudt et al., 2020). The obsession with 'physical type' of Khoena women (see also Somerville, 1799) is well known through the story of Sarah Baartman. The period in which Khoena women were paraded as part of freak shows in Europe coincided with the time when Heinrich Lichtenstein and others were collecting indigenous human remains for museums in Europe. Lichtenstein took the head of a Karoo Khoekhoe woman from her body to Europe in 1805 (Morris, 2008: 222). Dubow (1996) refers to this time as the 'age of typology'.

In terms of colonial physical typology, the indigenous woman is both excessive (in a carnal sense), as well as cognitively, spiritually and maternally deficient. Due to this intrinsic disruptive idiosyncratic symbiosis within her, the hysterical indigenous woman has to be silenced and tamed. In this process of erasure, it is hoped that she ceases to be the knowledgeable and agency-driven *Taras* or *Ausi* and becomes the enslaved and oppressed *meid* or the framed sexually promiscuous slut (loose woman). Krotoa (*c.*1643–1674), the young Goringhaiqua Khoena woman who worked in Jan van Riebeeck's fort, and as an interpreter and peacemaker, represents generations of indigenous women in colonial contexts globally. Absent from these colonial representations is these indigenous women's high human and cognitive consciousness in relations to land, landscape, memory, and of wellbeing. In this context, what would cognitive justice[6] therefore mean? How do we negate the negation (as in Marxist theory) and enact that process as decoloniality?

Cape indigenous slave woman knew about plants and healing, but

---

5   Denoting the crude reference, in the creole local Afrikaans, to (predominantly) 'coloured' women's genitalia, although in contemporary times, it has become more inclusive (referring also to any gender in a derogatory way) and also appropriated by feminist anti-gender-based violence activists. See Hartmann, 2019: 74–83.

6   Cognitive justice is the right of multiple forms of knowledge to be co-created and to co-exist, including as ways of life. Also see De Sousa Santos, 2015.

we do not get a glimpse into these narratives derived from the colonial observations and archives, nor from the interpretations by the male historians (both Black and white, including Marxists and liberals), who use the colonial archive as the exclusive source of knowledge, even for 'decolonising' purposes; a paradox in itself – a form of feminism-cide. Today, the terms *Taras* and *Ausi* are little known in descendant communities.

One widely promoted misrepresentation is that of *Taras* Krotoa who was portrayed as the neglected niece of her Goringhaicona uncle, Autshumao, and who in turn neglected her own children through irredeemable drunkenness. Wells (1998: 419) discusses the Khoena clan conflict between the gathering activities of the Goringhaicona and the cattle-herding Goringhaiqua. Taken into Van Riebeeck's household at the age of 12, Krotoa dies and is represented as a drunken prostitute after the death of her Danish surgeon husband, Meerhoff. The story of *Taras* Krotoa as the narrativised neglectful 'married mother whore' who had a 'dishonourable' death is well known. Another example is the Khoena woman *Taras* Sara who, in 1671, committed suicide, with judicial action taken against her dishonoured corpse by the Dutch East India Company's Council of Justice. *Taras* Krotoa's representation in South African historiography represents the colonial framing of the quintessential indigenous Cape Khoena people – particularly through the bodies of women.

Despite these acts of erasure of all sorts that came with the violent colonial encounter and invasion, the process of compulsive extermination never fully succeeded. Remnants of what once existed, do remain and are part of our everyday life, though much invisibilised, such as the knowledge of plants. Botanicide was not a completely intended process, as later, with industrialisation in Europe, indigenous plants from the colonies fulfilled the opportunistic agendas of the colonials as they looted them for use in their growing pharmaceutical industries. Other knowledges have nearly vanished because of geological and landscape changes and the loss of the narratives through oral tradition as a direct result of the impact of Dutch colonialism, British imperialism and later Apartheid. This epistemicide of the cultural knowledge of the people at the Cape cannot be fully appreciated without a wider understanding of the landscape of plants and wildlife, and how the process of erasure was enacted. It was always acknowledged in white scholarship that the process by which the 'KhoiSan'[7] lost their culture in the Cape is only 'sketchily known' (Elphick and Shell, 1979). There is, of course, a need for far greater understanding of the rituals and practices depicted in these later rock paintings (see Yates, Manhire and Parkington, 1993) by working more closely in interpretations with women of the descendant communities in both local and urban areas (who hold related intergenerational knowledge), and those who lived in spaces around wetlands where much of the ritualistic, hybridised knowledge and practices survived until much more recently than was previously assumed.

Much of this indigenous feminist knowledge erasure of landscape, plants, flora and fauna is reflected in early European male travellers' accounts within the wider Cape region. Le Valliant's (1796) travel writing at the time of the 18th-century French Revolution is of particular interest. Travelling from Holland to the Cape in 1780 to collect specimens of birds and animals, he recounts in his *Travels into the Interior of Africa via the Cape of Good Hope*, his romance with a 'beautiful Gonoqua woman', whom he gratuitously and proprietorially describes as 'my young savage' (1796: 166), whom he 'took pleasure' in dressing. He casually de-baptised her and named her 'Narina', 'which means flower in the Hottentot language'. 'I begged her to keep this beautiful name which suited her in a thousand ways ...' (Le Vaillant, 1796: 167). He also gratuitously and randomly gave this name to a bird, disregarding local indigenous names. Notable in these colonial texts is the consistency of the proprietorial 'my' in describing Cape indigenous people as European possessions. For instance, 'my Hottentots' (Sparrman in Forbes, 1975: 180; 318) and another instance of the generous collective appropriation of 'our Hottentots' (Forbes, 1975: 226). These European imaginations of the Cape and its people influenced later visitors, such as British socialite, Lady Ann Barnard, who shared in her diaries her gaze during 'zoo-like' expeditions into the interior 'in search of Hottentots' (Morris, 2008) when she visited in 1798 to 'observe' 'Hottentots' (in their natural environment) and 'watch them closely'. In reading Barnard's diaries, it is clearly of interest that she took particular delight in observing indigenous women – yet, nowhere does she indicate an observation of their immense knowledge or agency; they are static figures within landscapes.

---

7   A now widely rejected term due to its origins within genocidal scientific acts in southern Africa coined by a German male scientist Schultze in 1928.

There could be several reasons why these travellers knew so little about women and their roles in these early Khoi and San societies at the Cape. One could be the lack of access that the indigenous locals gave to inquisitive European invaders to their homes, and their well kept secrets of plants. De Houtman explains in 1595: 'We could find none of their dwellings, far less any of their women' (Raven-Hart, 1967: 18). These invaders were also unsure of who were women and who were men as they imposed their European and gendered sense of dress on them – 'the women dress like the men' (Nicholas Downton, 1610, 1613, quoted in Raven-Hart, 1967: 47).

In 1687, Tavernier (a traveller) paid tribute to 'KhoiKhoi' healing skills but gave no indication of the plants used. Another traveller, Bergius, complained of the 'secrets' of the Cape people in 1767. An image of *wildedagga* is provided by Hermann in 1672, recorded at the time for the same purposes as it is still used today by *Ausidi* on the Cape Flats. Oldenlands spoke of the '*kruidboek*' and '*kruie vroue*' on the Cape Flats. Although they refused to treat the sexually transmitted illnesses of European sailors, it is recorded that during the 18th century there were, indeed, established Khoe and San remedies for venereal disease. Medicinal formulations, based on botanical knowledge, were also recorded in the period 1650–1710.

Early European travellers' extensive observations on Cape indigenous women were about them being 'savage'. For instance, the women are described by Downton as eating flesh and raw intestines and guts' (Raven-Hart, 1967: 47). Quite notable is the observation of the independence of Cape Khoi women, which must have been astonishing for the male European gaze at the time coming from very patriarchal European societies. 'Each wife had her own hut ... regarded as the mistress of the hut ... and so far from being dominated by her husband appears to have had a good deal of independence' (Dapper quoted in Schapera et al., 1933). Not only were women in charge of household resources and played a central role in livestock management, veld education and ceremonies, they were also incredibly independent and not subjected to the husband's authority within the family structure (at least from observations). Kolbe (1731: 163) indicated the responsibility women had for education; something which she does while smoking 'dacha'. The wind blows the 'dacha' into the child's face which 'she minds not this' (Kolbe, 1731: 164). Even in romance she was free as marriages, according to Kolbe (1731: 157), were not entered into for political reasons. Kolbe described the great respect men had for their wives and women (1731: 162).

Because indigenous women were considered vacuous and lacking in knowledge – judged as being considered as part of fauna and flora rather than recognised for their profound knowledge of the landscape and its entire ecology of plants, flowers, healing, livestock and astronomy – the European missionaries thought they would rescue them from themselves through the imposition of patriarchal Christianity, and in the process erased their diverse indigenous spirituality and identities. Colonial photography of indigenous women was a form of epistemicide and feminism-cide. A curious case is that of the work of the English photographer, George Angas, who specialised in capturing the mission to 'civilise' the indigenous people of South Africa, Australia and New Zealand – from savage state to 'educated'. The missionaries at Genadendal welcomed Angas 'to sketch the Khoikhoi' during his visit there in 1847. Angas's images of the 'civilised Khoikhoi' in European dress were sent back to England to report on the progress of the 'savages'. Some of Angas's work illustrated 'An old Hottentot woman with half-caste grandchildren'. The elder indigenous woman knowledge holder (*Taras* or *Ausi*) is presented as vacuous – a lifeless body devoid of knowledge, with offspring that are not fully human. Bredekamp (1997: 46) points out that the scholarship on the early history of the Genadendal Mission and its indigenous history occurred only after the 1930s. Yet, Genadendal is known for its ongoing ancient indigenous knowledges of plant and healing archives (see Parker, 2015). Similar studies have been done on indigenous knowledge in Elim as previous mission station (see Thring and Weitz, 2006).

Erasure of the wider ecology of wildlife and plants was enacted concomitantly. Sarah Baartman as a Khoe woman was put on display in London in 1810 as part of the Cape's fauna and flora, and dissected as a sub-human 'curiosity' in Paris in 1815, as part of this historical European world of trafficking people, and plundering plants and animals. Her iconic story is one of brutal erasure as part of the colonial extermination ecology, turning the indigenous female body into a dehumanised, vacuous entity, disavowed of any knowledge of landscape. This was an epistemicidal act in its most graphic and brutal form.

Scholars have also focused largely on the extractive archives of Lloyd and Bleek's collections from the /Xam people in the 1870s and 1880s (Skotnes, 2007; see Vollenhoven's reinterpretation of this archive in chapter 1) and on rock narratives to understand early indigenous Cape histories. Important women's voices have been left out, which we should include in new innovative research methodologies going forward. This trend of peripherisation of indigenous women in knowledge creation and interpretation of archive is global. In other words, we work with deficit models inherited from the masculine Eurocentric and Western-originated disciplines, which involve the systematised destruction of feminist indigenous knowledge ecologies and of epistemological self-determination.

When Andries Stoffels (a prized, indigenous male, Christian convert) appeared before the House of Commons Committee on Aborigines in London during his visit in 1835–1836, he praised the missionaries: 'The Bible charmed us out of the caves, and from the tops of the mountains ... made us throw away all our old customs and practices, and we lived among civilised men. We are tame men now' (Ross, 2017: 69). A civilised indigenous man meant one who understood his place after colonial defeat, converted to Christianity, had patriarchal authority over his wife and children as his property (most likely the case of Europeans at the time) and accepted the superior authority of the European patriarch as his master in the gendered and racialised hierarchy. Sparrman described meeting 'Hottentot Captain Rundganger', who 'answered with a sly sarcastic smile that his command extended no farther than to his wife and children and that he might be called with equal propriety Major (Opper-Captens), or what else you please (Forbes, 1975: 229). A similar tactic was used in creating and deepening divisions among the Khoe and San and to instil colonial patriarchy on indigenous women through indigenous males by belittling their indigenous culture and ways of knowing, 'A Hottentot had caught and had in his custody three old Boshies-women with their children with the intention to take them home to his master for slaves' (Forbes, 1977: 34). 'His master had given him a gun. His female captives had threatened to bewitch him but he had no faith in witchcraft and equal contempt for their savage manners' (1977: 34–35).

The potency of oral history in restoring this knowledge implies a total reassessment of 'history', given that our written archive is colonial, male, and white dominated, both in its content and research method. Oral history of plants and landscape of Cape indigenous women as knowledge keepers enriches us by introducing new creative methodological approaches while also promoting the study of indigenous languages, essential for the understanding and interpretations of a more inclusive and complex southern African herstoriography. Though there have been concertedly powerful attempts under colonial occupation and Apartheid to obliterate this ancient past of intergenerational knowledges, my research on the Cape Flats (2015–2020) shows that the present generation still holds traces of the 'precolonial' feminist indigenous knowledge and memory, and they remain and linger in all sorts of ways in the everyday, especially in healing rituals and plants and the wider ecology of dreams and visions. It is the *Ausis* (a term that has survived phonetically and is still used in some Cape Flats households)[8] that hold these ancient landscape knowledges, which could veritably be triangulated with the specificities of the stories of those of the knowledge holders recorded in the early European travellers' archives on the Khoe people's knowledge, rituals and practices in the 1400s to 1700s, and their contestations. Oral tradition in medicinal knowledge and practice is profoundly strong on the Cape Flats, although not visibilised or narrativised as part of the mainstream history of the Cape Peninsula because it is outside the official record and archive (*anarchive*).[9] There exists 150 years of unrecorded indigenous medicinal knowledge in the colonial archive alone, which remains inaccessible, but points to tremendous research capacity through stories in the anarchive. *Taras'* and *Ausi's* Cape indigenous knowledge became appropriated into the Western canon, classified and typologised. Male professors in Leiden in the Netherlands, 300 years ago (and more since), became leading botanists of their day by extracting botanical and medicinal knowledge from *Taras'* and *Ausi's* archive, laying the foundations for associated gigantic pharmaceutical profits that evolved later. The capitalist pharmaceutical extraction of the indigenous knowledge of the hoodia plant is a prime example (see Wynberg, 2004).

In recent years, Prada-Samper (2007) in the 'The plant lore of the /Xam San: //Kabbo and ǂKasiŋ's identification of "Bushman medicines"' indicated the neglected area in research on plant knowledge as indicative of precolonial social history. But their work focuses, like many others, on the /Xam in the Bleek and Lloyd archives as disconnected from contemporary descendant communities on the Cape Flats. Earlier

---

8   The Khoekhoegowab term *Taras* as singular for respected woman has re-emerged in Khoi revivalism.

9   'seeing what is not there' (Zaayman, 2019). As scholar, Zaayman writes as a direct descendant of Krotoa.

works, such as Deacon (1986; 1988), looked at the contextual elements of place. What of this deep and wide knowledge of an ancient archive remains in unassumed places and living on in descendant communities, and what are the associated rituals in this surviving ecology?

Taras' and *Ausi's* indigenous knowledge system was part of a large network in the community and the wider Cape. Through the self-narrativised stories of the indigenous-descendant women at the Cape, we will be able to find that larger ecology, which has elements that can be traced to colonial observations of Khoe people some 600 years ago. These observations have remained in those texts and assigned for limited interpretation by 'ethnobotanists' and anthropologists. Very rarely has the knowledge recorded in those texts been used as a basis for historical interpretation by the Cape Khoena and San descendant women themselves. Khoe histories have been written more from the point of view of political conflict and self-determination in political leadership, and identity formations into the present. The archaeological occupation has been predominantly about the hunter-gatherer versus herder debates. Alternative histories have focused largely on male Khoe leaders and two women – Krotoa (1600s) and Sarah Baartman (1800s) – both predominantly presented as victims and European colonial male casualties with tedious reinterpretation (an industry in itself), though diverse, within this paradigm. We do not get to know these women as indigenous knowledge keepers. They represent the silent mass of faceless and nameless *Ausis* they come from, even in the imposed 'hysteria'.

The lives and herstories were part of a larger epistemological ecology as exposed in Le Vaillant's summation of European ignorant ignorance (De Sousa Santos, 2009) when he recounted:

> They [the indigenous women] looked at me with surprise as they could not understand why I killed the birds to skin them and then immediately restore their form. I did not waste my time explaining the merits of the cabinets of collections and the fuss made about them in Europe. They would rightly have been surprised that I have come from so far only to collect animals. And the question Narina [as he had now baptised her] asked whether there were no birds in my own country, seemed to me a very simple question and a just one (Le Vaillant in Glenn, 2007: 172).

By the time the trekkers moved inland with the so-called 'Great Trek' during the 1830s, the knowledge they gained from the Khoe and San about the landscape and plant medicines put them on a road to independence for survival against disease in a significant way (Pretorius, 1987: 20). Kolbe (1727: 154–155) illustrates cupping by the Khoikhoi at the Cape.[10] This is a practice often exclusively associated with ancient Chinese medical practices.

Ausis had herbs from the veld and mountain, constantly on the boil on the fires throughout the day as stories were told and forecasts were made. Early travellers (geographers, missionaries or 'leisured men of culture'), from which the grand narrative for South Africa's precolonial and early colonial past was drawn, knew very little about indigenous women, and what they did write is often grossly misleading, patriarchal and racist, or a distortion of the truth. Ignorant ignorance. Rock rabbit urine – the 'master of medicines' for epilepsy and other illnesses administered by Cape indigenous women until recent times (it has now largely been appropriated by the global pharmaceutical industry) – is described by Sparrman as merely 'dassen-pis' in a footnote (Forbes, 1975: 285), totally decontextualised from its ritual context. Women are described in their gathering activities, but not as knowledge transfer keepers; only as engaging in fixed 'foraging' activities in the 'wild'. Although Khoekhoegowab was lost at the Cape through colonial occupation and suppression, traces of those meanings remain, especially in medicinal practices such as in words like *buchu*, and *dagga* which became ubiquitous into the present day because of its powerful recognised healing properties and link to trance rituals and dream prophecies. Knowledge of plants was and remains integrally connected to learning about prophecies, visions and dreams. Some plants were used to induce the dream state for visions, such as wilde dagga. Buchu was used for rituals in childbirth which continue today; for cleansing, for welcoming visitors. It symbolised hospitality and cleanliness. When Europeans appropriated buchu through the pharmaceutical industry, buchu became treated as 'without narrative' and ritual archive; as only a profit-making medicinal commodity (see Low, 2007). Some women on the Cape Flats taught their boy children to collect *kukumakranka*[11] (which kept its original Khoekhoegowab name, although debated) found on the mountains and now most likely extinct. It was noted as a 'celebrated

---

10 Illustration titled 'Manier van Koppen en Aderlaaten'.

11 Online at: http://planet.botany.uwc.ac.za/nisl/bdc321/ekapa%20cape%20towns%20lowlands/module7/kukumakranka.htm (Accessed 11 October 2020).

little plant' in 1931 'having a perfumed odour of ripe fruit, for which it is chiefly valued, prized in the old days for its medicinal knowledge' (Luckoff, 1951: 43). The triumphant invincible spirit of *Taras* and *Ausi* existed in these archives of the landscape, on the mountains and on ocean beds, in rituals and linguistic traces outside of mainstream knowledge on the Cape Flats, despite attempts at erasure through colonialism and Apartheid. This knowledge offers us an opportunity to decolonise historiography towards herstoriography, by applying decolonial research methods, such as through the lens of the knowledge of plants. Such new approaches will take us beyond biodiversity studies for economic capitalist-driven profit, towards attaining indigenous, feminist, cognitive justice in (re)writing the past.

References

Abrahams, Y. 1994. 'Resistance, pacification and consciousness: A discussion of the historiography of Khoisan Resistance from 1972 to 1993 and Khoisan resistance from 1652 to 1853'. Master's thesis, Queen's University, Kingston, Canada. Unpublished

Abrahams, Y. 2000. 'Colonialism, dysfunction and dysjuncture: The historiography of Sarah Bartmann'. PhD dissertation, History Department, University of Cape Town. Unpublished.

Alam, N., Shinwari, Z.K., Ilyas, M. and Ullah, Z. 2011. 'Indigenous knowledge of medicinal plants of Chagharzai Valley, District Buner, Pakistan', *Pakistan Journal of Botany*, 43(2): 773–780.

Bam, J.C. (Forthcoming 2021). *Knowing on the Wind, ǂoaba ǂans*. Cape Town and Johannesburg: Jacana Media and Texture Publishing.

Botha, C.G. 1926. *Place Names in the Cape Province*. Cape Town: Juta and Company.

Bradlow, E. 1979. *William Somerville's Narrative of his Journeys to the Eastern Cape Frontier and to Lattakoe 1799–1802*. Cape Town: Van Riebeeck Society.

Bredekamp, H.C.J. 1997. 'Construction and collapse of a Hernnhut mission community at the Cape, 1737–1743', *Kronos*: 46–61.

Cheikhyoussef, A., Shapi, M., Matengu, K. and Ashekele, H.M. 2011. 'Ethnobotanical study of indigenous knowledge on medicinal plant use by traditional healers in Oshikoto region, Namibia', *Journal of Ethnobiology and Ethnomedicine*, 7(1): 10.

Deacon, J. 1986. '"My place is the Bitterpits": The home territory of Bleek and Lloyd's /Xam San informants', *African Studies*, 45(2): 135–155.

Deacon, J. 1988. 'The power of a place in understanding southern San rock engravings', *World Archaeology*, 20(1): 129–140.

De Sousa Santos, B. 2009. 'A non-occidentalist West? Learned ignorance and ecology of knowledge', *Theory, Culture & Society*, 26(7-8): 103–125.

De Sousa Santos, B. 2015. *Epistemologies of the South: Justice against epistemicide*. London: Routledge.

Dubow, S. 1996. 'Human origins, race typology and the other Raymond Dart', *African Studies*, 55(1): 1–30.

Fauvelle-Aymar, F.X. 2005. 'Four wordlists of extinct Cape Khoekhoe from the 18th century', *Studies in African linguistics*, 34(2): 159–178.

Forbes, V.S. (ed.). 1975. *Sparrman, Anders. A voyage to the Cape of Good Hope towards the Antarctic Polar Circle around the world and to the country of the Hottentots and the Caffres from the year 1772–1776*, Vol. 6. Cape Town: Van Riebeeck Society.

Forbes, V.S. (ed.). 1977. *Anders Sparrman*, Vol. 7. Cape Town: Van Riebeeck Society.

Glenn, I. (Trans. and ed). 2007. *Francois Vaillant: Travels into the interior of Africa via the Cape of Good Hope*. Vol. 1. Cape Town: Van Riebeeck Society for the Publication of South African Historical Documents.

Harris, D. 1999. 'The postmodernization of landscape: A critical historiography', *The Journal of the Society of Architectural Historians*, 58(3): 434–443.

Hartmann, L. 2019. '"Los my poes af" – the fine line between being radical enough and being too radical', *Agenda*, 33(2): 74–83.

Joshi, A.R. and Joshi, K. 2000. 'Indigenous knowledge and uses of medicinal plants by local communities of the Kali Gandaki Watershed Area, Nepal', *Journal of Ethnopharmacology*, 73(1/2): 175–183.

Kolbe, P. 1727. *Naaukeurige en uitvoerige beschryving van de Kaap de Goede Hoop: behelzende een zeer omstandig Verhaal van den tegenwoordigen toestant van dat vermaarde Gewest, desrelfs Gelegenheit, Haven, Sterkte, Regeringsvorm, Uitgestrektheit, en onlangs ontdekte aanleggen de Landen.* Vol. 1. Amsterdam: Balthazar Lakeman.

Kolben, P. 1731. *The present state of the Cape of Good Hope: Or, A particular account of the several nations of the Hottentots: Their religion, government, laws, customs, ceremonies, and opinions; their art of war, professions, language, genius, &c. Together with a short account of the Dutch settlement at the Cape*. Vol. 1. Translated from the original by Mr Medley. London: W. Innys.

Le Grange, L. 2019. 'A comment on critiques of the article age- and education-related effects on cognitive functioning in Colored South African women', *South African Journal of Higher Education*, 33(4): 9–19.

Le Vaillant, F., 1796. *New Travels into the Interior Parts of Africa, by the Way of the Cape of Good Hope, in the Years 1783, 1784 and 1785*. Translated from French. In three volumes (Vol. 3). London: G.G. and J. Robinson.

Low, C.H. 2007. 'Different histories of buchu: Euro-American appropriation of San and Khoekhoe knowledge of buchu plants', *Environment and History*, 13: 333–361.

Mahwasane, S.T., Middleton, L. and N. Boaduo, N. 2013. 'An ethnobotanical survey of indigenous knowledge on medicinal plants used by the traditional healers of the Lwamondo area, Limpopo province, South Africa', *South African Journal of Botany*, 88: 69–75.

Mendez, X. 2015. 'Notes toward a decolonial feminist methodology: Revisiting the race/gender matrix', *Trans-scripts*, 5: 41–56.

Moodie, D. (ed.). 1838. *The Record; Or, a Series of Official Papers Relative to the Condition and Treatment of the Native Tribes of South Africa*, Vol. 3. Cape Town: AS Robertson.

Morris, A.G. 2008. 'Searching for "real" Hottentots: The Khoekhoe in the history of South African physical anthropology', *Southern African Humanities*, 20(1): 221–233.

Nieuwoudt, S., Dickie, K.E., Coetsee, C., Engelbrecht, L. and Terblanche, E., 2020. Retracted article: 'Age- and education-related effects on cognitive functioning in Colored South African women', *Aging, Neuropsychology, and Cognition*, 27(3): 321–337.

O'Flynn, S. 2009. 'Challenging the Cartesian self: Autobiography as an intertextual/interrelational discourse in the works of Aritha van Herk and Kristjana Gunnars', *Rethinking History*, 13(1): 65–78.

Omobuwajo, O.R., Alade, G.O. and Sowemimo, A. 2008. 'Indigenous knowledge and practices of women herb sellers of southwestern Nigeria', *Indian Journal of Traditional Knowledge*, 7(3): 505–510.

Parker, H. 2015. '"Doing" diabetes: A focus on local experience, medical knowledge systems and herbal management of Type 2 diabetes among individuals in Genadendal, Western Cape'. Master's dissertation, University of the Western Cape.

Pidatala, K. and Rahman Khan, A. 2003. 'Women and indigenous knowledge: A South–South perspective'. Online at: https://openknowledge.worldbank.org/handle/10986/10774 (Accessed 1 December 2020).

Prada Samper, J.M.D. 2007. 'The plant lore of the/Xam San: //Kabbo and ≠Kasiŋ's identification of Bushman medicines', *Culturas Populares. Revista Electrónica* 4 (Accessed 18 February 2020).

Pretorius, J.C. 1987. 'Medicine at the Cape in the 17th and 18th centuries'. *South African Journal of Cultural History*, 1(1): 17–22

Prigioniero, A., Scarano, P., Ruggieri, V., Marziano, M., Tartaglia, M., Sciarrillo, R. and Guarino, C. 2020. 'Plants named "lotus" in antiquity: Historiography, biogeography, and ethnobotany', *Harvard Papers in Botany*, 25(1): 59–71.

Raper, P. 2010. 'The ethnonyms "Bushman" and "San"', *Acta Academica*, 42(1): 168–186.

Schapera, I., & Farrington, B. 1933. The Early Cape Hottentots Described in the Writings of Olfert Dapper (1668). *Willem ten Rhyne (1686) and Johannes Gulielmus de Grevenbroek (1 695)*. van Riebeeck Society, Cape Town.

Schlag, B.J. 2015. 'Historiography of North American ethnobotany'. Online at: https://usso.uk/historiography-of-north-american-ethnobotany/ (Accessed 10 October 2020).

Schultze, L. 1928. *Zur kenntnis des Körpers der Hottentotten und Buschmänner*. Stuttgart: Gustav Fischer.

Skotnes, P. 2007. *Claim to the Country: The archive of Lucy Lloyd and Wilhelm Bleek*. Johannesburg: Jacana Media.

Thring, T.S.A. and Weitz, F.M. 2006. 'Medicinal plant use in the Bredasdorp/Elim region of the Southern Overberg in the Western Cape Province of South Africa', *Journal of Ethnopharmacology*, 103(2): 261–275.

Van der Spuy, P. 1997. 'Silencing race and gender?' *South African Historical Journal*, 36(1): 256–263.

Wells, J.C. 1998. 'Eva's men: Gender and power in the establishment of the Cape of Good Hope, 1652–74', *The Journal of African History*, 39(3): 417–437.

Wynberg, R. 2004. 'Rhetoric, realism and benefit-sharing: Use of traditional knowledge of Hoodia species in the development of an appetite suppressant', *The Journal of World Intellectual Property*, 7(6): 851–876.

Yates, R., Manhire, A. and Parkington, J. 1993. 'Colonial era paintings in the rock art of the south-western Cape: Some preliminary observations', *Historical Archaeology in the Western Cape*, 7: 59–70. Goodwin Series.

Zaayman, C. 2019. 'Seeing what is not there: Figuring the anarchive'. PhD dissertation, Faculty of Humanities, University of Cape Town.

The bones

Diana Ferrus

the white-dried bones weep dusty tears
they have been naked for two hundred years.

if these are the gifts that your fathers left you
if these are the souvenirs that you now cling to
if these are the medals that their victories brought
if these are the trophies for which they have fought
then show me the lines where the battles were drawn
paint me the hills as it stood at dawn
recount the cries that slashed through the night
disclose your reason for that one-sided fight

if logic is the law that we live by
if evolution made our fortunes multiply
why do you hold on to bones that cannot talk
is it with their pain and agony with which you wish to walk
if abundance is only found in the grass-green fields
why hunger for crops that the scorched earth yields

the white-dried bones weep dusty tears
they have been naked for two hundred years.

Camissa

Khadija Tracey Carmelita Heeger

Coab, blood
Coab means blood or milk in khoekhoegowab
Blood is tricky, defiant
Blood is contradiction
It messes the historical rule with the exception
Savages the spaces between the lines and bibliography marked expert,
fouls the air where identity equals one bloodline
Once upon a time at the Cape someone distilled your roots down to rape
managed the magma and roughage transported on rivers, seas, across stone and sand to this thing

Coloured
It does not carry sweet in the name
Coloured means secret, means better, means worse
You live in the great sea of old ships with bloody secrets chained up in silent memory
You live in the great absence of Khoikhoi, San
You live inside the great mouth of too many roots in a place where the lie has become the truth
there the lords of history have cut-throat passions

Coloured
Nothing about it comes cheap

It comes with a debt too hefty and a tide that carries no good blood in it, they say
190 bloodlines fail truth in the present
And the stone star watches the children devil their eyes with divide 'n rule.

Coloured
It is the blood of untimely history
It is a woman spread legs akimbo across Buuren and Katzenellenbogen
She murmurs from the clouds the name, Camissa
She is a devastated monologue on a ghost river tongue salvaging the riddles of San, Khoena, the Xhosa, the tides of Nguni tribes leaning southwest to southeast
She is many skins of the //Ammaqua
She is //Ammaqua greeting the stolen, the buyers, the truants, the travellers of sea and land
She is //Ammaqua steeping rivers of blood in the Krooman, the indentured
Swaddling the drifters, Maroons, the Manillas, those refugees of labour
Lavishing the many, the needy, the hunted, the lost, the freed ...
She is Bengali indigene mix, her name is Angela
Her name is Anna. Daughter of Angela – her blood mitigated by marriage to a white man
She is unknown her name lost in the sea of perils
She arrives flavoured with the smell of Nil Manel plucked from the fields of Sri Lanka
She is a trinket stolen from the Kampong Meji, offering to the ocean where nothing returns
She is China compassing the Indian Ocean in ages before colonies
some 960 years AD in the times of Song and Laio Chinese feet touched the eastern coastline
She is moments with Khoikhoi and AmaXhosa suffering in invisible ink
Her name is Krotoa
Her name is Autshumao
Her name is Sarah, Susanna, Pieternella, Johanna, Amosijn, Nzinga, Elsie, Zara, Christina
Her name is Angola, Timor, Japan, Cirebon, Ethiopia
Her name is unknown, there will be no gravestone

Coloured
She is the tide that rolled in from every side of our great mountain and river collecting blood and words set in the stone tablet of Hoerikwaggo's Rosetta
she is the story of you and me before and beyond
from the cradle circle of the Thoathoa to the Keiskamma
come the feet planted in the soils of many places
come the children of //Hui !GAeb
unburdening these stories from labels aggressive with greedy history and the stink of dirty pure-blood ideas
now the time is here
when the parrot of lessons learned will speak unburdened truth into wombs
this is a story as old as all stories as we shake the devil from our eyes
this is the Ama, freedom walking strong across centuries
come the children //Hui !Gaeb
we are a multitude of voyages in blood.

call to art
Shelley Barry

for people with disabilities

if we want
to be part of this story
we have to write
our own chapters
we have to paint
our revolution across blank spaces
we have to dance
and stomp upon our space on the land
and make it sacred
we have to cross the stage
and speak from the centre
not the side, not the back
we have to capture our images
and rid ourselves
from the tinshaking-streetsitting-pityme-pictures

we have to embroider our history
on coloured cloth
and wave flags of freedom
we have to name this apartheid
crush it with our art
prise open a new way
with our pens/brushes/feet/voices/cameras
embracing the space we carve
the place we sculpt

5

Valuing the increased and invisible workload

Indigenous women, labour and the COVID-19 pandemic

Sharon Groenmeyer

INVISIBILISATION OF WOMEN'S WORK: A BRIEF HISTORICAL CONTEXT

As a feminist and indigenous[1] woman, and in line with Walklate's discussion on experiential knowledge (Walklate et al., 2011: 107) that globally, women perform many roles in the formal and informal economy because they are often employed in 'womanlike' (Groenmeyer, 2011) work as domestic workers, hairdressers, nurses, teachers, waste pickers and home caregivers. In precolonial societies,

---

1   Indigenous peoples are not a homogenous group, and there is no official definition of indigenous peoples. Informally, they are described as groups of people descending from the original inhabitants of a defined territory, who share distinct cultural, social, economic and political systems and institutions, and a will to preserve their identities, which are often linked to a collective relationship to lands and resources. Indigenousness lacks an official definition because the concept 'is not capable of a precise, inclusive definition which can be applied in the same manner to all regions of the world'. The international community decided, therefore, to adopt a 'flexible' version that would not require the adoption of a definition. This decision is reflected in the United Nations Declaration on the Rights of Indigenous Peoples (UNDRIP), which established the criterion of self-identification (art. 33). Since then, indigenous peoples officially have the right to determine their own identity and membership in accordance with their own customs and traditions. Online at: (https://www.un.org/esa/socdev/unpfii/documents/5session_factsheet1.pdf (Accessed 27 November 2020).

such as at the Cape, these roles were equally varied and included gathering *veldkos*, milking cattle and herd management. Even though precolonial indigenous societies were more egalitarian, caring for the ill using environmental knowledge was common practice, as is the case globally in indigenous communities. In contemporary times, globally, the balance of labour has shifted to women[2] in terms of them having to carry out at least twice more unpaid care work than men and COVID-19 has increased the burden for women by a further 30 per cent (FSG, 2020).

Pandemics are not new, and nursing the sick and aged are equally not new roles for indigenous women at the Cape. As Shell (1992) notes, the choices indigenous and enslaved women made and the constraints they lived under, shaped the families, households and society of the colonised Cape. The first evidence of care in Cape settler households by enslaved women was recorded in the smallpox epidemic in 1713. Historian Theal (cited in Van der Spuy, 1992: 11) noted that by then there was not a single settler household without someone sick or deceased, yet it was impossible to pay nurses, which meant the further exploitation of enslaved women. Feminist historian Van der Spuy critiques the invisibilisation of the enslaved women at the Cape by white male historians, who give them no recognition in historiography by discussing them in terms of 'fertility', 'breeding' and 'ratios'. The fact that reproduction was particularly low in enslaved people, has not been given adequate interpretation from the perspective of indigenous women; for example, see chapter 6 in this volume by Bam and Humphreys on the indigenous practice of abortion in precolonial times. Male historians have ascribed this phenomenon exclusively to 'poor diet' and the practice of 'wet nursing' in settler households (referring to Shell's 'wet nurse argument'); 'their economic role rendered negligible' (Shell, 1992: 43–44). Wet nurses were hired out to breastfeed children of colonisers in the 19th-century Cape (Shell, 1992: 11):

> Nevertheless, quite different types of primary evidence endorse both the existence and importance of the Cape wet nurse; for example, many of the requests for manumission of slave women mention that they were or had been nurses or even 'foster mothers', and were considered 'part of the family'.

---

2   This gendered imbalance of labour is not observed in colonial records of the precolonial period at the Cape.

Slave women were said to be 'constantly lactating' (Shell, 1992: 51), which could also have indicated their agency in the well-established precolonial indigenous practice of abortion,[3] not noted in such analyses. Van der Spuy does refer to the incident of the 'Khoisan' woman, Ana, who gave evidence of the use of coal and snake skin, which killed both the mother and the fetus (Shell, 1992: 54) as a fact of a possible means of resistance to enslavement (see also Christiansë, 2006). These are discussed by non-indigenous historians as 'underclass-deprived contraceptive practices', rather than as established indigenous culture long before the Cape colony was established. The 'nanny thesis' (Shell, 1992: 54) masked the economic role of enslaved women and their contribution to the formation of the Cape political economy. Part of this invisibilisation of indigenous and enslaved women has been the obsession of sexual relations with settler men without noting their often violent nature (Shell, 1992: 46), although Van der Spuy claims that precolonial 'Khoisan' societies were male-dominated (Shell, 1992: 46), which implied in this argument a continuation of a historical pattern of unproblematised patriarchy. However, Bam, Humphreys, Muthien and others in this and other volumes argue the contrary, that the Khoi and San were not historically patriarchal.

The invisibilisation of indigenous women in global colonial historiographies of political economies is commonplace. Part of this erasure is the neglect of analysis of their economic roles in disease management through their knowledge and care roles, and equally, the impact that diseases and epidemics have had on their lives. Historically, women globally have been affected by many epidemics including smallpox (see, for instance, Viljoen, 1995), cholera, Spanish flu, Ebola, Zika, HIV and AIDS, and recent outbreaks of SARS, swine flu and bird flu. The Ebola virus in West Africa increased the risk for women in particular, in terms of access to both maternal- and childcare, and in their roles as carers and as primary role players in traditional funeral rites (see Menéndez, et al., 2015: 130). There has been extensive scholarship and writing on the impact of HIV and AIDS on women's lives and livelihoods in Africa, dealing also with the impact on gendered power relations, unpaid care labour and the prevalence of associated gender-based violence (Jewkes et al., 2010).

Notwithstanding the fact that every epidemic affects both men and

---

3 Derived from the ubiquitous, everyday, oral tradition among women on the Cape Flats on which herb to use for which reproductive condition (my own experience).

women's ability to work or earn an income, the balance of power often shifts negatively towards women. For instance, many women rent rather than own their homes because of a lack of economic power. During the COVID-19 lockdown, these women were unable to earn income and pay rent, and many were asked for sex in lieu of rent by their landlords (Vallejo, 2020; Milne, 2020) Given the structural nature of racialised economies, it can be assumed that this form of exploitation and violence impacts particularly indigenous-descendant women globally. Given that women typically earn less than men, there is a growing risk that Black domestic workers will be sacrificed with consequent homelessness, leading to a drop in participation in both the formal and informal women's workforce. Initially during the COVID-19 lockdown, the City of Cape Town bused all homeless people to a makeshift camp in Strandfontein, a case discussed in chapter 6 in this volume. Several instances of rape and other gender-based violence were reported by girls and women interned in the camp. The camp was eventually closed due to humanitarian concerns, yet it continues to serve as an illustrative case study of the devastating impact of pandemics on the homeless (many of them indigenous women and their young daughters).

Past pandemics saw an increase in undesirable health outcomes for women and girls, especially a rise in teenage pregnancies and domestic violence. For instance, the United Nations Population Fund (UNFPA) (see Ayenew et al., 2020: 13) predicted in 2015 that the Ebola outbreak was projected to cause 120,000 preventable maternal deaths due to pressure of health services and fears among parents of contracting the disease in hospital (see Peterman et al., 2020). The same estimate has not yet been calculated in terms of both abortions and births during COVID-19 as hospitals are similarly associated with contracting the virus.

WHAT IS WOMEN'S WORK?

As indicated earlier, drawing on experiential theory, as a feminist and indigenous-descendant woman, I *know* that pandemics cause a health crisis; a health crisis causes a pause in everything – a pause that increases women's invisible workload.

But the fundamental question is, *what* is women's work? Women's work is changing with every epidemic because of the workload linked to paid and unpaid work. The formal–informal continuum changes every time we encounter an epidemic. For example, a woman may have formal employment as a concierge in a restaurant, but with lockdown, the same woman works at an informal job in her home making biscuits. Consequently, many women experience further invisibility and marginalisation, both in the public and private spheres, because the informal continuum grows longer without workplace security and benefits. Women typically earn less, save less and work in precarious jobs with little security protection. More than two million working-class women are classified as homemakers but say they would prefer a decent job to full-time unpaid work in the home (SAFTU, 2020). Before the COVID-19 pandemic, South Africa's official unemployment rate was 30 per cent, but in reality the level of unemployment was closer to 50 per cent just before lockdown (SAFTU, 2020). This raises a further set of questions around the significant decrease in 'decent work' opportunities for working-class women, and indigenous women in particular.

> Decent work sums up the aspirations of people in their working lives. It involves opportunities for work that is productive and delivers a fair income, security in the workplace and social protection for families, better prospects for personal development and social integration, freedom for people to express their concerns, organize and participate in the decisions that affect their lives and equality of opportunity and treatment for all women and men.[4]

As the COVID-19 pandemic upends work and home life, women's caring roles are likely to increase, and many women are likely to lose their jobs and shoulder greater unpaid workloads because schools and daycare centres are closed and will only reopen gradually. The gradual reopening of education and care centres will not solve problems, but rather compound them, by forcing women out of the labour market into unemployment or part-time jobs, including taking on more responsibility at home. Many who studied these episodes found that they had deep, long-lasting effects on gender equality, even though the pandemic could be an opportunity to value women's work (Abirafeh, 2020; Sewall 2020).

HISTORICAL TRAUMA OF PANDEMICS AND THE DISPROPORTIONATE IMPACT ON WOMEN

As indicated earlier, nursing everyone, especially the sick or aged, during pandemics is not new for women. Patriarchal social norms dictate

---

[4] International Labour Organisation, 'Decent Work', https://www.ilo.org/global/topics/decent-work/lang--en/index.htm (Accessed 8 April 2021).

the various roles men and women hold in society. Historically, women have been affected and have nursed the sick through many epidemics. Epidemics often accentuate many features and beliefs present in society, as well as accelerate processes already underway (Phillips, 2012: 10).

With the dismantling of Apartheid laws, South Africa became a signatory to the Convention on the Elimination of All Forms of Discrimination against Women (CEDAW) because the country promotes and protects non-discrimination and gender equality in its Constitution. South Africa is also a signatory to the International Labour Organisation (ILO) Convention No. 169 on the governance of indigenous people, the United Nations Universal Declaration on the Rights of Indigenous Peoples (UNDRIP), as well as Article 23 of the Universal Declaration of Human Rights (UDHR), which guarantees the right to, and conditions of, work, including equal pay for equal work.

When the South African Constitution was promulgated in 1996, its compilers used 1913 as the cut-off date for addressing the land question. However, Khoi and San activism over the past 20 years has ensured increased state recognition of land loss since the arrival of colonial settlers in the Cape in 1652. Nevertheless, the systematic loss of indigenous identity as a result of the dispossession of land is not part of the mainstream discourse (discussed in Richards, 2017). In the absence of land restitution, indigenous people look to workplace legislation like the Employment Equity Act of 1998, which was promulgated to give effect to section 9(3) of the Bill of Rights. The purpose of the Act is to ensure equity in the workplace by way of equal opportunities and fair labour practices. Workers adhere to the Basic Conditions of Employment Act 75 of 1997/2002 (BCEA). However, employers often circumvent the BCEA by, for example, paying employees commission rather than basic salaries, conditions that affect women workers in particular.

Although the South African Constitution officially recognises women's equality in society, women are more marginalised and invisible than ever. Global and domestic economic recessions and structural adjustment programmes have meant less fiscal investment in social welfare. As a result, South Africa has become increasingly inequitable, and women, many of whom are single mothers, face deep-seated, structural socio-economic problems, exacerbated by living in shacks or small government subsidised houses, or being homeless and living on the streets. In the informal urban sector, many women work as cashiers, domestic workers, waitresses and shop assistants. If the statistics are examined by sector, the majority of women (78 per cent) work in services, 22 per cent in manufacturing, and 1 per cent in agriculture (Rogan, 2019: 2). Women not only face gender-based discrimination in relation to the control and ownership of land, indigenous women also face triple discrimination on the basis of their gender (as women), their ethnicity (as indigenous peoples) and their economic class (economically poor). In terms of property ownership, 38.54 per cent of women own commercial property, 34.23 per cent are farm or smallholding owners, 43.05 per cent own free-standing home, 48.69 per cent own apartments and 49.03 per cent are holiday homeowners (Fourie: 2020).

Before the COVID-19 pandemic, 300 years of brutal colonialism resulted in land dispossession, 50 years of Apartheid capitalism and 30 years of neoliberal macro-economic policies exacerbated inequality and trauma due to dispossession and inequality. It is this historical trauma that Black and indigenous women experience. It is dehumanising and degrading, and subjects them to treatment as second-class human beings, despite the existence of national legislation that discourages such practices.

The Disaster Management Act (57/2002) announced on 27 March 2002 complicated issues further. The distinction between essential and non-essential workers made women essential unpaid workers in the home because of the differentials in power relations between men and women.

Women as essential and important workers

In precolonial times, the Khoi division of labour was not necessarily gendered, and usually tasks were chosen irrespective of sex or gender. However, in education it is generally described that most women and girls did domestic chores closer to the kraal and hunted for edible plants and small animals in the surrounding countryside. Women are therefore described as key in making decisions about the family's herd and took responsibility for butchering livestock and distributing the meat.[5] In colonial times, looking after the sick was linked to women's work.[6] This revelation or exposure still rings true today because the South African government, through its neoliberal policies, has informally (yet structurally) outsourced care services, which are now done by women in their homes.

---

5   Women in World History. Online at: http://chnm.gmu.edu/wwh/modules/lesson7/lesson7.php?s=0 (Accessed 13 July 2020.)

6   Women in World History: Cultural contact in southern Africa, Module 7.

From historical records, one reads that indigenous Khoi were treated differently by colonial authorities, especially the Khoi women who died of notifiable[7] diseases, such as smallpox during the 18th century (Arnott, 2019: 17). One of the reasons for the Khoi's lack of immunity to smallpox was their poor quality of life, because during the Dutch occupation, they fenced off the settlements thus preventing indigenous people and their cattle from accessing clean drinking water (Shell and Guelke, 1992). The vulnerable were considered a nuisance. The sexual division of labour continued. Many indigenous women worked as independent washerwomen at Platteklip Stream on Table Mountain and used this opportunity to socialise, trade and share with one another (Arnott, 2019: 21). The mountain washerwomen were also critical links in the escape routes of the enslaved. These anecdotes are gleaned from archaeological records, which are few; this silence indicates that an underclass of women arose in the colonial period outside of the legal framework of labour relations. Following statutes like Ordinance 50 of 1828 and the Slave Emancipation Act of 1833, historians find that free Khoi women, while confined to 'women-like work', were denied welfare services and became homeless. This ordinance which freed Khoi women from slavery, did not recognise them as knowledge bearers of rituals and medicinal herbs in the local environment, let alone their invaluable contribution to building the colonial pharmaceutical industry.

Today woman's work is classified as either essential or non-essential. In the formal services sector (essential work) many women work as nurses and teachers on the frontline. Women may work as managers or decision-makers, but the sexual division of labour continues, and the majority of women perform 'women-like' work, much of it considered 'non-essential'.

With the lockdown came regulations linked to the Disaster Management Act (57/2002), which restricted movement, and there was a growing risk that female workers were being sacrificed with consequent unemployment and homelessness, leading to a drop in both formal and informal participation in the workforce. Many domestic workers had their working week cut from five to two days, or no work at all, as employers preferred domestic workers to live on the premises because many women travel to work on public transport, a vector of infection

---

7 Notifiable illnesses compel medical officials and others to notify government of the presence of an illness to stem infections and pandemics.

and transmission. However, many domestic workers have families of their own. Furthermore, the hours worked per week by informal workers decreased by half. This was confirmed by speakers who mentioned that 'decreases in typical working hours were particularly reduced for women and workers in self-employment and for informal casual workers'.[8]

Domestic workers care for the elderly and children but, without their assistance, these additional chores fall on the women in these households, since women are expected to care for the elderly, the young and the sick. Entrenched social norms around care work mean that women bear much of this additional care load. Given that elderly people are more vulnerability to the virus, healthcare services for the elderly were dramatically scaled back, which created a double burden of unpaid household and care work.

In the informal sector in urban areas, casual female workers have been calling their trade unions because they have been intimidated and threatened by their employers with reduced work and unemployment. This virus appears to have given employers an opportunity to dismiss workers, especially women workers.[9] However, negotiating job guarantees in terms of Article 23 of the Universal Declaration of Human Rights states that everyone has the right to work (Fraser et al., 2020: 3).

In rural areas, where Department of Labour offices do not exist or are few, many farmers closed the harvest season when the announcement for lockdown Level 5 was made and workers were unable to file for unemployment grants or other benefits. In the Klapmuts rural area of the Western Cape province, women farmworkers experienced a reduction in hours of work. Many farmworkers considered this action by the farm owners as an unfair labour practice. However, labour offices were shut and workers had to rely on non-governmental offices for support. While there was a moratorium on evictions during the lockdown, when lockdown regulations were eased to Level 3, farm owners continued forced evictions or constructive evictions by cutting electricity and water supplies to households.[10]

---

8   The National Income Dynamics Study (NIDS) Coronavirus Rapid Mobile Survey (CRAM), which assesses the impact of the COVID-19 pandemic on employment and welfare of a representative sample of 7,000 South Africans. The study surveyed participants between 7 May and 27 June.

9   Simunye Workers Advice office (for casual workers) Zoom meeting with the Women's Legal Centre (Accessed 15 July 2020).

10 Women Legal Centre, Food Security during COVID-19: voices from below on 30 June 2020 and Womxn Working on the frontline during COVID-19 Zoom meeting on 30

Men and women experience the negative effects of economic crises differently. In the short term, male workers are more affected by unemployment, but women bear the brunt of austerity and cutbacks in public services such as social grants, free or subsidised healthcare and unemployment insurance. However, a guaranteed job offers each person access to work that allows them to live with dignity. Guaranteed employment would enable women who rent their homes to pay their rents during the national shutdowns and not be asked for sex or payment-in-kind by their landlords. This health crisis raises many questions of the Department of Labour to create awareness of the virus and the rights of workers.

Gendered essential unpaid work

Work was destabilised in the paid economy, but unpaid work for women increased. Women working full-time were logging 10.1 hours per day or 70.7 hours per week on housework and caregiving, while men in the same situation logged 51.5 hours per week. The majority of single parents logged even longer hours, which included grocery shopping.[11] This virus added an additional task to women's unpaid work because patriarchal social relations encouraged the sexual division of labour to flourish.

All schools, early childhood development centres and childcare facilities were shut, and domestic and childcare workers were unable to work in private households. Globally, governments closed schools to slow the spread of disease in the face of the pandemic. While during precolonial times, indigenous women at the Cape played the key role in the education of children, with the advent of colonialism, this role shifted significantly to an unsustainable one, particularly visibilised by the current impact of COVID-19. While schools were closed, it was the mothers – as primary carers – who had to manage their children's distance or online learning. Many women struggled with their children's education, which they received on their cell phones. Many women who work outside the home, were forced to work remotely online during the day, so they could care for the children. Ensuring that children did their learning daily became the mother's responsibility. Whether it was

---

June and 15 July, 2020.

11 'Women are maxing-out and burning-out', Surveymonkey Poll, 4/13/20 – 4/17/20 (findings from a survey of 3117 adults over 18 years of age living in the United States). https://media.sgff.io/sgff_r1eHetbDYb/2020-05-07/1588873077242/women-are-maxing-out-during-covid-19_1.pdf (Accessed 8 April 2021).

a Zoom call, WhatsApp messages on a cell phone or study material dropped at the door, the primary caregiver now managed or taught their children at home. During lockdown, working at home forced teachers to choose between paid work and their families. As teachers, they had to alternate between asking pupils to repeat themselves and snapping at their families to keep quiet. Female teachers struggled to maintain focus on their schoolwork as their own children needed help with assignments while their own household chores piled up.

Gendered homelessness and violence: The case study of Strandfontein Camp

At the start of lockdown, the City of Cape Town voluntarily and involuntarily transported many homeless people to a rudimentary tented camp in Strandfontein (Charles, 2020) Local permanent residents objected to the camp for homeless people on their doorsteps (McKaiser, 2020). Homeless people were fenced inside the camp, which was under constant security surveillance.

The fenced-in tented site had three main large tents: 'The Haven' for street-based people from the metropolitan area, 'The Ubuntu Tent' for street people from the Strand area, and 'The Oasis Tent' for street people from Muizenberg to Fish Hoek. The three tents were overcrowded and there was no social distancing, as determined by global and national COVID-19 regulations. National regulations stipulated that there not be more than 50 people per tent, but in The Haven Tent, there were more than 600 people. A few days later, markings were made on the floors to indicate social distances (Cruywagen, 2020). The South African Human Rights Commission noted that female occupants reported feeling unsafe and asked for a female-only tent separate from the men. Several rapes of girls and women were reported. Many other incidents of gender-based violence were never reported. Still under investigation is the rape of an 18-year-old girl, which occurred at the Strandfontein camp on Good Friday in April 2020 (IOL News, 2020).

Many camp occupants mentioned that the lack of safety measures at the camp created fear and anxiety among inhabitants. Mattresses arrived days after camp residents were transported there, and a few blankets were handed to people who slept on the ground. Social media (IOL News, 2020) showed queues of women and men waiting for food or to use the ablution facilities. Thus, the fear and intimidation were exacerbated by the authorities, who pretended to concentrate on abiding by the health restrictions and overlooked the welfare and safety issues raised by the camp occupants. As shown in the Strandfontein case study, the pandemic highlighted the levels of inequality in housing and healthcare of ordinary citizens in the country.

The pandemic also highlighted the crisis in food sovereignty. During lockdown Level 5, the army was in the streets preventing neighbours from supporting one another, including sharing food (see chapter 4 in this volume on precolonial sharing of food and the central role indigenous women played in this social etiquette.) State violence was high and there were no plans to feed communities. Often frontline workers, who were nurses or doctors, would come home from work to share stories of empty pots and no food parcels. Long queues of women and children forced women-headed, non-governmental organisations to feed the queues of hungry people, many of them children.[12] While there are many reasons for handing out food parcels, the vulnerable elderly received food parcels via 'knock and drop'.[13] Humanitarian relief by government was not forthcoming for the majority of residents living on the Cape Flats as social media showed long queues of hungry men, women and children at often impromptu community kitchens. Moreover, global mass unemployment caused the world's highest levels of income inequality, which exacerbated hunger. Locally, food prices increased, somewhat alleviated by a COVID-19 special grant of R350 per month during lockdown for unemployed people who were not on existing social grants. This modest financial relief would not buy a basket of nutritious food for a family. Women, who participated in the Women's Legal Centre Zoom meetings, cried because they had to tell their hungry children that they would have 'to go to bed on an empty stomach'.[14] While many families received food parcels during lockdown, these food parcels, as relief, are not sustainable because local economies have to be rebuilt by communities to grow food gardens.

Pandemics have historically orphaned and impoverished many children globally. In South Africa, with COVID-19 during 2020, the closure of schools increased hunger because feeding schemes could not operate; food security became a significantly highlighted right to dignity and emphasised the considerable importance of 'education with

---

12 Women's Legal Centre, Zoom meeting on 30 June 2020.

13 Women's Legal Centre, Zoom meeting on 30 June 2020.

14 Women's Legal Centre food security: Voices from below. Zoom meeting on 30 June 2020.

production' that should form an essential part of the school curriculum going forward (Shillington, 2020).

Due to COVID-19, schools in Africa were closed for six to eight months during 2020. In the wake of Ebola, orphans whose parents had died of the disease were taken in by extended family networks, and the quality of care provided to each child in resource-scarce environments declined. With the outbreak of the H1N1 flu epidemic, schools closed across a range of diverse countries. Even short-term school closures can impact children's long-term opportunities and create demographic shifts, because many girls do not return to school. Many older girls care for their younger siblings because their mothers have to find employment outside the home. In many settings, women and girls living in poverty encounter pressures to engage in intercourse with sexual partners in exchange for financial or in-kind support, ranging from transportation to food and clothing. In South Africa there is a phenomenon of much older men purchasing sex from girls and very young women, men called 'blessers', with concomitant HIV infections between the older men and younger girls and women. Even some members of the country's Cabinet are said to be 'blessers', not unlike male leaders of other countries with their wives and mistresses. Probably due to lockdown, pandemics also drive increased fertility rates, and early onset of sexuality for girls, which in turn creates a cascade of undesirable health outcomes for women and girls, especially a rise in teenage pregnancies and domestic violence.

During the Ebola outbreak in 2014, adolescent pregnancies in parts of Sierra Leone increased. In Sierra Leone, the lack of intervention to ensure out-of-school girls spent time engaged in productive activities with other girls within their age group meant time spent with older men increased significantly, pregnancies outside of marriage increased, and girls' enrolment in school decreased once schools reopened (Peterman et al., 2020: 13). In the longer term, early marriage and adolescent pregnancy are associated with increased threats of violence, both during pregnancy and over a lifetime (Peterman et al., 2020: 13). Taken together, while increases in risk due to demographic shifts in mortality and fertility (transitions to sexual behaviour) are often overlooked in developed countries, underlying vulnerabilities, particularly in developing countries, make this an important area of mitigation, particularly for young children and adolescent girls.

Conclusion: Pandemics redefine women's work

Historically under capitalism and now under neocolonialism, pandemics have revealed global inequalities, especially the sexual division of labour. Due to the impact of colonialism, capitalism and Apartheid, many indigenous women have become intergenerationally homeless and deskilled outside the social relations of labour relations. Exclusion and isolation from social relations for Black women mean that pandemics appear to have deepened the existing social division of labour. The division between the public and private spheres continues. Many women continue to work as domestic workers or carers in private homes as a form of employment. While many women consider formal equality as a right, substantive equality disappears when health pandemics occur.

Job guarantee schemes would also provide work, albeit for a short period, but would protect the right to work, as stipulated in the South African Constitution, and enable working people to live with dignity, by decreasing the risk of homelessness and unemployment for women.

As the economy opens up, local municipalities would be able to allocate work time to unemployed work seekers, including the homeless, for a period of time so they can plan accordingly. 'Education with production', as part of their retraining, would add skills to unemployed work-seekers' bucket of abilities on offer for employment.

Pandemics and the associated socially inequitable resource management in contemporary capitalist societies can be blamed for many of the deepest socio-economic problems, such as the extreme violence, particularly against women and girls, as well as drug and alcohol abuse that afflicts so many communities.

The silence of the archival records is deafening because the question, '*what is women's work?*' remains problematic. As indigenous women, we have lost the security of livelihoods and our agency in intergenerational environmental and knowledge management since precolonial times, and we need to explore ways and innovative methods to reclaim that important space as *valued* women's work.

References

Abirafeh, L. 2020. 'Patriarchy and the pandemic: rethinking "women's work" in a post-covid world', 29 May. Online at: https://www.mei.edu/publications/patriarchy-and-pandemic-rethinking-womens-work-post-covid-world (Accessed 19 November 2020).

Arnott, T. 2019. 'Gendered Silence: Female slave imports and Khoikhoi women in the Dutch Cape Colony,' Indian Ocean World Centre Working Paper Series, No. 6.

Ayenew, B., Pandey, D., Yitayew, M., Etana, D., Binay Kumar, P. and Verma, N. 2020. 'Risk for surge maternal mortality and morbidity during the ongoing corona virus pandemic', *MedLife Clinics*, 2(1): 1012.

Cape Slavery & Indigene Heritage. *Camissa People*. Online at: https://camissapeople.wordpress.com/2014/03/31/t (Accessed 25 July 2020).

Casale, D, and Posel, D. 2020. 'Gender and the early effects of the COVID-19 crisis in the paid and unpaid economies in South Africa'. In *The National Income Dynamics Study – Coronavirus Rapid Mobile Survey* (NIDS-CRAM). School of Economics and Finance, University of the Witwatersrand, 15 July 2020. Online at: https://cramsurvey.org/ (Accessed 15 July 2020).

Charles, M. 2020. 'Concern after Cape homeless camp out in Strandfontein'. Online at: https://www.iol.co.za/capeargus/news/concern-after-cape-homeless-camp-out-in-strandfontein-area-48123402. (Accessed 3 July 2020).

Christiansë, Y. 2006. *Unconfessed*. Cape Town: Kwela.

Cruywagen, V. 2020. 'Strandfontein homeless camp poses health threat, doctors warn', *Daily Maverick*. Online at: https://www.dailymaverick.co.za/article/2020-04-20-strandfontein-homeless-camp-poses-health-threat-doctors-warn/#gsc.tab=0.

Dieng, R.S. 2020. 'Tired all the time: Caring, parenting and home working during Covid-19'. Online at: : https//www.coronatimes.net/parenting-home-working-covid-19/ (Accessed 25 July 2020).

Eyford, R.C. 2006. 'Quarantined within a new colonial order: The 1876–1877 Lake Winnipeg smallpox epidemic', *Journal of the Canadian Historical Association Revue de la Société historique du Canada*, 17(1). Online at: https://id.erudit.org/iderudit/016102ar (Accessed 25 July 2020).

Fourie, B. 2020 ' Property owners by women surges in SA'. Online at: https://www.iol.co.za/lifestyle/home-garden/property-ownership-by-women-surges-in-sa-9574cb33-cb32-42ec-9407-3bd84a91d051 (Accessed 18 November 2020).

Fraser, N., Neiman, S., Mouffe C., Sassen, S., Muller, J., Rodrik, D., Pikkety, T, Zucman, G. and Chang, H. 2020. 'Humans are not resources. Coronavirus shows why we must democratise work', *The Guardian*, 18 May. Online at: https://www.theguardian.com/commentusfree/2020/may/15/human-resources-coronavirus-democrtise-work-health-lives-market?CMP=Share-andriod (Accessed 25 July 2020).

FSG. 2020. 'Seven issues affecting women and girls during Covid-19 pandemic'. Online at: https://www.fsg.org/sites/default/files/7%20issues%20affecting%20women%20during%20covid-19_0.pdf (Accessed 17 June 2020).

Groenmeyer, S. 2011. 'Women and social policy: Experiences of some Black working women in contemporary post-apartheid South Africa'. PhD dissertation, Norwegian University of Science and Technology, NTNU, Trondheim, Norway.

International Labour Organisation (ILO). 2002. 'National Labour Law Profile: South Africa contribution'. Online at: https://www.ilo.org/ifpdial/information-resources/national-labour-law-profiles/WCMS_158919/lang--en/index.htm (Accessed 29 June 2020).

IOL News. 2020. 'Cops investigating rape of 18-year-old'. Online at: https://www.iol.co.za/news/south-africa/western-cape/cops-investigating-rape-of-18-year-old-girl-at-strandfontein-temporary-shelter-46587343 (Accessed 20 February 2021).

Jenkins, T. 2020. 'Report Monitor C-19 Report', 12 April: T. Jenkins (member of an independent task team comprising medical health, legal, social services, gender experts, and civil society invited by the South African Human Rights Commission to report on the relocation camp at Strandfontein Sports Complex).

Jewkes, R.K., Dunkle, K., Nduna, M. and Shai, N. 2010. 'Intimate partner violence, relationship power inequity, and incidence of HIV infection in young women in South Africa: A cohort study', *The Lancet*, 376(9734): 41–48.

Lebus, F., Amalya, L., Rathi, S. and Gupta, H., 2020 'Seven issues affecting women and girls during COVID 19 Pandemic - and What you can do about them'. Online at: FSG/7%20issues%20affecting%20women%20during%20covid-19_0.pdf (Accessed 29 June 2020).

Marson, F.A.L. and Ortega, M.M. 2020. 'COVID-19 in Brazil'. *Pulmonology*, 26(4): 241–244.

McKaiser, E. 2020. 'Human Rights Commission criticises Cape Town's Strandfontein site', Cape Talk. Online at: www.capetalk.co.za/podcasts/125/the-best-of-the-eusebius-mckaister-show/313842/human-rights-commission-report-criticises-cape-towns-strandfontien-site (Accessed 25 July 2020).

Mellet, P.T. 2020. *The Lie of 1652: A decolonised history of land.* Cape Town: Tafelberg.

Menéndez, C., Lucas, A., Munguambe, K. and Langer, A. 2015. 'Ebola crisis: The unequal impact on women and children's health', *The Lancet Global Health*, 3(3): e130.

Milne, A. 2020. ' "I had no choice': Sex for rent rises with coronavirus poverty', Reuters, 21 May. Online at: https://in.reuters.com/article/us-britain-housing-harassment-trfn/i-had-no-choice-sex-for-rent-rises-with-coronavirus-poverty-idUSKBN22X2N7 (Accessed 17 November 2020).

National Income Dynamics Study-Coronavirus Rapid Mobile Survey (NIDS-CRAM). 2020. Online at: https://cramsurvey.org/s (Accessed 25 July 2020).

Peterman, A., Potts, A., O'Donnell, M, Thomspon, K., Saha, N., Oertelt-Prigione, S. and Van Gelder, N. 2020. 'Pandemics and Violence against Women and Children', Centre for Global Development Working Paper, No 528, April 2020.

Phillips, H. 2012. *Plague, Pox and Pandemics: A Jacana Pocket history of epidemics in South Africa.* Johannesburg: Jacana Media.

Redolfi, G., Pikramenou, N. and Algora, R.G. 2019. 'Raising indigenous women's voices for equal rights and self-determination', *New England Journal of Public Policy*, 31(2). Online at: https://scholarworks.umb.edu/nejpp/vol31/iss2/9 (Accessed 24 June 2020).

Richards, R. 2017. *Baastards or Humans: The unspoken history of Coloured people.* Cape Town: Indaba Publishing.

Rogan, M. 2019. 'Informal Workers in Urban South Africa: A statistical snapshot', WIEGO Statistical Brief, No 19.

Senthilingam, M. 2020. *Outbreaks and Epidemics: Battling infection and measles to coronavirus.* London: Icon Books.

Sewall, Rebecca. 'The pandemic brings the value of women's unpaid work into focus', 9 April 2020. Online at: https://www.creativeassociatesinternational.com/insights/the-pandemic-brings-the-value-of-womens-unpaid-work-into-focus/ (Accessed 8 April 2021).

Shell, R. 1992. *Tender Ties: Women and the slave household, 1652–1834*, Collected Seminar Papers, Institute of Commonwealth Studies, Vol. 42, pp. 1–33.

Shell, R. and Guelke, L. 1992. 'Landscape of conquest: Frontier water alienation and Khoikhoi strategies of survival, 1652–1780', *Journal of Southern African Studies*, 18(4): 803–824.

Shillington, K. 2020. *Patrick van Rensburg: Rebel, visionary and radical educationist.* Johannesburg: Wits University Press.

South African Federation of Trade Unions (SAFTU). 2020. 'SAFTU response to mass unemployment that has become a pandemic', 24 June, Debate forum. https://saftu.org.za/saftu-response-to-mass-unemployment-that-has-become-a-pandemic (Accessed 20 November 2020).

Tusk, B. 'The Rebuilders: Women are burning out from 71 hours of home labor a week', https://www.fastcompany/90504726/in-defense-0f-big-pharma-the =-innovation-engine-we-love-to-hatedated 14 May 2020. (Accessed 25 July 2020.)

Vallejo, J. 2020. 'Sex for rent schemes targeting tenants struggling financially during coronavirus shutdown', *The Independent*, 18 April. Online at: https://www.independent.co.uk/news/world/americas/sex-rent-landlords-coronavirus-tenants-a9471801.html (Accessed 17 November 2020).

Van der Spuy, P. 1996. '"What, then, was the sexual outlet for Black males?" A feminist critique of quantitative representations of women slaves at the Cape of Good Hope in the eighteenth century', *Kronos*, 43–56.

Viljoen, R.S. 1995. 'Disease and society: VOC Cape Town, its people and the smallpox epidemics of 1713, 1755 and 1767', *African Historical Review*, 27(1): 22–45.

Walker, C. 1990. *Women and Gender in Southern Africa to 1945*. London: James Currey.

Walklate, S. and Mythen, G. 2011. 'Beyond risk theory: Experiential knowledge and 'knowing otherwise', *Criminology and Criminal Justice*, 11(2): 99–113.

# 6

Decolonising the representation of indigenous women at the Cape during COVID-19

June Bam and Robyn Humphreys

The gendered global impact of COVID-19

Globally, by 30 November 2020, there were over 62 million confirmed cases of COVID-19, including 1.5 million deaths reported to the World Health Organization (WHO).[1] In Africa, the numbers have been significantly low (Harding, 2020). Of concern is that people of African descent in the diaspora have been disproportionately affected (Dune et al., 2020: 46) – a condition ascribed to poor access to health services and the already existing comorbidities as a result of historical disadvantages in these societies; a situation that is 'magnifying racial health inequalities' globally. In Brazil, indigenous people's deaths due to COVID-19 have been attributed to lack of access to medical care (Marson et al., 2020: 242) and the illegal exploitation of their land (Cupertino et al., 2020: 609). Similarly, the Maori people and Aboriginal Australians were more adversely affected by the 1918 Spanish flu pandemic (Power et al., 2020: 2737) due to displacement, forced assimilation, discrimination, exploitation, erasure of knowledge and culture, genocide and trauma. Although South Africa has not provided formal disaggregated statistics of the pandemic (as a result of

---

1   Online at: https://covid19.who.int/ (Accessed 30 November 2020).

its historically sensitive nature with regard to racialised demographics), it can be safely assumed that the majority of those adversely affected economically (because of their structural oppression, household and caring responsibilities within families and communities) would be Black indigenous women (in their inclusivity), as is the case globally.

The biggest impact of COVID-19 on the global economy has been on small business and the informal economic sector, where women have often been employed, including as unpaid carers in families and for domestic work. As a United Nations Women's report (2020) observes, women are bearing the brunt of COVID-19 in terms of economic impact, and of illness and the significant increase in domestic violence; 70 per cent of first respondents in the pandemic are women (Azcona et al., 2020). In South Africa, by April 2020, domestic violence reports had increased by 30 per cent compared to the same period in 2019.[2] This, the UN Women's report recognises, is a threat to attaining the 2030 Sustainable Development Goal 3 (ensure healthy lives and promote wellbeing), increasing poverty for already marginalised women in their respective societies globally – fewer resources, unsafe work environments and restrictions on mobility.[3] The impact of COVID-19 is, therefore, decidedly gendered. The UN prediction of the future poverty gap by 2030 is 232 million from 206 million pre-COVID for women and those living in poverty, while it is estimated that the figure for men will be 221 million. It is predicted that it could push 96 million people into extreme poverty by 2021. Peterman et al. (2020: 18) speak of 'intersecting vulnerabilities' visibilised by COVID-19 and relevant to indigenous women and other marginalised groups. Choice of termination of pregnancies also decreased as priorities during lockdown.[4]

Many women have lost livelihoods as a result of the pandemic, and do not enjoy social protection (pension, healthcare and unemployment insurance), a problem that will widen the gender poverty gap. More women have lost their jobs and the most impacted industries (food, retail and entertainment) have affected more women. South Africa lost three million jobs during lockdown (Staff writer, BusinessTech, 2020),

---

2   Doctors Without Borders, 7 April 2020. Online at: See https://www.msf.org.za/news-and-resources/latest-news/south-africa-sexual-and-gender-based-violence-concern-during-COVID (Accessed 15 November 2020).

3   See also https://www.unwomen.org/en/news/in-focus/women-and-the-sdgs/sdg-3-good-health-well-being (Accessed 8 November 2020).

4   See also https://www.msf.org.za/news-and-resources/latest-news/south-africa-sexual-and-gender-based-violence-concern-during-COVID (Accessed 15 November 2020).

two-thirds of which belonged to women (Tswanya, 2020), which has entrenched economic dependency on their male partners or other family members. As a result, many women have remained trapped in abusive relationships. Domestic violence was dubbed as South Africa's second pandemic in the midst of COVID-19 (Brown-Luthango, 2020). During global lockdowns, many domestic workers were abandoned by their employers due to a perceived risk of infection. Women also endured increased labour at home due to the closure of educational facilities. It is estimated that an additional 11 million girls may leave school by the end of the COVID-19 crisis,[5] putting them at increased risk of poverty and gender-based violence (see Oleschuk, 2020).

Indigenous women globally (of 476 million people) (ILO, 2020) will be at the centre of this devastating impact, as an already marginalised group with increased care responsibilities in extended families. Additionally, in the face of climate change, indigenous women suffer the significant impact on biodiversity loss, environmental degradation, loss of small-scale farming and food security. As a result of COVID-19, these women face increased homelessness, stigma, criminalisation, loss of children to social services, police brutality, racism, domestic violence,[6] femicide, social isolation due to lockdown, lack of sanitation, increased risk of infections and inadequate access to medical care and financial support.[7] During the pandemic, President Ramaphosa formally called for periods of national mourning for victims of COVID-19 and gender-based violence (Mlaba, 2020).

Lockdown also impacts the usual sharing of resources to retain food security networks. In other African countries, the impact has been equally devastating for certain indigenous communities. For example, COVID-19 has led to the closure of livestock markets by the Maasai

---

5   UN Women, 'Covid-19 and its economic toll on women: The story behind the numbers'. Online at: https://www.unwomen.org/en/news/stories/2020/9/feature-covid-19-economic-impacts-on-women (Accessed 1 April 2021).

6   A 2009 study showed that the highest incidents of femicide due to intimate partner violence were among 'Coloureds' in South Africa and 'Coloured' men had the highest perpetration rate.

7   Canadian Feminist Alliance for International Action (FAFIA) and Dr. Pamela Palmater, Chair in Indigenous Covernance at Ryerson University, 'Impact of the Covid-19 Pandemic on Indigenous Women and Girls in Canada', submitted for the report to the General Assembly on the impact of Covid-19 on indigenous people, 19 June 2020. http://fafia-afai.org/wp-content/uploads/2020/06/P.-Palmater-FAFIA-Submission-COVID19-Impacts-on-Indigenous-Women-and-Girls-in-Canada-June-19-2020-final.pdf (Accessed 8 November 2020).

of Kenya; other indigenous groups (especially women who design and make crafts and goods) have been impacted due to their reliance on tourism, which has been significantly impacted by global lockdowns. In countries like Chad, the challenge of communication in English as the COVID-19 hegemonic language[8] has been highlighted. For example, people do not know why borders are closed, with the result that they are disadvantaged in accessing food, and this impacts mostly on women. For example, women cannot sell milk at the markets and milk cannot be stored without refrigeration because it goes sour. When they are unable to sell their milk, they cannot feed the children, the sick and the elderly. It is the women in Chad who go to the mountain and nomadic pastoralists are also affected. Cattle are dying, which impacts food security, creating conflict in communities. The animals that die, in turn create other diseases in these affected communities. According to the Maasai activist, Agnes Leina, lockdown has created food insecurity because of its impact on pastoralism.

Children are learning online globally, but this has not been easy in African countries during lockdown. The only way children can learn in Kenya, according to Leina, is via mobile phones, even in villages. COVID-19 lockdowns and protocols are alien to African customs and cultures, especially with regard to social distancing and the now-forbidden way of greeting elders (handshakes are traditionally a sign of respect). In addition, communities do not have access to masks, and some have limited access to clean water and soap. Indigenous schools in African countries have access to electricity but no ready access to the internet.[9] According to Kaniyenke Sena,[10] COVID-19 has been chiefly associated in Africa with cities, but it is spreading to rural areas where there is little awareness. Women are at the centre of these impact factors, as a result of their central roles in caring for the elderly, families, schooling and small-scale farming.

---

8   Chad's official languages of French and Arabic are marginalised, for example, by the World Health Organization's main website, which is in English. See also https://www.ilo.org/wcmsp5/groups/public/---ed_norm/---normes/documents/genericdocument/wcms_739937.pdf (Accessed 8 November 2020).

9   IPACC: Podcast, The impact of Covid 19 on indigenous people in Africa. https://www.ipacc.org.za/blog/2020/07/27/podcast-the-impact-of-covid-19-on-indigenous-women-in-africa/ (Accessed 1 April 2021).

10 IPACC: Podcast, The impact of Covid 19 on indigenous people in Africa. https://www.ipacc.org.za/blog/2020/07/27/podcast-the-impact-of-covid-19-on-indigenous-women-in-africa/ (Accessed 1 April 2020).

THE PLACE AND ROLE OF WOMEN IN PRECOLONIAL CAPE

Since precolonial times women's roles have been sustained to some degree, and changed substantially. From exploring oral history and oral traditions on the Cape Flats,[11] supported by accounts in colonial texts (travellers' accounts), there emerges a different representation of indigenous women at the Cape and their place in social formations and as health managers. There are many misrepresentations of the place of indigenous women in the early precolonial Cape. For example, today it is widely believed and accepted that males of descendant communities are inherently violent. Yet, gender-based violence in the form of rape was severely punished in precolonial times at the Cape, which included the confiscation of property, and if the victim was a child, it was punished by the death penalty (Schapera, 1951: 242).

The sacrosanct role of women in the precolonial Cape household is commonly observed as 'supreme' and also with regard to the education of children. She could even forbid her husband to enter her home. She had her own property in cattle (inherited from her parents and through marriage), and this property was considered equally sacrosanct over which her husband had no authority. 'Each wife had her own hut, in which she lived with her unmarried children. She was regarded as the mistress of the hut ... and so far from being dominated by her husband appears to have had a good deal of independence' (Schapera, 1933: ix). Even if he traded his own cattle, he usually consulted his wife first. During his absence, she had the authority over his herds. She was in charge of all food provisions and the sharing of them according to needs in the community (Schapera, 1951: 251).

The Cape Khoi were, therefore, often described as the 'early socialists' and 'communists' because of the way in which they approached property and resources according to needs in the community – especially regarding the use of land with all members of a 'tribe' enjoying equal customary rights (Schapera, 1951: 319). Theft was even punishable by the death penalty and greed was considered offensive (Schapera, 1951: 320). Grevenbroek noted in 1695 (Schapera, 1933: 273) the 'generosity' of the Cape Khoi (particularly women) in how they 'all alike delight in this communion of goods ... Let the Christians learn from the natives to vie with one another in

---

[11] Research by Bam over the past four years on the Cape Flats and southern Cape (Mossel Bay and Kranshoek).

well-doing.' As observed by Ten Rhyne in 1686 (Schapera, 1933: 135, fn 27), women also played a central role politically in leading peace talks among Cape Khoi leaders. Krotoa herself was notable for this role at Van Riebeeck's fort in the early Dutch colonised peninsula of the Cape of Good Hope.

Women's use of herbs and roots as medicines is a well-established health practice among Khoi and San descendant women at the Cape since precolonial times, although considerably still at the margins of mainstream Western practices. In 1649 Tavernier observed that 'they ... have a special knowledge of herbs, which they know how to use against the sicknesses from which they suffer ... they can bring about a cure in a short time by means of herbs which they know how to select. Of nineteen sick who were on our ship, fifteen were put in the hands of these ... and in less than fifteen days they were all completely cured ... [they] go to seek for herbs according to the nature of his wound or ulcer ...' (Raven-Hart, 1967: 179–180). The use of cabbage for the sick, as observed in the 1600s, is still commonly practised by indigenous women at the Cape (see Schapera, 1933: 57). They were determined to keep their secret remedies to themselves and not share them with Europeans, such as how to cure colic quickly with 'a certain aromatic root' and other remedies that involved 'dacha' (referring here to cannabis, dagga or marijuana). Even midwifery practices involving the umbilical cord were kept secret – practices among women still common place on the Cape Flats today (see Schapera, 1933: 153).

Abortion was 'not infrequently practiced' through the use of dassiepis (rock rabbit urine) (Schapera, 1951: 260) – frequently still used today – when a woman did not want a child. Ten Rhyne noted in 1686 (Schapera, 1933: 147) that Cape Khoi women were 'sufficiently skillful in binding and severing nature's links ... they invoke the aid of a plant of wonderful efficiency, which happily expels the foetus'. Ten Rhyne complained that he could not purchase this plant 'at any price' as it was a jealously guarded secret kept by the indigenous women. 'Their reply always was that they were forbidden by law to share it' (Schapera, 1933: 147). Ten Rhyne noted in 1686 (Schapera, 1933: 151–153), 'They get rid of rheumatism ... know ... vegetable remedies ... these cannot be got from them for love or money ... they are determined to keep their secret remedies to themselves.' Abortion and contraception were common practices globally among indigenous women, 'administered by grandmothers and aunties'; women were the 'medicine people' and the plant knowledge was passed down generationally (Monchalin, 2020: 2). These precolonial gendered practices were not spiritually judged (Monchalin, 2020: 3), as came to be the practice during Christian missionary rule at the Cape. Indigenous reproductive health knowledge was strongly established by the time of colonial invasion.

Women had profound agency in their own health management and in sustaining others. The binding of the abdomen after having given birth and child expulsion is still practised today and described among indigenous descendant communities at the Cape (Schapera, 1951: 260). Regular massage with herbs and oils of the woman's abdomen by older women is still frequently practised on the Cape Flats. The beating of a pregnant woman was severely punished (Schapera, 1951: 261). To this day, children born with a caul are considered to have prophetic powers and might become a clever *!gei aob* (magician) or the *gebo aob* (seer) (Schapera, 1951: 265). Today, on the Cape Flats, descendants of the Khoi and San speak of '*met die helm gebore*' (born with the caul) and indigenous-descendant women accord the same significance to the wisdom and future role of such a child who is expected to share dreams and visions with mothers, and this ritual forms part of wellbeing for the community. Children are carried on the back (*aba*), while the mother works. The precolonial Khoi word *aba* is still commonly used on the Cape Flats today, like the many other words derived from the indigenous Khoekhoegowab.[12] Elders must be spoken to using special names; *Ousi* (*Ausi*) in the case of the eldest sister (Schapera, 1951: 271). Today, *Ousi* is still the traditional name for the eldest respected sister and even grandmother on the Cape Flats. *Ousi* denotes great traditional knowledge of plants, healing, spirituality and authority in the family. *Ausi* (plural as *Ausidi*) must be spoken of in respectful ways, especially by men. According to Grevenbroek in 1695 (in Schapera, 1933: 196), women were free to love and even if she slept with a married man, no one could speak of her 'dishonourably' (disrespectfully). Men, whose sisters, daughters or other female relatives, were spoken of in disparaging ways, were said to leave such company immediately to demonstrate their disapproval.

Scarification at the Cape was a form of inoculation against disease: herbs and other ingredients for healing were rubbed into a cut in the flesh. Cupping (popularly thought of today as being exclusively of

---

12 Thanks to Bradley van Sitters and Pedro Dausab for guidance on Khoekhoegowab (Nama) language usage.

Chinese origin) was also commonly practised, as observed in the 1600s (see Norwich, 1971). Scarification was evidently practised until at least the 1940s among indigenous 'Cape Coloureds'.[13] 'Healing or noxious plants and their qualities they know extremely well. I remember their pointing out a flower to me and telling me that, when it sprouts from the earth, their women every year in the month of September during several days fall into a deep sleep and drowsiness ... they are also able to foretell the weather ... the various movements of the stars and constellations ...' (Grevenbroek, 1695 in Schapera, 1933: 245). Poison treatments, involving the dog or snake responsible for the bite inflicted, have been practised into contemporary times. 'Experience has shown them the great worth of this remedy' (Grevenbroek, 1695, in Schapera, 1933: 247).

COLONIAL REPRESENTATIONS OF CAPE INDIGENOUS WOMEN

These narratives of health practices and vast medicinal knowledge at the Cape, and survival of disease through the powerful agency of women, were gradually erased as colonial invasion and permanent settlement advanced. By the 1960s during Apartheid, in the writings of South African white males such as Marais (1962), the descendants of these indigenous communities at the Cape are described within paradigms of ignorance, alcohol, vagrancy and slavery. They were represented structurally through the Apartheid political economy discourse of 'acts of emancipation' of the Cape Ordinance 50 of 1828 and the British Act of 1833. Although considered 'freed' by these Acts, Cape Khoi women and men were certainly not free but were a severely land-dispossessed people after almost 200 years of colonial invasion. With land dispossession Khoi women became particularly vulnerable (Arnott, 2019:10) in a domestic situation of servitude in which their children could also be used to serve the ends of manipulation (threats of separation, for example) by the colonial enslaver. Enslaved Khoi women variously worked on farms and as washerwomen. Indigenous environmental knowledge could be exploited by farmers (Arnott, 2019:12), as well as in the domestic realm for healing and child rearing. The Khoi were highly skilled with cattle, slaughter procedures, the creation of meat products, milking and the making of leather hides (Arnott, 2019: 11–12).

The respective Acts of 1828 and 1833 became the cornerstones on which the indigenous history of the Cape people was represented and

---

13   Research by Bam (forthcoming publication in 2021).

permeated both university and school education during Apartheid through ubiquitous themes, familiar to those who schooled at the time, such as on 'the history of South Africa's population groups', which included that of 'Coloureds'.[14] In this representation of South Africa's 'population groups', slaves from the East were represented as the 'skilled' architects, builders and tailors while the indigenous locals were represented as 'unskilled'. Indigenous Khoi and San were described as 'savage' and illiterate, though along with the enslaved from the East they were conflated into the demographic category of 'Cape Coloured'.

This 'savage' paradigm of the indigenous people was further entrenched with Cape indigenous women being designated under Apartheid as *meid* (maid), not a 'woman', and a girl was a *kleinmeid* (small maid) (Marais, 1962: 5). They were further described as 'creatures' who offered no agency or resistance to colonialism and invasion; they fought 'two little wars' against the Europeans (Marais, 1962: 7), after which there was no resistance against land invasion and the Cape indigenous people were exterminated by smallpox by the late 1700s (shown by archaeologist Andrew Smith as a distortion) (see Arnott, 2019: 19). They had a 'wandering' existence and were 'incurably lazy' and 'like most primitive races...readily succumbed to the temptation of strong drink'...and 'would soon become extinct' (Marais, 1962: 7–8). By 1809 they were simply in contracted labour with Europeans, had lost their land 'over which they had been thinly scattered as nomads' and got their access to land through the 'assistance of the missionaries, who were prepared to try and convert the nomadic Hottentots ... into agriculturalists...' (Marais, 1962: 123). 'A few, a very few, might indeed earn a livelihood as wood-cutters...the others must work for the farmers or live as vagrants' (Marais, 1962: 123). By the 1820s, 'a Hottentot found anywhere without a pass was a vagrant', and was jailed 'until his master claimed him' and if he had none, one would be found. 'No Hottentot was exempted from the necessity of carrying a pass' (Marais, 1962: 126). Children were by then no longer carefree in the veld to learn about medicines and plants under their mother's tutelage; they were tied to white masters in oppressive and exploitative labour relationships. In quintessential Afrikaner nationalist racist style of the time, Marais (1962: 183) noted that 'vagrancy, unauthorised squatting... remained endemic in the Cape Colony'.

---

14 This was part of all Apartheid-era school curricula from primary through to high school, especially in history and geography subjects. It is accepted as common knowledge.

Early European writers admitted that disease was often brought to the Cape colony by them. 'Epidemics ... a loathy impetigo and venereal disease have, I am afraid, been caught from us' (Grevenbroek, 1695, in Schapera, 1933: 241). With the outbreak of the smallpox epidemic in 1748, Khoi washerwomen, who handled the infected laundry from the ships, were targeted by officials as spreading the disease. Segregated and quarantined from the rest of the population, they were told they would be shot if they should try to leave (see Viljoen, 1995: 27). They were left to infect one another, while European ships were still allowed to dock even if they brought in disease. During the 1755 smallpox outbreak, regulations again targeted Khoi women, in which they were stigmatised for their lifestyle as responsible for spreading disease (Arnott, 2019: 19). Yet historians such as Ross (1977: 416–428) showed that Khoi women were in all likelihood resistant to smallpox because, as they did the milking of cows in precolonial times, they would have had immunity to cowpox. They were also nomadic pastoralists and, hence, would have had more resilient immunity than they were represented to have had in history. Khoi women also survived the smallpox epidemic in greater numbers than men (Guelke and Shell, 1992: 823). The smallpox extinction discourse on the Khoi and San also implies that indigenous people had little or no contact with the outside world prior to European contact. Archaeological evidence and oral narratives reveal the contrary – that the early Chinese circumvented the Cape, which is being researched increasingly in contemporary scholarship. An ancient human disease, smallpox was recorded as early as the 4th century in China and in the 7th century in India. Possible smallpox can also be traced to ancient Egyptian mummified remains of 1200–1100BCE (Fenner et al., 1988: 210). Smallpox was commonly used in warfare, such as during the Crusades in Europe at the end of the 12th century (Fenner et al., 1988: 215). By the time the Dutch settled at the Cape in the 17th century, the region appeared as yet free of smallpox – although this in itself does not suggest that it was an unknown disease when it was brought by the Dutch East India Company en route from the East and Europe in the 18th century. However, what is certain is that smallpox was definitely spread by colonists to the indigenous people at the Cape and further inland in southern Africa by the 1700s.

COVID-19 AND REPRESENTATION OF CAPE INDIGENOUS WOMEN

Consistent with the racist Marais (1962) discourse on 'Cape Coloureds', contemporary representation of indigenous women in the media during the COVID-19 pandemic is one of helplessness and victimhood, of the ignorant and uninformed – in short, the 'nuisance factor' in cities. In Cape Town itself, this representation needs to be historicised to get a more informed understanding of the context in which such public representation of indigenous women has emerged in our society today. Abrahams (1997) has written extensively on the misrepresentation of Cape indigenous women as a 'long insult' through pornographic images of Khoi women, which disavowed the public from learning about their real lives and own narratives of the past.

Indigenous people have had a long history of battling pandemics and disease brought by European colonisers, and which also impacted on their livelihoods and gender. The smallpox epidemics of the 1700s at the Cape being a good example of the impact on people, the erasure of their language and loss of the land. Those epidemics came through women's labour – enslaved washerwomen at the Cape who washed the infected clothes of colonists.

Indigenous communities also need to be mindful of how they are perceived by scientists who do epidemiological research. Often indigenous communities were identified as important test subjects for vaccination trials. With scientists believing that they had a unique biological response, which required further investigation, with some even going as far as to say that some populations need to diversify their gene pool because their current genetic profiles and biological responses proved inadequate to cope with certain 'new' diseases to which they would be exposed. Globally, because of the historical correlation between medicine and racism, levels of trust in vaccines and Western medical or pharmaceutical interventions are low among indigenous people (see Jamison et al., 2019: 87–94).

Pandemics have also been used to explain declines in indigenous populations after colonial settlement and contact. In addition, the 'virgin soil hypothesis' (see Smith, 1990)[15] and 'vulnerability to disease' tropes have been used to explain declining populations. However, these epidemics would often occur long after first contact and they would often lead to high death tolls, which were not due to vulnerability but rather

---

15 The debate among scholars centred on the cause for the 'extinction' of the Khoi at the Cape as related to the soil degradation due to colonialist agricultural exploitation versus the smallpox epidemic of the 1700s.

socio-economic conditions under colonial settlement, exploitation and oppression, which made communities more susceptible to disease. Less nutrition and inadequate access to clean drinking water (along with other factors brought on by colonialism) meant that communities would die at higher rates, not only of new diseases, but also of diseases that were already found in the population prior to colonialism. Thus COVID-19 offers an opportunity to rethink the narratives about indigenous communities and disease, and to fully take stock of how marginalisation results in the disease disproportionately affecting indigenous communities. Narratives of disappearing indigenous communities due to contact with colonists also surfaced and contributed to how these communities were perceived, further contributing to the racist narrative of disappearing indigenous populations, which still lingers today. Narratives of biological susceptibility means that government and other policy institutions can be less accountable in terms of discriminatory and unequal health policies and the historical context of these intergenerational structural patterns. Thus, it is important to understand the socio-economic factors that affect Khoi- and San-descendant communities today, such as tuberculosis on the Cape Flats (see Richardson et al., 2016; Wood and Becker, 2017), and their contextual susceptibility to diseases that are poverty-related.

In April 2020, Anne Nuorgam reported to the UN Permanent Forum on Indigenous Issues for the need to attend to the rights and specific needs of indigenous people globally.[16] It is reported globally that indigenous women are of the worst affected by COVID-19 involving health, social and economic risks such as poor nutrition, elder isolation and inadequate housing.[17] South Africa witnessed Black people, including women, being violently evicted from their homes in winter during lockdown. In South Africa, particularly in Cape Town, there has been confusion among indigenous-descendant and marginalised

---

16 United Nations Department of Economic and Social Affairs: Indigenous Peoples, Statement by the Chair of the Permanent Forum on Indigenous Issues on Covid-19, 6 April 2020. Online at: https://www.un.org/development/desa/indigenouspeoples/news/2020/04/chair-message-on-COVID-19/ (Accessed 30 November 2020).

17 United Nations Department of Economic and Social Affairs: Indigenous Peoples, 'Covid-19 and Indigenous Peoples' Cultural Survival, 'Covid-19s Growing Impact on Indigenous Communities Globally', 09 April 2020. Online at: https://www.un.org/development/desa/indigenouspeoples/COVID-19.html (Accessed 30 November 2020); See also https://www.culturalsurvival.org/news/COVID-19s-growing-impact-indigenous-communities-globally (Accessed 30 November 2020).

communities regarding COVID-19, exacerbated by brutal crackdowns by the police and military. While Sena notes that in some African countries COVID-19 is dubbed 'the disease of the city', similarly, for the marginalised people on the Cape Flats it is called 'the disease for rich people'[18] or 'white people's disease'.[19] These sceptical approaches that people have to COVID-19 and government policy became highlighted in the notorious Strandfontein 'COVID camp' which was established at the start of the national lockdown in late March 2020. The Strandfontein COVID camp presents a prime example of brutal responses to a pandemic by local government in their treatment of indigenous and marginalised communities during a global crisis.

Doctors Without Borders (MSF) reported during 2020 on this 'quarantine' temporary shelter for the homeless set up by the City of Cape Town. An independent Human Rights Commission investigation was conducted on 11 April 2020, which highlighted violations of international humanitarian standards, which put the homeless at risk of increased COVID-19 infections and other infections such as tuberculosis.[20] The fenced shelter, which encamped 1,500 people, reportedly failed the protection principle, exposing indigenous women and others to further harm, such as sexually transmitted illnesses, rape and other forms of gender-based violence. The homeless were, in fact, at higher risk in the 'quarantine camp' than free on the streets. Those quarantined were brought there by the police and local government, and the camp was under constant police and security guard (including an armoured vehicle). The use of these high-handed security measures was interpreted by those held in the camps as not for the safety of them as the homeless, but to prevent them from leaving. In other words, they were involuntarily interned or jailed by local government. One large tent contained 500 people with no medical staff in the tents and after 4 pm no masks were worn and inadequate sanitation was provided.[21] Poor infection and prevention control have been the key COVID-19 challenges for the homeless (the often land-dispossessed indigenous people) of

---

18 Conversation with a Lavender Hill resident in October 2020.

19 Informal conversation with a township resident in July 2020.

20 A video by the government paints a rosy picture of a 'professional' camp. See https://www.youtube.com/watch?v=bp_kMXoFt28 (Accessed 15 November 2020) – pictures of showers, matrasses, food, medical staff and a 'happy' minstrel figure with an umbrella.

21 See Gilles van Cutsem, M.D., 'Health in Strandfontein shelter' (n.d.).

South Africa – due to 'erratic healthcare facilities and overcrowding'. MSF therefore called for the decommissioning of the camp in favour of smaller community-based shelters with adequate medical care.[22] Due to civic protests by indigenous groups like the A/Xarra Restorative Justice Forum, the camp was closed in May 2020, roughly a month after it was established. Civic activists drew similarities to the Cape Colony's response to the bubonic plague of 1901, which removed 6,000 Africans to 600 tents in Ndabeni. What occurred in Strandfontein is similar to the removal of homeless Khoi women who lived in colonial Cape Town during the outbreak of smallpox in 1755. They were considered a health hazard because their lifestyles were viewed as irregular and filthy (Viljoen, 1995). Subsequently a placaat was promulgated, which prevented them from living this way and they were coerced into working on farms. They were told to leave the city during the smallpox epidemic because their living conditions were unsanitary. In this instance, the Khoi women whose lives had been severely disrupted by colonialism were blamed for their living conditions and the spread of disease. Strandfontein Beach was itself created as a barren 'Coloured' recreation area under Apartheid forced removals during the 1960s, later followed by the establishment of the neighbouring Apartheid-designated residential areas of Mitchells Plain (late 1970s) and Khayelitsha (early 1980s). As a journalist put it, 'The Strandfontein camp was to restructure where people live, to resegregate the city whose street population defies racial and economic boundaries.'

The women of the notorious COVID camp were evidently from the Cape's intergenerational homeless Khoi and San women communities (the well-known *bergies*, or mountain dwellers, who have been around in the colonised city since the time of the colonial Vagrancy Laws).

Chantal, a homeless woman from Camps Bay, shared her feelings about the COVID camp in a video interview:

> I am just a little bit confused. Why did they take us from our safe place to come and sleep here on the floor? I was asleep, the next thing I was forced out of our space to come sleep here ... They don't take notice of the sick people inside ...

---

22 Doctors without Borders, 'South Africa: Covid-19 Pandemic demands safer temporary shelters', 15 April 2020. https://www.msf.org.za/news-and-resources/press-release/south-africa-COVID-19-pandemic-lockdown-demands-safer-temporary (Accessed 15 November 2020).

Another woman, Wanita Davids, explained the brutal process of displacement:

> On Sunday, they just come with the vans with the inforcements [sic], they said come come let's go ... by force ... [we] did not have time to get our clothes ... I still have the same underwear on ... we are human beings man![23]

An unnamed homeless elderly woman exclaimed as she sobbed uncontrollably:

> [They] only talk lies ... we don't want to be here ... I don't want to be here. We are not safe. You know how many gangsters are here ... every night ... we have families ... we have families to go to.[24]

Eyford (2006) has shown how epidemic quarantines have been used to create new colonial orders in which to entrench the 'reserve system' for indigenous people, as was the case of the people of the Canadian Northwest during the smallpox epidemic of 1876–1877. While they were effective in the treatment of the spread of illness, such quarantine measures shifted power and created stigmas and boundaries among communities. Quarantine, in the instance that Eyford describes, was used as a form of appraisal for how indigenous people could be assimilated into accepting Western medicines and healing practices to encourage 'new modes of behaviour' (Eyford, 2006: 60); what Thomas calls the 'sanitizing colonising' project (2006: 61) through 'brute force public health measures' (2006: 71) – used 'to justify dispossession and marginalisation'. Similarly, the Cape Colony used the Public Health Act of 1883 to rationalise, on the basis of the smallpox epidemic of the time, to segregate the African population from other demographic groups such as 'Coloureds' and 'Indians'. Although the smallpox deaths among Capetonians far outnumbered those of the plague of 1901, according to Swanson (1977) it was used to move Black Africans to Uitvlugt (later named Ndabeni).

---

23 Online at: https://www.youtube.com/watch?v=5Q_DOTaU7UQ (Accessed 15 November 2020).

24 Online at: https://www.youtube.com/watch?v=EcBJd9SUp4k (Accessed 15 November 2020).

WHAT INDIGENOUS WOMEN DO AND COULD DO TO SUSTAIN RESILIENCE AMID COVID-19

Most at risk are indigenous women elders and, in the event of their death, there is a significant loss of indigenous knowledge of plants and healing, loss of knowledge of biodiversity and intergenerational teaching of endangered and erased languages. Lack of food security among indigenous communities is also a direct result of land loss[25] due to colonialism. Communities draw on the customs, rituals and wisdoms of the past. The indigenous people of Thailand rely on the ancient practice of 'Kroh Yee' (village closure). The people of the Amazon have considered closing entries to tourists, land grabbers and miners.[26] To other indigenous activists like Maria Tuyuc in Guatemala, women should create economic empowerment from the crisis, find confidence in their own creativity and resources in communities which will help to combat both poverty and gender-based violence; working on economic independence is key.[27] Other recommendations made by activists, such as the A/Xarra Restorative Justice Forum[28] in South Africa, is the provision of long-term alternative housing and shelter for victims of domestic violence and abuse.

Engaging in flexible and diverse income streams is important, as indigenous women have often similarly adapted to the impacts of colonialism and capitalism. For example, as research by Bam (forthcoming 2021) shows, with the impact of land dispossession and Apartheid, the Cape Flats indigenous women who were small-holding cattle keepers and milk traders, diversified their income streams by selling traditional medicinal plants and vegetables. Indigenous women who rely on tourism to sell crafts could return to the power of their own knowledge and cultural systems that have creative income opportunities,

---

25 United Nations Department of Economic and Social Affairs: Indigenous Peoples, 'Covid-19 and Indigenous Peoples'. Online at: https://www.un.org/development/desa/indigenouspeoples/COVID-19.html (Accessed 8 November 2020).

26 United Nations Department of Economic and Social Affairs: Economic Analysis, UN/DESA Policy Brief #70: The impact of Covid 19 on Indigenous People, 8 May 2020. Online at: https://www.un.org/development/desa/dpad/publication/un-desa-policy-brief-70-the-impact-of-covid-19-on-indigenous-peoples/ (Accessed 1 April 2021).

27 UN Women, 'In Guatemala, investing in indigenous women's economic empowerment is key to building back better after COVID-19', 29 June 2020. Online at: https://www.unwomen.org/en/news/stories/2020/6/feature-empowering-indigenous-women-in-guatemala-in-COVID-19-response (Accessed 8 November 2020).

28 WhatsApp Housing Commission group dialogues during 2020 lockdown.

while at the same time visibilising and centring lost knowledge and its restoration. Women from southern to eastern Africa, such as the Maasai, make soap for sale, and indigenous technologies.[29] Indigenous women need to reclaim their knowledge of biodiversity, conservation, food security and the spiritual relationship with earth and sky. Indigenous women's rights to land, water and resources for food sovereignty are crucial and are non-negotiable rights. Women should be compensated for the immense value their indigenous knowledge of ecosystems and healing practices contribute in a post-COVID world.

Mindou Oumarou, a Mbororo pastoralist from Chad, advocates that indigenous communities should collaborate and share indigenous knowledge. Leina argues that social protection should increase and should centre on sharing of resources, since indigenous people themselves know what they need.[30] These 'solidarity exchanges' are crucial for collective community survival. Kenya's Maasai communities lead information campaigns on COVID-19 in their indigenous languages – an issue also highlighted by the International Labour Organisation (ILO). Women-led groups organise communication events, challenging 'traditional beliefs and practices' that may inadvertently also spread the virus. Women have also challenged indigenous patriarchy around their roles in communication on culture to prevent the spread of the pandemic. Indigenous revivalist movements in South Africa tend to be patriarchal, and there are claims in everyday conversation that the men with these mindsets consider themselves 'immune' to disease and pandemics.[31] Such patriarchal attitudes leave indigenous women, elders and the children in impoverished townships increasingly vulnerable to the spread of COVID-19 and the associated economic hardships.

Against the challenge of patriarchy in contemporary indigenous revivalism, we need to centre the work and knowledge of women. Participatory research frameworks, such as applied by Aboriginal

---

29 Climate and Development Knowledge Network, 'FEATURE: Kenya – Indigenous women overcome discrimination to lead community Covid-19 responses', 24 August 2020. Online at: https://cdkn.org/2020/08/feature-kenya-indigenous-women-overcome-discrimination-to-lead-community-COVID-19-responses/?loclang=en_gb (Accessed 8 November 2020).

30 IPACC, Podcast: The impact of Covid-19 on indigenous women in Africa. Online at: https://www.ipacc.org.za/blog/2020/07/27/podcast-the-impact-of-covid-19-on-indigenous-women-in-africa/ (Accessed 8 April 2021).

31 Referring here to a recent informal encounter with a township community group that refused to wear masks and to sanitise.

Australians during COVID-19, centre indigenous women's health knowledges that encourage the principle of women as agents of their own health, using both indigenous epistemologies and methodologies. We should advocate competent programmes for Africans by Africans (Dune et al., 2020: 47).

What would be the indigenous women's meaning of the South African philosophy of ubuntu ('I am because you are') in a post-COVID world? Could we chart our own *Uluru Statement of the Heart* (see McKay, 2017)? Such a statement could connect indigenous women's long and ongoing sovereign connection with the land and its ecology, which should affirm our African, deep-listening and women-centred practices (that also tackle indigenous patriarchy parading as 'precolonial').

Our deep listening practices, through ritual and reclaiming our erased indigenous languages, similar to Miriam-Rose Ungunmer's[32] Aboriginal Australian practice and theory of *Dadirri* – 'the deeper inner spring inside us' – should move to the heart. In southern Africa, in the context of epistemicide, a sustainable future lies with indigenous-descendant 'Women of the Heart',[33] in reclaiming our knowledge of the environment for health and wellbeing as the *!gei aob* (to be interpreted as today's spiritual sorceress) and the *gebo aob* (to be interpreted as today's intuitive knowledge seer) in our ritualistic ecological relations with earth, water and sky. Women of the Heart know differently; they 'know on the wind' – *ǂoaba ǂans*.

REFERENCES

Abrahams, N., Jewkes, R., Martin, L.J., Mathews, S., Vetten, L. and Lombard, C. 2009. 'Mortality of women from intimate partner violence in South Africa: A national epidemiological study', *Violence and victims*, 24(4): 546–556.

Abrahams, Y. 1996. 'Disempowered to consent: Sara Bartman and Khoisan slavery in the nineteenth-century Cape colony and Britain', *South African Historical Journal*, 35(1): 89–114.

Abrahams, Y. 1996. 'Was Eva raped? An exercise in speculative history', *Kronos*, 23: 3–21.

---

32 See https://www.miriamrosefoundation.org.au/about-dadirri (Accessed 10 December 2020). See also Ungunmer (2017).

33 A concept proposed by June Bam, which could help in decolonial research methods and rethinking in Africa, in keeping with indigenous knowledge and practices, both locally and around the world.

Abrahams, Y. 1997. 'The great long national insult: "Science", sexuality and the Khoisan in the 18th and early 19th century', *Agenda*, 13(32): 34–48.

Arnott, T. (2019). 'Gendered Silence: Female slave imports and Khoikhoi women in the Dutch Cape Colony', Indian Ocean World Centre Working Paper Series, No. 6.

Azcona et al., 2020. 'From insights to action: Gender equality in the wake of Covid-19', UN Women. Online at: https://www.unwomen.org/en/digital-library/publications/2020/09/gender-equality-in-the-wake-of-COVID-19 (Accessed 8 November /2020).

Brown-Luthango, M. 2020. 'South Africa's 2nd Pandemic: reflecting on gender-based violence during and beyond Covid-19'. Online at: http://aidc.org.za/south-africas-2nd-pandemic-reflecting-on-gender-based-violence-during-and-beyond-COVID-19/ (Accessed 15 November 2020).

Cogger, J. 2020. 'The Strandfontein shelter touches a societal and political nerve', *Mail and Guardian,* 27 May. Online at: https://mg.co.za/opinion/2020-05-27-the-strandfontein-shelter-touches-a-societal-and-political-nerve/ (Accessed 15 November 2020).

Cupertino, G.A., Cupertino, M.D.C., Gomes, A.P., Braga, L.M. and Siqueira-Batista, R. 2020. 'COVID-19 and Brazilian indigenous populations', *The American Journal of Tropical Medicine and Hygiene*, 103(2): 609–612.

Dune, T., Gesesew, H.A., Hiruy, K., Udah, H., Lee, V., Kwedza, R. and Mwanri, L. 2020. 'Use of indigenous informed epistemologies can inform intervention models to fight COVID-19 in Africa', *African Journal of Reproductive Health*, 24(2): 46–48.

Eyford, R. 2006. 'Quarantined within a new colonial order: The 1876–1877 Lake Winnipeg smallpox epidemic', *Journal of the Canadian Historical Association/Revue de la Société historique du Canada*, 17(1): 55–78.

Fenner, F., Henderson, D.A., Arita, I., Jezek, Z. and Ladnyi, I.D. 1988. 'The history of smallpox and its spread around the world'. In *Smallpox and its Eradication*. Geneva: World Health Organization, pp. 209–244.

Guelke, L. and Shell, R. 1992. 'Landscape of conquest: Frontier water alienation and Khoikhoi strategies of survival, 1652–1780', *Journal of Southern African Studies*, 18(4): 803–824.

Harding, A. 2020. 'Coronavirus in South Africa: Scientists explore surprise theory for low death rate', *BBC Africa*, 3 September.

International Labour Organisation (ILO). 2020. 'Urgent action needed to tackle poverty and inequalities facing indigenous people'. Online at: https://www.ilo.org/global/about-the-ilo/newsroom/news/WCMS_735575/lang--en/index.htm (Accessed 8 April 2021).

Jamison, A.M., Quinn, S.C. and Freimuth, V.S. 2019. '"You don't trust a government vaccine": Narratives of institutional trust and influenza vaccination among African American and white adults', *Social Science & Medicine*, 221: 87–94.

Marais, J.S. 1962. *The Cape Coloured People*. Johannesburg: Witwatersrand University Press.

McKay, D. 2017. *Uluru Statement: A quick guide*. Law and Bills Digest Section, Parliament of Australia: Canberra, Australia.

Mlaba, K. 2020. 'South Africa's Ramaphosa calls for 5 days of Mourning for Victims of Covid-19 and Gender Violence', Global Citizen, 13 November. Onlline at: https://www.globalcitizen.org/en/content/ramaphosa-5-day-mourning-south-africa-COVID-gender/ (Accessed 15 November 2020).

Monchalin, R. 2020. 'Novel coronavirus, access to abortion services, and bridging western and indigenous knowledges in a post-pandemic world', *Women's Health Issues*, 31(1): 5–8.

Norwich, I. 1971. 'A chapter of early medical Africana', *South African Medical Journal*, 45(5): 501–504.

Oleschuk, M. 2020. 'Gender equity considerations for tenure and promotion during COVID-19', *Canadian Review of Sociology*, 57(3): 502–515.

Peterman, A., Potts, A., O'Donnell, M., Thompson, K., Shah, N., Oertelt-Prigione, S. and Van Gelder, N. 2020. 'Pandemics and Violence Against Women and Children', Center for Global Development Working Paper, No. 528.

Power, T., Wilson, D., Best, O., Brockie, T., Bourque Bearskin, L., Millender, E. and Lowe, J. 2020. 'COVID-19 and indigenous peoples: An imperative for action', *Journal of Clinical Nursing*, 29(15/16): 2737–2741.

Raven-Hart, R. 1967. *Before Van Riebeeck: Callers at South Africa from 1488 to 1652*. Cape Town: Struik.

Richardson, E.T., Morrow, C.D., Ho, T., Fürst, N., Cohelia, R., Tram, K.H., Farmer, P.E. and Wood, R. 2016. 'Forced removals embodied as tuberculosis', *Social Science & Medicine*, 161: 13–18;

Ross, R.J. 1977. 'Smallpox at the Cape of Good Hope in the eighteenth century', *African Historical Demography*: 416–428.

Rubenstein, K. 2018. 'Power, control and citizenship: The Uluru Statement from the Heart as active citizenship', *Bond Law Review*, 30(1): article 3.

Sacks, J. 2020. 'Blindness: How the Strandfontein camp was set up to fail', *Mail and Guardian*, 15 May. Online at: https://mg.co.za/coronavirus-essentials/2020-05-15-blindness-how-the-strandfontein-camp-was-set-up-to-fail/ (Accessed 15 November 2020).

Schapera, I. 1951. *The Khoisan Peoples of South Africa: Bushmen and Hottentots* (Vol. 1). London: Routledge & Kegan Paul.

Schapera, I. and Farrington, B. 1933. The Early Cape Hottentots Described in the Writings of Olfert Dapper (1668). *Willem ten Rhyne (1686) and Johannes Gulielmus de Grevenbroek (1695)*. Cape Town: Van Riebeeck Society.

Smith, A.B. 1990. 'The origins and demise of the Khoikhoi: The debate', *South African Historical Journal*, 23(1): 3–14.

Staff Writer, BusinessTech. 2020. 'Don't expect SA jobs lost to Covid-19 lockdown to bounce back:study', 1 October. Online at: https://businesstech.co.za/news/business/437559/dont-expect-sa-jobs-lost-to-COVID-19-lockdown-to-bounce-back-study/ (Accessed 30 November 2020).

Swanson, M.W. 1977. 'The sanitation syndrome: Bubonic plague and urban native policy in the Cape Colony, 1900–1909', *Journal of African history*, 18(3): 387–410.

Tswanya, Y. 2020. 'Lockdown cost 3 million jobs, caused widespread hunger', *The Cape Times*, 16 July. Online at: https://www.iol.co.za/capetimes/news/lockdown-cost-3-million-jobs-caused-widespread-hunger-51062845 (Accessed 8 April 2021).

Ungunmerr, M.R. 2017. 'To be listened to in her teaching: *Dadirri*: Inner deep listening and quiet still awareness', *EarthSong Journal: Perspectives in Ecology, Spirituality and Education*, 3(4): 14–15.

Van Barneveld, K., Quinlan, M., Kriesler, P., Junor, A., Baum, F., Chowdhury, A., Junankar, P.N., Clibborn, S., Flanagan, F., Wright, C.F. and Friel, S. 2020. 'The COVID-19 pandemic: Lessons on building more equal and sustainable societies', *The Economic and Labour Relations Review*, 31(2): 133–157.

Viljoen, R.S. 1995. 'Disease and society: VOC Cape Town, its people and the smallpox epidemics of 1713, 1755 and 1767', *African Historical Review*, 27(1): 22–45.

Wood, R. and Bekker, L.G. 2017. 'An epidemic uncurbed: Tuberculosis in Cape Town, South Africa, 1910–2010', *Transactions of the Royal Society of South Africa*, 72(3): 234–241.

7

Repositioning *!uiki IInaosa/aia/*

gertrude fester-wicomb

/gui, /gam, !nona, haka, koro, !nani, hû, //khaisa, khoese, disi ...
- Aunt Una is counting in Khoekhoegowab.
- *'Ja my kind. Toe ons klein was het ons dit gepraat. Aus Sank het ons lekker geleer.'*[1]
- (Wicomb[2] family lunch, 20 October, Ottery, Cape Town, 2019)

In this chapter, i[3] shall explore words in indigenous languages relating to women/older women and grandmothers. This starts very much from my personal experience as a woman and a descendant

---

1 'Yes my child. When we were little we spoke Khoekhoegowab. Aus Sank taught us well.'
2 My maternal grandparents, Robert and Gertrude Wicomb had a smallholding at the foot of the Swartberg mountains, near the Cango Caves, district of Oudtshoorn in the Eastern Cape province. Swartberg is part of the Outeniqua Range, named after the Khoi people who originally lived there. My grandparents had 14 children of which my mother was the third eldest. As subsistence farmers, they farmed cattle, sheep, tobacco and walnuts. Aunt Una is the youngest and only living sibling. She shared that, as children, Aus Sank looked after them and taught them. Aus Sank could speak many languages, including English and Afrikaans. They had a smallholding in Vinknesrivier with the river running through their property. There were weeping willow trees on the banks of the river. Situated at the foot of the Swartberg, it was a very picturesque place. It was declared a white area in the late 1960s and grandpa came to the city for the first time, where he waned to death. Fortunately, Grandma was saved from this uprooting as she had passed on earlier.
3 I consciously use the first personal pronoun as a lower-case letter. In Afrikaans and

of indigenous and enslaved people. The chapter is divided into three parts: Language and *Ilnaosa, aia* and *!uiki* (Khoekhoegowab and Nama words for woman/older woman); visual texts and *Ilnaosa/aia/!uiki*, and lastly, repositioning and reclaiming (which comprises prose/poems to maternal and paternal grandmothers).

LANGUAGE AND *ILNAOSA/AIA/!UIKI*

Black feminist thought is central to this analysis. However, i disaggregate 'Black' as i am a descendant of Aboriginal Khoi and San and enslaved indigenous people from the East. This hybrid indigenous global identity informs my Black feminist standpoint in this chapter.

Another which also informs my scholarly position on *Ilnaosa/aia/!uiki* is the African Feminist Charter (2006: 4), which avers:

> We assert our space as African feminists. We also draw inspiration from our feminist ancestors who blazed the trail and made it possible to affirm the rights of African women ... We reclaim and assert the long and rich tradition of African women's resistance to patriarchy in Africa. We henceforth claim the right to theorise for ourselves, write for ourselves, strategise for ourselves and speak for ourselves as African feminists.

In repositioning *!uiki*, i build on the theory of Magoqwana (2018) in which she explores the rich institution of *uMakhulu* (grandmothers in isiXhosa) by challenging narrow conceptions defining *uMakhulu*. According to Magoqwana, *uMakhulu* embodies knowledge which she transfers via 'history through *iintsomi*' (stories, folktales) as well as a body of indigenous knowledge that transfers and propagates knowledge and values. The *uMakhulu* also directs the lives and spiritual aspects of the clan. Magoqwana bases her theories on Oyēwùmí (1997) who emphasises the spiritual analysis of *uMakhulu* as a 'productive but invisible institution that shapes our spiritual awareness in the African household' (Khondlo (2015) quoted in Magoqwana, 2018: 75). Khondlo (2015) uses the concept, *isazela* (conscience) as part of 'desired public leadership values'. To further decolonise our knowledge promoting indigenous theory, it is also important to integrate the local languages

---

Khoekhoegowab, 'tita' is written with a lower-case letter as is the case in many other languages, like Nama, N!uu, French, Dutch, etc. The exception is at the beginning of a sentence, as is the convention.

and values of *uMakhulu*. These can help to confront political, social and economic aspects of African societies. Mahmood Mamdani (2017) and Ngũgĩ wa Thiong'o (1986) emphasise the centrality of local languages in the decolonising project. However, they do not mention the gender aspects thereof. Furthermore, Magoqwana (2018: 76) draws on Ntuli (2002: 54) in her theorisation of *uMakhulu*, 'language represents a specific worldview and ontology', which is why the term *uMakhulu* rather than 'grandmother' is maintained throughout her chapter. Referring further to the work of Adésínà (2006), Mgoqwana asserts that the use of the term *uMakhulu* attempts to contribute to local concepts rather than adopting 'imposed categories, theories and paradigms that tend to be unfit for local conditions' (Magoqwana, 2018: 76). This assertion aligns with Mafeje's argument for endogenous epistemologies (see Adésínà, 2008) against Eurocentric 'alterity and extroversion' through the promotion of engaging with authentic interlocutors in Africa, such as *uMakhulu*.

Similarly, in relation to the argument for endogeneity and authentic interlocutors, Vossen (1984: 33) contends that 'For Africa the significance of linguistic research for ethno-historical reconstruction can nowhere be estimated higher than in the Khoisan[4] speaking area'.[5]

It is important to use indigenous languages as *languages that contain deep implications and aspects of the culture and values of the people*. Pittman and Naciri (2013) explain how, for example, they organised their comprehensive regional coaction-building campaign for nationality and citizenship for women across the Middle East and North Africa – the Campaign to Reform Arab women's nationality. This included countries from Morocco to Iraq. In Arabic, *citizenship is a masculine word, hence reserved for men only*. They then coined the slogan 'My nationality: A right for me and my family' (Pittman and Naciri, 2013: 123). Closer to home, isiXhosa linguist Pamela Maseko (2018: 35) argues how African languages have been misinterpreted and, in this process, undermined the interpretations of peoples' pasts through prejudiced understandings of the African lexicons. She asserts that, like all languages, African

---

4   The term 'KhoiSan' is currently under review and rejected by many. See Mellet (2020: 35, 49). I use it only in direct quotation. The term is also used interchangeably by Richards, alternating with Qua/KhoiSan (Richards, 2017: 7). He states that the Khoekhoegowab language is the language of the KhoiSan.

5   Quoted by Khoekhoegowab linguist Wilfred Haacke, UCT Summer School Lectures, January 2020.

languages encode the thoughts of the people who speak them (Maseko, 2018: 36). Drawing also on Oyēwùmi (1997), she argues that it is through the hegemonic Eurocentric languages that the process of distortion of interpreting the African past occurs. One notable form of this distortion is linked to the constant engendering in the English language, which is not the case in isiXhosa. Language through oral tradition is text, and Nomalanga Mkhize (2018) makes an argument around distortion in southern African historiography in her chapter, 'The missing idiom of African historiography', to illustrate how distortions in interpretations in historical writing took place.

As i am a descendant of First Nations[6] of southern Africa, in the Cape, i focus specifically on the Khoi and San languages. I derive this First Nations identity from *the first indigenous social formations the Europeans encountered when they invaded and settled at the Cape, and the first people they waged war against for the land.* It is, therefore, not a claim to assert being the 'first people' of southern Africa, or the only Africans who had social organisation in the form of clans as political governance at the time of contact with Europeans.

Various words are used for the Khoi and San indigenous people. At my primary school i was informed of the *Strandlopers* or beachwalkers and how lazy they were. Of course, we soon understood the concept of independence of indigenous populations[7] and their subsistence economy.

This was the masters' narrative: *'Tant que les lions n'auront pas leur propres historiens, les histoires de chasse continueront de glorifier le chasseur.' Proverbe d'Afrique.* [Until lions have their own historians, hunting stories will continue to glorify the hunter].[8] Hence it is important that we

---

6 The use of the term 'First Nations' has attracted much debate in recent times in South Africa, critiqued by South African Patric Mellet (2020) in *The Lie of 1652* as 'firstism', which he argues is historically inappropriate in southern Africa. A pioneer in this debate in contemporary global scholarship is Flanagan (2019), who argues against 'aboriginal orthodoxy' in Canada. However, indigenous peoples in Canada informed me that they prefer the term First Nations (personal interaction as well as papers presented at the Sexual Justice/Cultural Justice: Critical Perspectives in Theory and Practice conference, University of British Columbia, Vancouver, Canada, May 2004.) Papers are published in Arneil et al. (2006).

7 The indigenous peoples were completely self-sufficient and independent; hence they did not need to work for the colonialists. In fact, many writers, including Richards (2017: 323), comment on how the indigenous peoples, 150 years before 1652, provided fresh provisions to passing ships.

8 In an interview with Chinua Achebe, Paris Review 1994. Online at: https://www.npr.org/sections/thetwo-way/2013/03/22/175046327/chinua-achebe-and-the-bravery-of-

research and write our own histories and herstories. This research and documentation is a political and historical imperative.

It is essential that part of the decolonisation process is to unearth many of the lost aspects of our ancestors' cultures, knowledge and heritage. Krauss (1992) alerted us to the world's languages in crisis. Mufwene (2002) pointedly linked the crisis and loss of languages to colonisation and globalisation. Many Khoi and San languages have waned,[9] as during colonisation indigenous people were not allowed to speak them. The same applies to the languages of the enslaved: Diane Ferrus (2006) eloquently expounds the situation of enslaved peoples and laments the loss of the names and languages of our slave ancestors. While the indigenous San experienced extremely brutal genocide (see Adhikari, 2010), the Khoi also suffered linguicide (loss of languages) and loss of cultures. Many attempts are now being made by Khoi and San descendants to preserve their languages and explore those lost cultures. Grandmother/*Ouma* Geelmeid (Katriena Esau) teaches N|uu, one of the few surviving 'KhoiSan' languages, at a private school initiated by her in Rosedale, Upington, Northern Cape province in the Kalahari.[10] In this search to locate and preserve indigenous South African languages thus far, the most successful is the Nama language, which is taught at many Northern Cape schools.

According to Nama scholar Bradley Van Sitters (interviewed 20 June 2018) the *Ilnaosa*[11] */auma/!uiki/aia* is like *uMhakulu* – a spiritual leader embodying wisdom and 'history through *iintsomi*'. Similar to *uMakhulu*, which embraces the elements of spirituality and wisdom so, too, do we

---

lions (Accessed 27 November 2020).

9   According to Xri researcher, Martin Mossmer, working with speakers of Xri, there are only three Xri speakers left in the Northern Cape (communicated via e-mail 5 May 2020). 'Based on my many weeks of field work over two years, I reached the conclusion that there are only three *individuals* who can be classed as 'speakers'. Even so, they have not used the language for many decades and possibly have an incomplete acquisition of the language. There are also a few dozen individuals who know words and phrases of Xri.' See http://www.cca.uct.ac.za/martin-m%C3%B6ssmer (Accessed 27 November 2020).

10 I was privileged to visit the school. Her work and that of Claudia Du Plessis and Mary-Ann Prins is published in *Ouma Geelmeid ke kx'u//xa//xaN/uu* (Ouma Geelmeid teaches N/uu) by Sheena Shah and Matthias Brenzinger, Centre for African Language Diversity, University of Cape Town, 2016.

11 Grandmother (Haacke, Eiseb and Gericke, 2010). Access to this and information regarding the vocabulary of grandmother was assisted also by Headman Joe Damons. *!uiki* is grandmother in N//uu.

find it in older women in Nama, *gã-aikhoes*, according to Van Sitters. He also argues that matriarchy is central to Nama culture and that *Ilnaosa* /older women are powerful. When one compares the power and position of *Ilnaosa* today, I argue that the matriarchal cultures and practices of many of the Aboriginal groups have been eroded and distorted by colonial and indigenous patriarchy and capitalism.

This wisdom, spiritual leadership, power and guidance of grandmothers/mothers are not restricted to African cultures and languages, but also occur elsewhere, for instance, in Marathi, in India. Chhaya Datar (an Indian feminist and Marathi scholar, interviewed on 16 May 2018) says that, in Marathi, motherhood/older women/grandmothers, called *Matrutva*, exemplify wisdom and spiritual leadership, and are disseminator of values. According to Datar:

> What is significant is that there is a whole lot of Mother Goddess imagery in the Hindu religion. However, once the patriarchy got established, all the Goddesses became the consorts of the male Gods. Mies and Kamala and many other writers emphasise the Mother Goddesses in their writings. Indian anthropologists, too, have written a lot about them.[12]

I want to argue that this erosion of *Matrutva*, *uMakhulu*, *Ilnaosa* – elder women/grandmothers – is the result of both colonial patriarchy and indigenous patriarchy. In the women's struggles in South Africa, key references highlight the significant power, leadership and militancy of women, both mothers and grandmothers. Wells (1998) wrote on women in the early 1900s. Lodge (1985: 142) concludes that 'as state oppression increased so women's defiance increased', and Fester (2014a; 2014b; 2015) emphasised the 1980–2014 period.

However, although *Ilnaosa/uMakhulu* embodies the wise grandmothers/mothers in many cultures, this receptacle of knowledge has also been abused for narrow nationalist aims (see Brink, 1990; Fester, 2015).

Visual texts and *Ilnaosa/aia/!uiki*

Apart from the oral tradition, we should also explore other forms of knowledge and what they signify. The various precolonial traditions and

---

12 Datar, 16 May 2018, via e-mail.

art forms are important receptacles of knowledge. Ndebele artist, Gogo Esther Mahlangu, embodies the legacy of women as artists conveying stories through geometric shapes and colours. This is an unexplored area of work. Bead designs and colours also evoke different messages.

Rock art created by the San is found throughout southern Africa. Miller (1979) graphically illustrates the richness of the art forms. She comments that:

> The artists were also the invokers of the spirits and tellers of tales, but their true genius lay in the recording and bringing to life upon the enduring rock the ceremonies, rites and myths which their people whispered around fires at night (Miller, 1979: 11).

So we note from the above that both language, as in storytelling, but also rock art/rock engravings are canons of history of the indigenous peoples. Some of the most impressive rock engravings are at Driekopseiland,[13] Wildebeest Kuil[14] and Nooitgedacht[15] in the Northern Cape. Morris (2007)[16] highlights the androcentrism of archaeology and lauds the positive role women archaeologists have contributed to palaeontology and archaeology. According to Morris, it has been proposed that because of the particularities of the Driekopseiland topographies, they might 'indicate water or rain or have some connection with puberty ceremonies'. Similar aspects have been noted by Fock, who highlights G/wi girls' coming-of-age rites in Botswana (quoted in Morris, 2007:19; 2008; 2012).

The most striking aspect of Driekopseiland is this ebb and flow of the water over the basalt (Morris, 2007; 2012). The choice of this location is significant as this flowing of the water during different seasons and tides over these basalt glaciers is reminiscent of menstrual flow. New research and interpretations of the numerous art, engravings and geometric patterns at Driekopseiland have positioned women centrally in these artworks. This research promotes the idea of women-centred focus and significance with perhaps 'young women as the makers of

---

13 Online at: http://www.driekopseiland.itgo.com/ (Accessed 1 December 2020).

14 Online at: http://wildebeestkuil.itgo.com/ (Accessed 1 December 2020).

15 Online at: https://www.sa-venues.com/attractionsnc/nooitgedacht-glacial-pavements.php (Accessed 1 December 2020).

16 This paper was given at Wildebeest Kuil as part of the Northern Cape's official Women's Month programme on 21 August 2007. It is made available as part of a resource pack for schools and others by the McGregor Museum Archaeology Department.

those images' (Morris, 2007: 2). Apart from animals, abstracts and shapes, the prevalence of the drawings of apron-like loincloths, worn by women, is remarkable. I would like to argue that these loincloths could possibly be the signatures of the women. If, as argued, that the ebb and flow of the water over these drawings is associated with rituals linked to the menstrual flow of young maidens and their initiation, these rituals would most definitely be coordinated by older women. The geometric engravings dominate here and could possibly reflect the counting of people or animals, or even a list of the /Xam and Naron communities. At Driekopseiland, many abstract engravings are similar to the scarification on women's faces. This is as 'offering to !Khwa/water', itself indistinguishable from the water snake. So once again we see what could be the centrality of *Ilnaosa/aia/!uiki.*

Not only do we have to critically interrogate the theory and knowledge of the North, but also reject aspects of it. The following are the 'experts' visiting the Cape and their observations:

'These heathen are called Hottentots ... are barely human, short in stature, very scrawny and thin. Their speech is disagreeable, as if they were clucking like turkeys' (Johan Jacob Saar, 1660).

'The people of the Cape are the most savage and beastly people God has ever created' (Edward Michelbourne, British official, 1605, quoted in Richards, 2017: back cover).

The above illustrates why we should reject aspects of northern knowledge with contempt. It is hence imperative that: '[w]e ... claim the right to theorise for ourselves, write for ourselves, strategise for ourselves and speak for ourselves as African feminists' (African Feminist Charter, 2006: 4).

REPOSITIONING AND RECLAIMING ... TO MY TWO *ILNAOSA/* GRANDMOTHERS

- /gui, /gam, !nona, haka, koro, !nani, hû, //khaisa, khoese, disi ...

DRIEKOPSEILAND

(Dedicated to my paternal *Ilnaosa/auma/ouma* Christine Fester (c. 1870–1938), paternal grandmother whom I never met).

At Driekopseiland
I am standing at the river

I watch the ebb and flow of the water
I see the myriads of engravings, mostly geometric.
I wonder what they may have meant to you, my ancestor auma?

Scholars[17] share
the most striking aspect
of Driekopseiland
is this flow and ebb of the water;
one moment engravings on the basalt
are visible in the stark hot heat,
and then again
submerged under the water.
We are told
Water and the great mythical snake, *waterslang*,
are still central in older people's lives here.
What seems to be the case
According to Morris
using Fock's work.[18]

The geometric engravings dominant here
at Driekopseiland may
'indicate water or rain
or have some connection with puberty ceremonies'.
Speculation is:
Rhythms of the tides and seasons
may have been used in rites,
Some scholars believe those are linked to 'new maidens'.
Others speculate the ebb and flow
is linked
or symbolic of women's menstrual flow
We do not know ...
Driekopseiland, presumably,
may be one of the places

---

17 I am indebted to the impressive research and scholarship of Professor David Morris. He introduced my colleagues and me from Sol Plaatje University in Kimberley to the archaeological jewels of the Northern Cape, including Driekopseiland, painstakingly explaining the intricacies of these archaeological sites. I also draw from Morris's many texts, including his 'Women in Rock Art', presented at Wildebeest Kuil as part of the Northern Cape's official Women's Month activities, 21 August 2007.

18 Quoted in Morris (2007: 18).

that young maidens
with scars on their faces
engrave those same scars on the rocks
as 'offering to !Khwa/' water,
itself indistinguishable from the water snake.

Young maidens ceremonially court the
water and water snake
This after a long *stap*/walk to the river;
Then 'ochre and other offerings'
would be scattered on the water by women elders
They also splash or sprinkle water
wetting the initiates –
This would 'signify the watersnake's acceptance'.

Young maidens
with scars on their face
engrave those same geometric scars on the rocks

All speculation ...

Auma/ilnaosa Christine,
i wish you told your daughters
about what you had experienced.
They could pass it on to us ...
or was the Christian dogma too strong and all-encompassing that there was no room
for your traditions?

DEDICATED TO MATERNAL ILNAOSA GERTRUDE WICOMB
(NÉE MARTINUS BORN IN PRINCE ALBERT, 6 JUNE 1888–19 MAY 1961).

Ouma Truidjie as everyone called you
Healer, medicine woman, midwife.[19]
You with your white uniform and white isosceles triangular starched veil

---

19 Self-taught midwife to all, Interview with Aunt Una Munnik, 20 November 2020.

On your white horse, Rosmead,
traversing the plains and hills of Outeniqua[20] with its hamlets of
Zuurhoek, Gatplaas, Hotnotskloof, Vinknesrivier and Voorbedacht
Healing and delivering babies to all communities, including those you called 'baas en nooi',
Where did you learn your healing art and skills or was it just like your
!*uika* mother and sisters – ancestors self-taught indigenous knowledge?

Did you acquaint yourself, knowing the herbs, veld flowers and mountain bushes and what was to be used for which ailment?
You - farmer, subsistence survivor, maker of everything required for a full healthy life for your *kroos*[21] of 14
I watched you making butter, churning the still warm freshly milked milk.
I watched, fascinated, as you made sausage using the membranes of the intestines of recently slaughtered sheep or cow
The *solder*[22] filled with the fruits of your labour: dried fruits and biltong for the lean months.
How you spoilt us grandchildren all converging on you during the Christmas holidays with special sweetie nights,
For days we would be assisting you with the baking ginger, spiced and bitter biscuits all baked in the mud oven far from the house,
Also your special *melktert*[23]
Gran, with the long black plaits of your Indian Masbieker[24] heritage, curled twice around your head,
You were and still are the star in our lives.

REFERENCES

Achebe, C. 1994. 'Chinua Achebe and "the bravery of lions"'. Interview 22 March 2013. 2:42 PM ET. Online at: https://www.npr.org/sections/thetwo-way/2013/03/22/175046327/chinua-achebe-and-the-bravery-of-lions (Accessed 29 November 2020).

---

20 Named after the group of indigenous people who first inhabited that area.
21 Afrikaans, meaning descendants, offspring, progeny.
22 Afrikaans, meaning attic, loft, garret.
23 Afrikaans, meaning milk tart.
24 Chapman (1868: 182) noted that 'the prize negroes brought from the east coast' to the Cape were called 'Mosbiekers, 'a corruption of Mosambique' [sic]. 'Masbieker' was in fact a more familiar use at the Cape.

Adésínà, J.O. 2006. 'Sociology beyond despair: Recovery of nerve, endogeneity, and epistemic intervention', *South African Review of Sociology*, 37(2): 241–259.

Adésínà, J.O. 2008. 'Archie Mafeje and the pursuit of endogeny: Against alterity and extroversion', *Africa Development*, 33(4).

Adhikari, M. 2010. *The Anatomy of a South African Genocide: The extermination of the Cape San peoples*. Cape Town: UCT Press.

African Feminist Charter. 2006. http://www.africanfeministforum.com/feminist-charter-introduction/ (Accessed 1 December 2020).

Arneil, B., Deveaux, M., Dhamoon, R. and Eisenberg, A. (eds). 2006. *Sexual Justice/Cultural Justice: Critical perspective in political theory and practice*. London: Routledge, Taylor and Francis.

Chapman, J. 1868. *Travels in the Interior of South Africa: Comprising fifteen years' hunting and trading; with journeys across the continent from Natal to Walvis Bay, and visits to Lake Ngami and the Victoria Falls*. Vol. 2. London: Bell & Daldy.

Ferrus, D. 2006. *Ons Kom Vandaan*. Cape Town: Diana Ferrus Publishers.

Fester, G. 2014a. 'Citizenship and Christianity: Women slaves and descendants in South Africa (1853 to 2013)'. In G. Muganga (ed.). *Healing Wounded History*. Mbarara, Uganda: Bishop Stuart University Press.

Fester, G. 2014b. 'The feminist agenda: Challenges, complexities and contradictions, South Africa (1994–2014)', *Agenda: Empowering Women for Gender Equity*, 28(2): 74–82.

Fester, G. 2015. *South African Women's Apartheid and Post-Apartheid Struggles: 1980–2014*. Saarbrucken: Scholars Press.

Flanagan, T. 2019. *First Nations? Second thoughts*. Kingston, ON: McGill-Queen's University Press.

Haacke, W.H.G. 2020. Notes from Summer School lecture series, Khoekhoegowab, UCT Summer School Lectures, January 2020.

Haacke, W.H.G., Eiseb, E. and Gericke, C. 2010. *Khoekhoegowab-Afrikaans: Glossarium/ Midi Saogub*. Windhoek, Namibia: MacMillan.

Kondlo, K. 2015. 'Meaning and significance of conscience and consciousness in public leadership in the post-1994 South Africa'. *Journal of Public Administration*, 50(3): 485-495.

Krauss, M. 1992. 'The world's languages in crisis', *Language*, 68(1): 4–10.

Lodge, T. 1985. 'Women's protest in the 1950s'. In *Black Politics in South Africa Since 1945*. Johannesburg: Raven Press, pp. 139–152.

Magoqwana, B. 2018. 'Repositioning *uMakhulu* as an institution of knowledge'. In J. Bam, L. Ntsebeza and A. Zinn (eds). *Whose History Counts: Decolonising African pre-colonial historiography*, Stellenbosch:

African Sun Media.

Maseko, P. 2018. 'Language as source of revitalisation and reclamation of indigenous epistemologies'. In J. Bam, L. Ntsebeza and A. Zinn (eds). *Whose History Counts: Decolonising African pre-colonial historiography*. Stellenbosch: African Sun Media.

Mellet, P.T. 2020. *The Lie of 1652: A decolonised history of land*. Cape Town: Tafelberg Publishers.

Miller, P. 1979. *Myths and Legends of Southern Africa*. Cape Town: TV Bulpin Publications.

Mkhize, N. 2018. 'The missing idiom of African historiography'. In J. Bam, L. Ntsebeza and A. Zinn (eds). *Whose History Counts: Decolonising African pre-colonial historiography*, Stellenbosch: African Sun Media.

Morris, D. 2007. 'Women in rock art: The legacy of Maria Wilman and Dora Fock'. Paper presented as part of Women's Day celebrations, McGregor Museum, Kimberley, 21 August 2007.

Morris, D. 2008. 'Driekopseiland rock engraving site, South Africa: A precolonial landscape lost and re-membered. Rock Art of the Northern Cape'. Sol Plaatje University, Kimberley.

Morris, D. 2012. 'Rock art in the Northern Cape: The implications of variability in engravings and paintings relative to issues of social context and change in the precolonial past'. PhD. dissertation, University of Western Cape.

Mufwene, S. 2002. 'Colonization, globalization, and the future of languages in the twenty-first century', *International Journal on Multicultural Societies*, 4 (2): 162–193.

Ntuli, P. 2002. 'Indigenous knowledge systems and the African Renaissance'. In C. Odora Hoppers (ed.). *Indigenous Knowledge and the Integration of Knowledge Systems: Towards a philosophy of articulation*. Cape Town: New Africa Books, pp. 53–66.

Oyěwùmí, O. 1997. *The Invention of Women: Making an African sense of Western gender discourses*. Minneapolis, MN: University of Minnesota Press.

Oyěwùmí, O. 2002. 'Conceptualizing gender: The Eurocentric foundations of feminist concepts and the challenge of African epistemologies', *Journal of Culture and African Women's Studies (JENDA)*, 2(3). Online at: https://www.africaknowledgeproject.org/index.php/jenda/article/view/68 (Accessed 1 December 2020).

Pittman, A. and Rabée N. 2013. 'Voicing autonomy through citizenship; The regional nationality campaign and Morocco'. In M. Sultan and S. Nazneen (eds). *Voicing Demands: Feminists reflecting on strategies, negotiations and influence globally*. London: Zed Books.

Richards, R. 2017. *Bastaards or Human: The unspoken heritage of coloured people* (Vol. 1). Cape Town: Indaba Publishing.

Shah, S. and Brenzinger, M. 2016. *Ouma Geelmeid ke kx'u//xa//xaN/uu* (Ouma Geelmeid teaches N|uu). Cape Town: Centre for African Language Diversity, University of Cape Town.

Vossen, R. 1984. 'Studying the linguistic and ethno-history of the Khoe-speaking (central Khoisan) peoples of Botswana, research in progress', *Botswana Notes and Records*, pp. 19–35.

Wells, J.C. 1998. 'Maternal politics in organising Black South African women'. In O. Nnaemeka (ed.). *Sisterhood, Feminisms and Power*. Trenton, NJ and Asmara, Eritrea: Africa World Press.

8

Ancestral letter to unborn descendants[1]

Sarah Malotane Henkeman

Dear unborn grand- and great grandchildren

> Our starting point is a search for tools. A fine combing of historical archives and narratives, a fine-tuning of the ear, and the development of a wider non-linear vision that can be read backwards, sideways and at all levels at any given point. [...] The relationship between the universal and the particular is one with which feminist scholars must continuously engage (Gasa, 2007: 228).

In this introductory letter, I would like to talk to you about the need for descendants of colonised, oppressed and enslaved people to adapt and craft conceptual tools from below, to help us escape the interlinked, and pre-existing existential and conceptual traps into which we are born. Given my own life experiences, the *existential trap* can best be described as a structure of invisible/visible violence that governs our dehumanised existence across time, and in which the colonial academy is integrally involved. The multilayered *conceptual trap* is in my growing understanding, broadly about barriers to accessing existing knowledge,

---

[1] This chapter draws on previous research and summaries from the following publications noted in references (Henkeman, 2010; 2012; 2016 and 2018).

and to the democratisation of knowledge production from the standpoint of the oppressed. Without producing the visceral, tacit, vicarious and explicit knowledge about the transtemporal[2] and intersectional[3] facts and impacts of our dehumanisation as a result of colonisation–Apartheid–market democracy, we remain forever trapped, and we bequeath these interlocked traps to future generations. If nothing else, this letter is about 'making links' across artificial conceptual boundaries that carry the design of the conceptual/existential trap in which we find ourselves. As Bauwens and Ramos (2020: 127) state:

> Through time, societies have experienced cultural and even civilizational transformations. Such transformations are recorded as collective memory, imbued in song, poetry, art, stories, and histories. For the individual, it is as difficult to get outside their own time frame and to experience historical social change as it is difficult for an ant foraging for food to realize that they are in someone's kitchen.

Thus, history, as a story about the past, does not ordinarily take account of the invisibilised trans- and intergenerational impacts of past events on dehumanised people. The onus is thus on us to collapse time and other artificial boundaries so that we can distil transtemporal knowledge, which crosses the political boundaries of the day. For example, transitional justice and other scholars insert discontinuity between past and present by naming South Africa a 'post-conflict' society. This constitutes a conflation of political and knowledge boundaries – a dilemma that they appear unable to resolve, so they simply ignore it, as it calls their very field into question. What this arbitrary Berlin-style[4] carving up of time and space signals to descendants of colonised, oppressed and enslaved people, is that our transtemporal knowledge about the structural nature of our shared existential trap, remains marginalised – and dismissed.

At the risk of having my contribution to this book viewed as out of place since it is not a narrative about a 'prominent person' or 'event', I still attempt to convey a standpoint about transtemporality in this

---

2   Not bound by ideas of past-present-future delineation of time.
3   Where different elements intersect, similar to crossroads. Can refer to multiple identities, simultaneous experiences, behaviours, conditions, and so forth.
4   This refers to both the carving up of Africa during the Berlin conference of 1884–1885, as well as to the Berlin Wall as examples of the arbitrary and constructed nature of 'borders'.

act of passing on a transdisciplinary conceptual framework from below, across time. This framework honours the unity-of-all-things worldview that our ancestors are reported to have embraced via the pan-African term ubuntu, also known as *Unhu* by the Sotho people and as Khoe!Na by the KhoeSan (Muthien, 2008: 6). Muthien suggests that this can be summed up as 'I am because I belong', rather than the Cartesian 'I think, therefore I am' of Descartes (2008: 6).

Taken together, the form *and* content of this letter, which constitutes a boundary-crossing bricolage, is also a personal battle to convey how I am attempting to come to terms with the fact that I am going to die structurally oppressed within this multifaceted existential trap. At the same time, I attempt to achieve conceptual freedom by constantly thinking of ways out of the conceptual trap to warn you about interlocked invisible mechanisms that many of us only became aware of after political liberation in South Africa. Political liberation, while absolutely necessary, was in the end not sufficient to provide a humane society for all of us. And since I know nothing about what happens once we cross over, I will write a series of letters to you on this matter, while I am still alive.

Personal and collective

Over decades of learning, unlearning and relearning, I am able to read my incomplete journey towards the conscious shared standpoint from where I view the world, as a process of decolonisation from the atomisation of our existence. My particular life experiences are located within a universal, transhistorical dance between a quest for humanity while experiencing dehumanisation at different levels of experience and analysis. I often think about the Zen proverb: 'it is the silence between the notes that makes the music. It is the space between the bars that cages the tiger.' I have learned that it is possible to exercise agency even under structural constraints. Standpoint feminists like Bowell understand that

> the epistemic process by which a standpoint emerges enables the occupants of that standpoint to gain an element of power and control over knowledge about their lives. In becoming occupants of a standpoint, they also become knowing subjects in their own right, rather than merely objects that are known by others.[5]

---

5   Online at: https://iep.utm.edu/fem-stan/ (Accessed 18 February 2021).

To build conceptual tools from below, and to produce and co-produce knowledge about the manifestations, patterns and cultures that produce our lived experiences, *is* a transtemporal act of gaining 'power and control' within this existential trap, so that one day this trap must and will implode. I write as a desperate prospective ancestor, even before I transition.

Brief background

I only became aware of my shared blind spots, a decade after political liberation, and while analysing a conflict which confronted me with South Africa's colonial past in the present, barely an hour's drive from Cape Town. This confrontation by the mirror of history, about the continuity of colonialism–Apartheid–market democracy dehumanisation, made me aware of the conflation of knowledge and political boundaries, and the denial it generates. This triggering moment, and growing awareness of a chasm in my praxis led to focused multiphase action research (including a PhD phase). The research yielded an adaptable framework within which to answer the questions that I had no conceptual tools for, despite already being in possession of multiple tertiary qualifications at the time (Henkeman, 2010). It took years to understand the message in my visceral, tacit, vicarious and explicit knowledge that came to my awareness, and that I now deploy to craft conceptual tools and arguments explicitly from the standpoint of the oppressed. I would like to pass on this overarching adaptable theoretical/methodological framework to you, for further refinement, ground-truthing, calibration and use during your lifetime.

The framework, adapted from veteran peace researcher Johan Galtung's (1996) triad of violence, serves as a heuristic device to continuously generate, manage and analyse data. Ongoing analysis of data in turn provides the means to ground-truth and calibrate the framework to make it responsive to context. This then becomes the means through which a herstorical story can be narrated, without adherence to any temporal and artificial boundaries to knowledge production, as erected in the colonial academy. To loop back to Nomboniso Gasa, it is about the particular, the universal, *and* the relationship between all of these, in perpetual non-linear motion, but also inclusive of the linear, as I came to understand the unity of knowledge, and the spaces and bars that cage the tiger.

This growing understanding of the unity of knowledge/unity of all things (Max-Neef, 1985) was considerably enhanced by the work of Yvette Abrahams and Bernedette Muthien. Abrahams (2007) and Muthien (2008) suggest that local groups, who encountered the first colonisers in South Africa, had a spiritually based social structure that was geared towards harmonious existence with one another and nature. Abrahams, a Khoekhoe historian, argues that not much of the social structure of the historical Khoekhoe has survived after '350 years of colonialism, 250 years of slavery, 48 years of Apartheid and ten years of structural adjustment' (Abrahams, 2007: 217). She suggests that, over time, colonialism distorted the Khoekhoe way of life and existence. For example:

> The taking of a life indiscriminately was just not done. It is probably one of the reasons we were so easily colonized. It took about 150 years for the Khoekhoe to get over killing one colonist; it just wasn't part of our culture. It was only around the mid-nineteenth century that the Khoekhoe began to understand the capitalist idea of taking life, as opposed to sharing life (Abrahams, 2007: 218).

While Abrahams believes that there is nothing left of the historical Khoekhoe social structure, recent research by Muthien suggests that traces of peaceful coexistence in some KhoeSan practices still exist. Using an interdisciplinary, intersectional approach to the study of a peaceful and gender egalitarian society, Muthien's research revealed that the KhoeSan – historically, and as assessed through modern KhoeSan oral history and practices – are a peaceful society for whom non-violence and gender egalitarianism are norms (Muthien, 2008: i). Even in groups where patriarchy was practised, the notion of ubuntu filtered through in everyday practices that were designed to restore wrongdoers to harmony.

History + Herstory = Ourstory

The invitation to write a chapter for this book came during the 2020 lockdown period due to the COVID-19 pandemic. This period forcefully confronted us with our vulnerability and mortality as relatively young people in our networks died one after the other. Strangely, the combination of watching the Zondo Commission[6] videos and thinking

---

6 A public inquiry launched to 'investigate allegations of state capture, corruption, fraud and other allegations in the public sector including organs of state in South Africa'. Online at: https://pmg.org.za/call-for-comment/694/ (Accessed 1 February 2021).

about death, caused me to act on an intensifying desire to communicate with you in some way. As I listened to people who were implicated in corruption and fraud, I wondered what caused many, who were prepared to lay down their lives for liberation, to now steal from those whose shared dehumanisation propelled them before. State capture and the COVID-19 pandemic have arguably brought our country to its knees, yet many even stole money that was intended to save lives during the pandemic. Beyond the legal story of criminality and the world of realpolitik, we have to wonder: What happened to us as human beings? What lessons can be drawn from this dark period so that future generations can be forewarned?

The preoccupation with history as a story about 'the past', as seen mainly through white, middle-class and male lenses, blinds us to the fact that for dehumanised people, the past remains present – and silenced. Our task is to collapse all artificial boundaries to understanding this key truth, and to fully grasp that one aspect and form of dehumanisation gives way to another with regard to what becomes salient over time. The invitation, for which I put two other book projects on hold, made me realise that 'history' as a discipline is about 'the past', so it follows that 'herstory', which is transdisciplinary,[7] should be about past–present–future (transtemporality) as this approach more accurately describes the reality for dehumanised people. For me, labouring for a humane and caring world lies at the root of feminist intersectional theory, and its sub-theory standpointism, which I put to use in this chapter. This transdisciplinary approach enables me to collapse and lump, rather than split a herstory according to geographic, disciplinary, political, social, economic and other artificial boundaries according to which our minds are deliberately shaped. When we collapse artificial boundaries to understanding, we are in a better position to grasp that transhistorical dehumanisation lies at the root of multiple forms, manifestations and patterns of dehumanisation in the present (and future). We become clearer that this is what we need to uproot, even in ourselves, so that a more just and humane society and world can be possible across time.

I thus argue that there is a false dichotomy between the universal and the particular of the past, present and future, but that the particular

---

[7] Micro/macro, past/present, agency/structure and nature/nurture linkages are made for the purpose of attaining social justice. Transdisciplinarity refers to the unity of knowledge as described by Max-Neef (2005: 5) and, thus, there is resonance between transdisciplinarity and a feminist approach – a herstory.

is a microcosm of the universal (macrocosm), and thus the two intersect and interact in perpetuity. The question about fraud, corruption and state capture then becomes, about each person I listen to: 'what are you teaching us about our society that we will bequeath to unborn descendants?' At the heart of this question lies the understanding that for individuals to change, the entire society eventually should, and must, change. Unorthodox[8] students of violence (of which I am one) argue that there is an interaction between individual propensity and structural factors that (co)produce harm or harmony.

It took more than half my lifetime to understand that the *null, hidden* and *official* curricula that constituted my education, rendered me blind and deaf but not so silent, as I was always confronted with vexing questions but not the framework within which to craft an adequate response. I now understand more fully that this dissonance arose as a result of my lived experiences *within a category of dehumanised people in a particular geographic location,* and not only as experienced by me as an individual. So too your everyday experiences in the future will not only be about you and those temporal moments, but will be part of the transtemporal experiences of the oppressed. Thus the notion of history as a discipline that focuses on 'the past' is one of many invisible mechanisms that inserts discontinuity where there is none, and it seeks to deny uninterrupted dehumanisation at different levels of analysis. Feminist intersectional and standpoint theories help us to abstract and attempt to 'theorise our own realities', and to act in line with our knowledge from below.

If history is largely a white, middle-class and/or male perspective about the past, it follows that herstory is an attempt to focus on our collective humanity across time. It cannot be exclusively about women, as we give birth to men and have no desire to write them out of existence; nor can it only be about the oppressed or the oppressor, because then we miss the transgenerational impact of the underlying dehumanisation (as act and impact) that stalks this nation. On the face of it, our oppression was largely based on the colour of our skin, which the United Nations declared a 'crime against humanity'. Yet colonialism, slavery and Apartheid were also economic, political, psychological and social projects that completed our dehumanisation. So, too, is market

---

8 Orthodox scholars of violence tend to focus mainly on visible, physical violence and on individual propensity. Unorthodox scholars take symbolic, structural, psychological and physical(ised) violence into account.

democracy, where inequality (structural violence) along constructed racial lines, has increased. We thus need a more comprehensive framework within which to disrupt, delink from and dismantle the old, and build the new more consciously. As Muncie and Goldson (2006: 104) have suggested, 'there appears to be little analysis of historical, political and economic contexts within which social life occurs' and that 'much of risk literature is mainly understood as individual and family failure' – therefore the micro-level approach. Thus, Apartheid in South Africa after the Truth and Reconciliation Commission (TRC) can become a story about racism or about specific, individual rights violations rather than about long-term, systemic abuses born of a 'colonial project with economic objectives', as Miller (2008) observes.

I hope the following brief transdisciplinary framework will be helpful to understand transhistorical trauma, which I narrowly focus on thereafter. While these aspects of violence are analytically distinct due to theoretical abstraction, they intersect and interact in the realm of experience. I shall write about other aspects and forms of the structure of invisible/visible violence in future letters elsewhere, after this chapter.

Conceptual framework

In this section I briefly describe the basic conceptual framework of dehumanisation (the structure of invisible/visible violence) to show how transhistorical trauma/psychological violence fits within it. I then move to discuss transhistorical trauma and its masked manifestations and patterns, by drawing on examples from different dehumanised groups (the universal), and examples closer to home (the particular) in a bid to connect manifestations–patterns–cultures of dehumanisation and denial. I hope this letter reaches you at a much earlier stage in your life, and that as for me, every encounter with this mind map will draw you into a deeper, wider and longer analysis of invisible mechanisms that shape our lives across generations. This exercise is not only for academic purposes, but so that we can disrupt, delink from, and together with others, dismantle these mechanisms, to contribute more consciously to the design and construction of more humane relationships, societies and world for future generations. More specifically, this particular communication is an attempt to disrupt the transmission of trans- and intergenerational trauma in our own family, and hopefully the broader community of dehumanised people.

Dehumanisation: The invisible/visible structure of violence, a summary

As stated earlier, the adapted basic framework consists of symbolic, structural, psychological and physical(ised) violence. The intersection and interaction of these aspects and forms of violence are routinely denied.

Symbolic violence

Symbolic violence collapses disciplinary and other artificial boundaries. According to Galtung (1996: 2) cultural violence is symbolic, it is exemplified by religion, ideology, language, art, empirical and formal science, and it 'legitimises or delegitimises and justifies structural and direct violence'. Bourdieu and Wacquant (1992: 271) take the concept of symbolic violence further to suggest that it results in unequal power relations that are 'naturalised'. On their part Iadicola and Shupe (2012: 52) argue that 'culture and its learning are important areas to investigate for an analysis of violence, particularly for conceptualizing the forms that violence takes'.

Key examples of symbolic violence in the South African context and elsewhere are:
- Oppression of indigenous people during the colonial and Apartheid eras, which found expression in a hierarchy of racial, economic, social and other forms of oppression based on the dispossession of land, its natural resources and loss of identity.
- Growing 'between' and 'within' group economic inequality which further entrenches 'othering' of people, mainly along racial or ethnic lines.
- Entrenched notions of superiority/inferiority, which inform every aspect of life.
- Inter-ethnic racism among colonised, enslaved and oppressed groups, which mimics the divide and rule strategy reproduced by the hierarchy of oppression.
- Gender oppression rooted in patriarchy.
- Homophobia and discrimination against LGBTQ and gender non-conforming people.
- Discrimination against people with disabilities.
- Epistemic violence in universities and other educational settings, that is, the dominance of Eurocentric knowledge and methods of knowledge production; and the destruction and/or marginalisation of the knowledge claims of indigenous and other oppressed groups.

Structural violence

Based on work done in Baltimore, Haiti, Rwanda and other unequal contexts, anthropologist Paul Farmer et al. (2006) suggest that: 'structural violence is one way of describing social arrangements that put individuals and populations in harm's way'. They argue that 'the arrangements are structural because they are embedded in the political and economic organization of our social world; they are violent because they cause injury to people'. These forces are stated to be 'historically given (and often economically driven) processes and forces [that] conspire to constrain individual agency'.

Structural violence crosses geographic and other artificial boundaries. According to Iadicola and Shupe (2012: 45), it occurs 'internationally in the positioning of nation-states and people within them and how these structures manifest themselves in differences in life chances'. They suggest that if we focus only on interpersonal physical violence, we 'fail to understand and see how the violence that is committed at the highest levels by those with the greatest power manifests itself in the violence of those with the least power in the society and the world' (2012: 49).

Psychological violence

According to Imbusch (2003: 23), psychological violence is inflicted on the mind, psyche and/or soul of people. It is argued to involve some forms of 'psychological cruelty and particular kinds of torture'. He argues that psychological violence is based on 'words, gestures, pictures, symbols, or deprivation of necessities of life, so as to force others into subjugation through intimidation and fear, or specific rewards'. The key observation he makes is that 'while it is difficult to detect', psychological violence is 'considerably more inhumane than physical violence'.

Transhistorical trauma falls within this category of violence, and I return to it later as a narrowed focus in this introductory letter.

Physical violence

Disciplinarity is largely responsible for the fact that visible (physical) violence is delinked from invisible (symbolic, structural and psychological) violence. However, if we take a transdisciplinary view of violence, we link manifestation to patterns, and patterns to cultures of violence, which collapse artificial boundaries to understanding. A principle suggested by Iadiola and Shupe (2012: 45) is that if we want to understand 'the causes of violence in a society, it is crucial to begin by assessing the society in terms of the patterns of interpersonal violence'. They argue that the corollary to this principle is that 'societies with high levels of structural violence also have high levels of institutional and interpersonal violence'. Physical violence is bodily harm that is self-inflicted (personal) and/or inflicted on others (interpersonal, intra- and intergroup, and international), and is intended to inflict pain and/or to end life in private and/or public settings. Physical violence can be understood to happen on a continuum of slow, attempted and successful suicide on the one extreme; and to intentional bodily harm or homicide on the other. There is a third form of physical violence, which I term dehumanisation or oppression-related illnesses, and because of its close link to symbolic–structural–psychological physical violence, I discuss it as part of transhistorical trauma hereunder. This phenomenon has been termed 'racial battle fatigue' (Smith, 2008), 'post-traumatic slave syndrome' (De Gruy Leary, 2005), a 'soul wound' (Duran, 2006) among other descriptive terms used by descendants of colonised, enslaved and oppressed people in other contexts.

In sum, this conceptual framework allows us to analyse the variety of ways in which the mechanisms that produce dehumanisation, manifest our everpresent reality transgenerationally. This allows us to see how the past remains present for dehumanised people via intergenerational transmission. It also shows how marginalisation and dismissal of our knowledge and modes of knowledge production keep us trapped in a past that remains present, with no hope of true freedom for our descendants beyond a continuation of 'marketisation for the minority and democratisation for the majority' (Chua, 2003). As one trap becomes more salient than another over time, it also serves to invisibilise other traps, as well as the links between traps.

TRANSHISTORICAL TRAUMA AND HOW IT MANIFESTS IN THE PRESENT

I now focus narrowly on transhistorical trauma, the 'soul wound' of colonised, oppressed and enslaved peoples, as this psychological/physical aspect of violence as an impact (and trigger) of dehumanisation, has largely been written out of history and remains denied. Over the years I have come to understand its impact on different members of our family, and my intention is to alert you to it, so that you can recognise its masked manifestations, and break the trans- and intergenerational curse more consciously. We cannot, however, delink this form of psychological violence from dehumanisation-related physical illnesses (referred to as a form of physical violence in the conceptual framework). For example, medical health professionals who study the links between racism and some patterned physical illnesses, alert us to this intersection between the disciplines of psychology and health.

What I prefer to name 'transhistorical trauma' is generally referred to as 'historical trauma' with the add-on 'lifespan trauma' by many scholars and practitioners, and particularly Brave Heart et al (2011) who coined the phrase. This split between 'historical' and 'lifespan' creates a false dichotomy and additive method between 'the past', present and future of dehumanised people, as if dehumanisation and its transgenerational impacts are divisible, and not intersectional. Yet reference is made to the intergenerational transmission of trauma. This is unnecessarily confusing, and it falls within the frame of those who have only vicarious knowledge about the content of our lives that refuses to confine itself to disciplinary boundaries. The lesson here is that we need to become clearer about the terminology we use, lest we fall into the disciplinary and siloed trap of knowledge production that has serious transtemporal consequences for dehumanised people. Examples of how these conceptual traps become existential traps for dehumanised people abound, and will be the subject of future letters as we study manifestations to discern patterns and cultures – from the particular to the universal – and more importantly, how these are connected, mainly invisibly, or ignored as they fall in between disciplinary cracks.

Manifestations–patterns–cultures = Particular–relationships–universal

During your lifetime you will become aware that descendants of colonised, oppressed and enslaved people are over- and disproportionately represented in society's stigmatised institutions. Each stigma falls into the domain of different disciplines where it is atomised, with individualised remedies according to narrowed specialisations. Instead of accepting that this is simply due to individual propensity, it is useful to consider the established processes (invisible mechanisms) of routine criminalisation of Blackness, and pathologisation of Otherness in the world, as well as the location from which this gaze is normalised. Seen from the standpoint of the oppressed, many of these behaviours are socially patterned as they are produced within the transtemporal structure of invisible/visible violence. Seen from a present that is delinked from a violent past, the 'soul wound'

(Duran, 2006) and unresolved transhistorical grief of dehumanised people are rendered invisible, and individuals are held solely responsible for their maladaptive behaviours. This becomes very easy when we consider that criminal law individualises harms. Proponents of 'law and order' largely ignore the role that uninterrupted structural violence plays in producing harms manifested by individuals, save as mitigation in some instances, but definitely not all. The 'rule of law', as it becomes the 'role of law' in keeping the status quo and status quo ante intact, requires further investigation.

Peace research offers a glimmer of hope because of its transdisciplinary approach. There are, however, many silences in peacebuilding discourse; what (Galtung, 1996: viii) refers to as causes and effects that are rendered invisible as 'externalities'. These silences centre mainly on the exclusion of the voices of ordinary people who have suffered the intergenerational effects of symbolic–structural–psychological–physical violence in its masked forms, on the one hand, and the continuity of pervasive structural inequality, on the other hand. Curle and Dugan refer to 'emotional, social, or educational deprivation' as 'unpeaceful' and suggest that 'social injustice, economic deprivation and political impotence tend to lead to physical violence' (Curle and Dugan, 1982: 19). They refer to the 'death-wielding impact of systemic, non-physical violence' and cite Apartheid South Africa as an example by arguing that

> it is not only that the freedom of the Black population is curtailed in a myriad of ways ranging from limited access to education and income from the forced separation of families, but that their actual physical lives are limited in just as real a way as planned execution. [...] These early deaths are the result of a systematic discriminatory distribution of social goods (medical care, sanitary conditions, subsistence, incomes, etc.) that contribute to longevity (Curle and Dugan, 1982: 20).

HISTORICAL TRAUMA = TRANSHISTORICAL TRAUMA

Manifestations of transhistorical trauma, and how to recognise and deal with it and its consequences, are the most neglected parts of state-level conceptions of peacebuilding and, indeed, of civil society peacebuilding in general. Brave Heart et al. (2011: 283) define 'historical trauma' as 'cumulative emotional and psychological wounding across generations, including the lifespan, which emanates from massive group trauma'. It has also been suggested that 'there is significant variation in how people experience, employ and intergenerationally transmit trauma experiences' (Denham, 2008: 391). Sotera's (2006: 99) conceptual model of historical trauma consists of the following elements: '(1) overwhelming physical and psychological violence, (2) segregation and/or displacement, (3) economic deprivation, and (4) cultural dispossession.' As Sotera (2006: 99) argues:

> Though overt legitimization of subjugation may be rescinded over time, its legacy remains in the form of racism, discrimination and social and economic disadvantage [...] Second and subsequent generations are affected by the original trauma through various means. Extreme trauma may lead to subsequent impairments in the capacity for parenting. Physical and emotional trauma can impair genetic function and expression, which may in turn affect offspring genetically, through in utero biological adaptations, or environmentally. Evidence suggests that disorders such as mental illness, depression and PTSD can be genetically transmitted to secondary and subsequent generations.

This suggests that the effects of intergenerational and lifespan dehumanisation in the form of discrimination, dispossession and oppression are compounded and shrouded in silence and denial, which makes it easy to individualise. The implication of this argument is that even those individuals who 'act out' in the form of social harm, are also unaware of the determinants and triggers of their actions. As Volkan (2006: 6–7) contends, when people become a deliberate target of the aggression of 'others', the victimised group have to cope with 'five interrelated psychological phenomena and others related to them'. He argues that these psychological phenomena 'attach themselves to real-world issues in the affected societies, such as continuing poverty, inexperience in the democratic way of life, corruption in the new political system, and international manipulations' (Volkan, 2006: 6). These psychological phenomena are argued to be

> a shared sense of shame, humiliation, dehumanization and guilt; a shared inability to be assertive; a shared identification with the oppressor; a shared difficulty or even inability to mourn losses; a shared transgenerational transmission of trauma (Volkan, 2006: 6–7).

I interpret this to mean that a two-way relationship is implied here. Firstly, where the traumatised person is retraumatised by the continuities of the traumatising event, and secondly, where traumatised people become the perpetrators of similar or other offences. Either way, a parasitic link can be inferred here by the use of the word 'attach'. According to Volkan, 'even when political and legal systems change and traumatizing elements within the society are removed, individual and societal responses to the previously existing and devastating political system do not disappear overnight'. This is an important aspect to take into account since he argues that 'depending on the severity of the traumatizing events and how long they lasted, the influence of the shared trauma on the victimised group *and their descendants* may continue for decades' (Volkan, 2006: 6).

Transhistorical trauma can, therefore, legitimately be understood from the standpoint of victims, as a conceptual/existential trap, the nub of which is expressed by Zolkos (2009: 270–271) as:

> Temporal immobility or the impossibility of passing through [...] in trauma theory, the traumatized person experiences the traumatic event as if it had a spectral quality of a continuous appearance after it had come to pass. Trauma complicates the relation between past and future in which what seems to belong to the realms of the past carries ontological weight in the present.

This suggests that transhistorical trauma is not an event, but a series of lived and relived events over time – a process that requires systemic rather than only individual intervention – and thus a transtemporal process that cannot be confined to 'history' as a story of 'the past'. This is incisively captured in the words of Khoekhoe historian Abrahams (2007: 422), who chronicled her struggle in a journal, which gives an idea of research on an aspect of South Africa's history, from a subjugated position:

> This diary is about my inability to be a disembodied academic dispassionately analysing some objectified specimen. My race and my gender follow me, even into my academic work. There is not, in the Sarah Baartman historiography which has been written by white males, any symbolic role model where Black = good, woman = righteousness, or Brown = beauty.

Here Abrahams alludes to the fact that she had to do a lot of '[r]estoring, recontextualising and rebutting' to rework the Khoekhoe history written from a white, mainly male perspective; and to replace this with an exploration of the triple intersection of the identity African/native/slave (Abrahams, 2007: 436).

Abrahams speaks to, and for many, if not all, indigenous women, when she demonstrates through her words, how the past remains present, for we are Sarah Baartman in a world that continues to either pathologise or criminalise us.

Dreaming the future[9]

There is no neat conclusion to this transtemporal bricolage as a herstorical account. It is first and foremost an act of self/community determination with regard to knowledge and knowledge production, then it can be read as a counterpoint to 'history' as stories about 'past events' or prominent men. It is ultimately about the *relationship* between selected particularities and what is considered to be universal. In this way, this transherstorical bricolage is also inclusive of history. My hope is that besides finding the conceptual framework useful for adaptation to your context, that you will also invert it, to make the implied opposite of every aspect and form of dehumanisation into incremental acts towards a more humane society and world. We cannot recreate the world of our ancestors, but we can learn from a worldview in which our lives are not atomised, but one in which we are interdependent and where being humane and respectful of the earth, benefits all of us.

'Worlding' (Spivak, 1985: 235) happens in the mind, before it is physically reproduced in 'the world'. Make your mind count!

References

Abrahams, Y. 2007. 'Ambiguity is my middle name: A research diary'. In N. Gasa (ed). *Women in South African History: Basus'iimbokodo, Bawel'imilambo / They Remove Boulders and Cross Rivers*. Cape Town: HSRC Press.

Bauwens, M. and Ramos, J. 2020. 'Awakening to an ecology of the commons'. In A. Grear and D. Bollier (eds). *The Great Awakening: New modes of life amidst capitalist ruins*. California: punctum books.

Bourdieu, P. and Wacquant, L.D.J. 1992. *An Invitation to Reflexive Sociology*.

---

9 I first encountered the notion of 'Dreaming the future' as a facilitator on women's workshops held around South Africa by the Desmond Tutu Peace Centre from about 2000–2004. Glenda Wildschut, a former TRC commissioner, was the director of this project. Afterwards several women and I co-wrote a book, edited by Ms Davis of *Agenda*, titled *Rainfire: Women in leadership in South Africa*, which was published in 2005.

Chicago, IL: University of Chicago Press.

Bowell, T. 2011. 'Feminist Standpoint Theory'. In J. Fieser and B. Dowden (eds). *Internet Encyclopedia of Philosophy.* Online at: https://iep.utm.edu/fem-stan/ (Accessed 15 February 2021).

Brave Heart, M.Y.H., Chase, J., Elkins, J. and Altschul, D.B. 2011. 'Historical trauma among indigenous peoples of the Americas: Concepts, research, and clinical considerations', *Journal of Psychoactive Drugs*, 43(4): 282–290.

Chua, A. (2003). World on fire: how exporting free market democracy breeds ethnic hatred and global instability. New York: Doubleday.

Curle, A. and Dugan, M.A. 1982. 'Peacemaking: Stages and sequences', *Peace and Change*, 8(2-3): 19–28.

Davis, C. (ed.). 2005. *Rainfire: Women in leadership in South Africa.* Cape Town: Desmond Tutu Peace House.

De Gruy Leary, J. 2005. *Post Traumatic Slave Syndrome: America's legacy of enduring injury and healing.* Milwaukie, OR: Uptone Press.

Denham, A.R. 2008. 'Rethinking historical trauma: Narratives of resilience', *Transcultural Psychiatry*, 45(3): 391–414.

Duran, E. 2006. *Healing the Soul Wound: Counseling with American Indians and other native peoples.* New York: Teachers College Press.

Farmer, P.E., Nizeye, B. Stulac, S. and Keshavjee, S. 2006. Structural violence and clinical medicine', *PLOS Medicine*, 3(10): e449.

Galtung, J. 1996. *Peace by Peaceful Means: Peace and conflict, development and civilization.* Oslo: International Peace Research Institute.

Gasa, N. 2007. 'Feminisms, motherisms and patriarchies in the women's struggle'. In N. Gasa (ed). *Women in South African History: Basus'iimbokodo, Bawel'imilambo /They Remove Boulders and Cross Rivers.* Cape Town: HSRC Press.

Henkeman, S.R. 2010. 'Mediator's dilemma: Mediation in South Africa – an unequal, deeply divided, transitional society', *Tidsskrift for Norsk Psykologforening*, Oslo, 47: 731–733.

Henkeman, S.R. 2012. 'Restorative justice as a tool for peacebuilding: A South African study. PhD dissertation, College of Law and Management Studies, University of KwaZulu-Natal, South Africa. Unpublished.

Henkeman, S.R. 2016. 'Open guide to a deeper, wider and longer analysis of violence'. Unpublished guide.

Henkeman, S.R. (ed.). 2018. *Disrupting Denial: Analysing narratives of invisible/visible violence and trauma.* Cape Town: New Adventure Publishers.

Iadiola, P. and Shupe, A. 2012. *Violence, Inequality, and Human Freedom*, 3rd edition. Lanham, MD: Rowman and Littlefield.

Imbusch, P. 2003. 'The concept of violence'. In W. Heitmeyer and J. Hagen (eds). *International Handbook of Violence Research*. Dordrecht, Netherlands: Kluwer Academic Publishers

Max-Neef, M.A. 2005. 'Foundations of transdisciplinarity', *Ecological Economics*, 53(1): 5–16.

Miller, Z. 2008. 'Effects of invisibility: In search of the 'economic' in transitional justice', *International Journal of Transitional Justice*, 2(3): 266–291.

Muncie, J. and Goldson, B. 2006. *Comparative Youth Justice: Critical issues*. London: SAGE Publications.

Muthien, B.F 2008. 'The Khoesan and partnership, beyond patriarchy and violence'. Master's dissertation, University of Stellenbosch. Unpublished.

Smith, W.A. 2008. 'Higher education: Racial battle fatigue'. In R.T. Schaefer (ed.). *Encyclopedia of Race, Ethnicity, and Society*. Thousand Oaks, CA: SAGE Publications, pp. 615–618.

Sotera, M.M. 2006. 'A conceptual model of historical trauma: Implication for public health and research', *Journal of Health Disparities and Practice*, 1(1): 93–108.

Spivak, G.C. 1985. 'Three women's texts and a critique of imperialism', *Critical Inquiry*, 12(1): 235–261.

Volkan, V. 2006. 'The next chapter: Consequences of societal trauma'. Online at: http://www.vamikvolkan.com/The-Next-Chapter%3A-Consequences-of-Societal-Trauma.php (Accessed 2 February 2021).

Zolkos, M. 2006. 'The conceptual nexus of human rights and democracy in the Polish Lustration Debates 1989–97', *Journal of Communist Studies and Transition Politics*, 22(2): 228–248.

9

The Falling Sky

Some notes about originary peoples in Brazil[1]

Ana Lígia Leite e Aguiar

> Whoever knows enough to have no fear
> And is strong enough to know that it exists
> And in the middle of their cogs and gears
> Makes plans against the one part that resists
>
> Who never falters even in defeat
> Who even when they've lost do not give in
> And severed, wrapped inside the storm,
> Between their clenched teeth hold onto spring.
>
> Secos e Molhados, *Primavera nos dentes*[2]

Brazilian literature, economy, politics and cultural life had always been studied from a colonised/colonising point of view. However, in the middle of the 20th century many studies have suggested a change of perspective. There was the option of valuing the local to

---

1 These notes are the result of a class for the Political Economy of Africa course, Centre for African Studies at UCT taught by Dr June Bam, in the midst of the COVID-19 pandemic during 2020. This study was financed in part by the Coordenação de Aperfeiçoamento de Pessoal de Nível Superior – Brasil (Capes) – Finance Code 001.

2 My sincere thanks to my sister, Ana Flávia Leite e Aguiar, and my friend, Bernard Belisário, for reviewing this paper, and Rob Packer for the poetic translation of the epigraph.

the detriment of the global (global versus local, which was not already a theorised discussion), the growth of cultural studies and the speech of people in vulnerable situations. Some special narratives, to name but a few important ones in Latin America, are: Rigoberta Menchú (*Me llamo Rigoberta Menchú y así me nació la consciência/ I, Rigoberta Menchú*, 1983, Guatemala); Carolina Maria de Jesus (*Quarto de despejo: diário de uma favelada/* Child of the dark: The diary of Carolina Maria de Jesus, 1960, Brazil); Domitila Barrios de Chungara (*Si me permiten hablar/* Let me speak, 1978, Bolivia). These narratives revealed the tenuous link in relation to literature, protest, sociology, portraying poverty-stricken people or human rights, anthropology, testimony, (auto)biography, symbolic analysis, etc. The speech barriers were blurred at that time. After decades we realised that contrasting literature would appear to demonstrate how we live in our land and deal with common issues, dissimilarities and disagreements. Awareness that such discourses have always existed, in different configurations, is what we today call 'decolonialism' or being decolonial.

SPEAKING OF DECOLONIAL PLACES us in a dilemma, which Stuart Hall (born in Jamaica) interrogated in his chapter, 'When was the post-colonial? Thinking at the limit' (1996). Colonialism doesn't end, and according to Hall and other prominent authors, such as Ella Shoat and Arif Dirlik – about whom he had a few reservations – the expression 'postcolonial' is confusing and cannot be applied in the same way to countries like Nigeria, Australia, India and Brazil because their different colonisation systems were different back then and, second, because of the fundamental changes that have occurred in these countries since colonisation took place around 500 years ago.

The postcolonial expression is ambivalent because, as McClintock (1992) says, our time – until now – has been European time, its periodism and its binarism. As postcolonial refers to something beyond colonial structures, there will naturally be many differences between them. In addition, Hall alerts us to a precarious and dangerous polarisation in the word *post*, since it can be interpreted as *after* or *continuum*; both interpretations raise issues, as the false idea that the word *after* cannot be sustained, because it implies an end to something; and the word *continuum* is not experienced by everybody equally. Hall writes that the idea of continuity, as a subtle transition between temporalities, is mistaken and this idea gains momentum from intellectuals who move from the First to the Third World. For Hall, these intellectuals enjoy a false sense of belonging, even though the barriers between the worlds have changed quickly and considerably, extrapolating the polarisations, here/there, colonised/settlers, etc. Postcolonialism is a secondary effect of colonialism (Hall, 1996: 110), which prevents us from fully mapping its implications. It is arguable, it contains tension and 'it shifts the history of capitalist modernity from European centring to its peripheries scattered across the globe' (Hall, 1996: 113).

TO UNDERSTAND THE UNRELENTING side of colonialism and its mentality, I am going to use Brazil to illustrate the current situation. It took almost five years after the publication of the French edition of *The Falling Sky: Words of a Yanomami Shaman* by Davi Kopenawa, before Brazilian readers were given the opportunity to read the Brazilian edition in Portuguese, even though Kopenawa is an indigenous leader from Brazil. Although a small proportion of the Brazilian population – intellectuals, artists, politicians, researchers and others – makes an effort to safeguard indigenous rights to their land, there are still disputes and disorientation regarding people's origins and rights to particular pieces of land, resulting in what we may call *auto-colonialism*. By *auto-colonialism* we mean a desire to reject, deny and transform this indigenous cultural heritage into an impoverished neighbourhood. For more insight into the subject, see Luciani (2016). A certain mentality continues to deforest, creates work in conditions similar to slave labour, and tries to perpetuate all the logic of a patriarchal society. Nowadays, this colonising behaviour is no longer perpetrated by foreigners, but by people from inside the country.

Brazilian anthropologist Eduardo Viveiros de Castro emphasises the idea of a landless Indian to deprive the indigenous people of their main attribute, land, which gives them their identity as Indians. Their values, customs and stories are connected to certain territories. Therefore, Indians without their territory are most likely Indians without their culture. Consequently, Indians without their traditions and cultural features become just like any other impoverished Brazilians, who will need government aid to survive. Additionally, farmers, land grabbers, prospectors and the tourism industry are not only the most ruthless promoters of poverty, but also to blame for the killing of native people and their culture.

Constantly struggling to acquire freehold tenure of their land, the Yanomamis and their leader, living in the furthermost north of Brazil, on the border with Venezuela, have decided to 'send some messages' to 'white episteme'. When we say 'white episteme', it is not to address skin colour, but rather a reference to a hegemonic class of people. Gold digging and mining currently widen the *napë's* (outsider or enemy) field,[3] which is 'the other indeed, the enemy par excellence and essence is white men' (Viveiros de Castro, 2015: 13). Enemy, foreigner, outsider – the world of white episteme emphasises that the exercise of indigenous alterity finds hostility in the world of white men. Another meaning for *napë*, which means the opposite of indigenous, is alien (Viveiros de Castro, 2015: 13).

Kopenawa's estimated date of birth is around 1956. Since the 1970s, he has tailored his life around the Yanomami people's rights to life and the protection of the people and their land. In his book, we observe the following: the denunciation, anger and stigmatisation of and by missionaries; the contrast between Brazilians and native indigenous people/forest people/traditional populations; furthermore, the portrayal of whites as thieves of indigenous children and bearers of plagues in general, such as pneumonia, measles, tuberculosis and influenza. Most importantly, he underlines that whites have their minds set on commodities. In his work, Davi Kopenawa introduces his own memories, his cosmogony and his relationship with *xapiri* (forest spirits, with whom only the shaman can communicate) since childhood. Today, he is recognised as a well-known writer and has challenged the world with reference to the dichotomous lectures given by white people. A shaman is an enchanted person, an entity, a man who talks with the world and nature on a different level to ordinary human beings.

Throughout the book, we enter Davi Kopenawa's trajectory, however we understand that it is an insurgency without illusions. Although he is against colonialism and he launches his myths of foundation, he wisely avoids being messianic. Kopenawa does not claim salvation as a shaman, because he understands that relationships demand continuous work. Therefore, listening is crucial. It is up to each one of us to acknowledge our own sensibilities and affections. He says:

Today white people think we should imitate them in every way. Yet this is not what we want. I learned their ways from childhood and I speak a little of their language. Yet I do not want to be one of them. I think that we will only be able to become white people the

---

3 "The word *napë* (plur. *-pë*) actually means 'outsider, enemy'" (Kopenawa and Albert, 2013: 490).

day white people transform themselves into Yanomami. I also know that if we live in their cities, we will be unhappy (Kopenawa and Albert, 2013: 22).

This is what I think. By wanting to possess all this merchandise, they were seized by a limitless desire. Their thought was filled with smoke and invaded by night. It closed itself to other things. It was with these words of merchandise that the white people started cutting all the trees, mistreating the land, and soiling the water-courses. First they started all over their own forest. Now there are few trees left on their sick land, and they can no longer drink the water of their rivers. This is why they want to do the same thing again where we live (Kopenawa and Albert, 2013: 327).

There is only one sky and we must take care of it, for if it becomes sick, everything will come to an end. This may not take place right now, but it could happen later. Then it will be our children, their children, or the children of their children who will die. This is why I tell the white people these words of warning that I have heard from very great shamans. Through them, I want to make them understand that they should dream further and pay attention to the voices of the forest's spirits. But I know very well that most of them will remain deaf to my words. They are other people. They do not hear us or do not want to listen to us. They think this warning is just a lie. But this is not the case. Our words are very old. If we were ignorant about these things, we would remain silent. But on the contrary, it is the thought of the white people, who know nothing of the *xapiri* and the forest, that seems full of oblivion (Kopenawa and Albert, 2013: 410).

FIRST OF ALL, WE HAVE our history recounted by foreigners, since *the arrival* of the Portuguese freight. *Arrival*, meaning *invasion* – these words have always been a subject of debate up to the beginning of the 20th century. With input from anthropologists, sociologists, artists and an array of knowledgeable people, some aspects have changed regarding our dependence on the global North. The Brazilian Modernism movement,[4] for example, reinstated our past national issues, starting a battle over images and restoring our cultural and economic idea of dependence on Western ideas and values, once more reinforcing prejudices and misconceptions, such as 'the only good criminal is a dead criminal'. It is of paramount importance to understand how

---

4   Brazilian Modernism is not the focus on this paper, but for a brief explanation, see: https://library.brown.edu/create/fivecenturiesofchange/films-and-literature/

people become impoverished and what drives them into criminality. It is equally important is to understand the indigenous population in the same way and stay away from the mentality that replicates the idea that 'the only good Indian is a dead Indian'. Coloniality is still prevalent, leaving the indigenous population regarded as over and done with. This mindset and the extreme lack of knowledge can only contribute to the increasing social inequality and the status quo that reinforces cultural genocides.

COLONIALITY IS STILL PREVALENT in Brazil and this stimulates defiance and confrontation. Currently, there are about one million indigenous people spread across Brazil and the numbers are increasing. Kopenawa's work reveals epistemic diversity, disengages from universalisms and recognises how the communities' canonical historiography has been provincialised and oversimplified.[5] Kopenawa's voice can be seen as the voice of a group; it is the collective that speaks; it is the voice of ancestry that is 'gone but not forgotten'. It is the struggle for a democracy, where many define the lives of many. Ramón Grosfoguel (2016:44) says:

> There are still non-Western epistemic perspectives, which retain a relative externality of Eurocentric Modernity. They were affected by the genocide/epistemicide, but they were not completely destroyed. It is this relative exteriority that, according to Enrique Dussel, provides hope and the possibility of a transmodern world: 'a world where many worlds are possible', to use the Zapatista slogan.

Relative exteriority is the key symbol of Kopenawa's work. Basically, we have to disobey (white episteme) in order to exist, he says. There is an urgency to piece together a world where differences do not have to be eliminated. Applying the ideas of Marisol de la Cadena, a Peruvian anthropologist, it is as if during every Anthropocene (see Chakrabarty, 2009) there was always an Anthropo-Not-seen, unable to see the functioning of the world through other relationships (Cadena, 2019). Assuming, on the one hand, the Anthropo-Not-seen struggles to eradicate disobedience, and on the other, classifying disobedience as human and non-human, once again separating nature and culture.

---

5   These concepts are better explained by Puerto Rican sociologist Ramón Grosfoguel (2011).

EPISTEMIC DISOBEDIENCE IS a concept that Walter Mignolo, a decolonial theorist from Argentina, uses to define some resistance systems. Such disobedience, however, does not reside at the theoretical or written level as we understand it, but includes a large number of actions (see Mignolo, 2009). For some time now, and more recently during the global COVID-19 pandemic, Brazilian shamans from over 300 indigenous villages have been warning the world and Brazil about diseases afflicting society, such epidemics caused by mosquitoes, in particular, Dengue, Zika and Chikungunya, and last but not least, as the gold fever, and the contamination of natural resources – rivers and seas – by greedy mining corporations. All things considered, these diseases are only an extension of the biological warfare to which indigenous people in Brazil have been subjected since the 1500s and since 1492 in the Caribbean and neighbouring areas. In addition, extraction of natural resources for export, excessive cattle breeding and monoculture have increased the existing self-colonisation that Brazil continues to self-inflict.

During the COVID-19 pandemic, Chief Cacique Babau and the Tupinambá indigenous group from Serra do Padeiro sealed roads and highways, enforcing their own sanitary barriers, as well as increasing the yield and the diversity of their crops to ensure that their people can be self-sustaining for the next two years. My research reveals a model of cooperation among members of the Tupinambá group. It shows their detachment from the Brazilian state, how their democratic process is nurturing, and their cultural autonomy and respect for their shamans and inherited knowledge. In the absence of a state that is committed to life, another state takes shape. Other possible worlds and ways of doing things were revealed as numerous contingency plans were executed by indigenous peoples during the pandemic in 2020. Juma Xipaia, an indigenous activist, has reported other examples from Médio Xingu. Actions such as this do not prevent the violence of an absent state from spreading along with the destructive virus – and this was understood long before 2020. An absent state, paradoxically, advances a project of destruction; which means that the state has always been there, lurking, and continuing the *auto-colonialist* war.[6]

Unquestionably capable of taking care of themselves, Chief Babau asserts that, the peoples can guarantee themselves sovereignty.[7] It is the

---

[6] Online at: https://www.youtube.com/watch?v=1JPSWGJG8JI (Accessed 12 October 2020).

[7] Online at: https://www.youtube.com/watch?v=oMFsmFme9lA&feature=youtu.be

indigenous way of life: 'you command while obeying' (Grosfoguel, 2016: 45). What does this mean? A society that understands the meaning of this is already a step away from that dreamed desire for equality that democracy promises us. What Cacique Babau reminds us, like Juma Xipaia, is that this democratic society already exists – and it is indigenous.

REFERENCES

Cadena, M. de la. 2019. 'Uncommoning nature stories from the anthropo-not-seen'. In P. Harvey, C. Krohn-Hansen and K. Nustad (eds). *Anthropos and the Material*. Durham, NC: Duke University Press, pp. 35–58.

Chakrabarty, D. 2009. 'The climate of history: Four theses', *Critical Inquiry*, 35 (2): 197–222.

Grosfoguel, R. 2011. 'Decolonizing post-colonial studies and paradigms of political-economy: Transmodernity, decolonial thinking and global coloniality', *Transmodernity: Journal of Peripheral Cultural Production of the Luso-Hispanic World*, 1(1): 1–38.

Hall, S. 1996. 'When was the post-colonial? Thinking at the limit'. In *The Post-colonial Question: Common skies, divided horizons*. London and New York: Routledge.

Hall, S. 1996. *The Post-colonial Question: Common skies, divided horizons*. London and New York: Routledge.

Kopenawa, D. and Albert, B. 2013. *The Falling Sky: Words of a Yanomami shaman*. Cambridge, MA: Harvard University Press.

Luciani, J.A.K. 2016. *Sobre a antimestiçagem*. Florianópolis: Cultura e Barbárie. Online at: http://culturaebarbarie.org/novo/wp-content/uploads/2016/05/antimesticagem.pdf (Accessed 6 October 2020).

McClintock, A.1992. 'The angel of progress: Pitfalls of the term post-colonialism'. *Social Text*, 31/32.

Mignolo, W. 2009. 'Epistemic disobedience, independent thought and decolonial freedom', *Theory, Culture & Society*, 26(7-8): 1–23.

Viveiros de Castro, E. (1992). *From the Enemy's Point of View: Humanity and divinity in an Amazonian society*. Chicago, IL: University of Chicago Press.

Viveiros de Castro, E. 2011. *The Inconstancy of the Indian Soul: The encounter of Catholics and cannibals in sixteenth-century Brazil*. Chicago, IL: Prickly Paradigm Press.

(Accessed 30 August 2020).

Conclusion

June Bam and Bernedette Muthien

'Why do you hold on to bones that cannot talk/
is it with their pain and agony with which you wish to walk'
– Dianna Ferrus

In a sense one can say we have written an implicit scholarly dedication to the memory of Sarah Baartman and other indigenous women ancestors, beyond the metaphor and predominant victimhood discourse, by transposing her negation to a serious rethinking of scholarship – not by focusing only on the colonial horrors that beset her, as scholarship has done without offering something new to her memory. Instead, as scholars, we have seriously considered what restoring her, their and our humanity would mean for decolonial, indigenous feminist, scholarly methods and research.

When we set out to write this book, we wanted to engage deep listening as part of the process to decolonise scholarship in an African feminist context. We all had very different ideas of what this would mean, coming from diverse disciplines, scholarships and forms of activism. We knew that the task could be attained only through transdisciplinary work and a reflection on praxis, by applying theory and practice in 'looking back' in deep time and its ongoing presence. We knew that we could not dislocate the present from the past or our personal experiences from scholarship. The one could not exist without the other, and this is a strong thread that runs throughout this book, as a dedication to our *Taradi, Ausidi (Ousis)* and *ooMakhulu*.

To the authors, this meant many things in going beyond conventional research methods and theorising. What the authors have in common is their long established praxis in the field in their respective capacities, which brought a range of authenticities to the particular perspectives they shared. New forms of narrativisation were brought to the surface, as storytellers within traumatised landscapes. They set out to interrupt the dismissive professor in his 'ignorant ignorance', to invite him to deep listening which can provide opportunities for a fuller, richer and more diverse, informed and inclusive scholarship. The authors made themselves vulnerable in the process by departing from Western canonical disciplines and regimes of what counts as scholarship and what does not. They disrupted the governability of what counts in epistemologies, taking forward the innovative work of Namibian historian Memory Biwa's 'women's quilt' as oral history to interrogate unreconciled narratives, breaking down the barriers so that we can understand who we are. Our intergenerational knowledge ecology is this ritual archive (Falola) of spirits, ancestors, languages, vibration of plants, water, sky and wind – of weaving quilts of knowledge that are infinite, dialogical and diverse. It is not finite, closed and limited, nor limiting. It does not judge and ridicule the knowledges outside the university – the homeless woman, the unemployed carer, the woman in the factory or on the farm. Deep listening requires inclusivity in dialogical processes; those stories that are told ancestrally on the wind.

In saying this, Paulo Freire's (1968) *Pedagogy of the Oppressed* has perhaps gained increased relevance during COVID-19. Senegalese anthropologist Francis Nyamnjoh (2017) speaks of conviviality that we require as Africans, to discount the foolish pretence of completeness, of 'knowing all'. There can be no fuller knowing without conviviality. Matricentrism has endured with conviviality (even in righteous rage) despite patriarchy and attempts at feminism-cide, *Taras*-cide, *Ausi*-cide (*Ousi*-cide), *uMakhulu*-cide – because that is the way of many women of the heart. It is through the dialogical of conviviality that we speak for and determine for ourselves on our terms, as deep listening requires a respectful stillness, an earthiness. We are interconnected and interdependent in crafting paths in new knowledge production processes; a necessary symbiosis in more complete and inclusive knowledge ecologies that draw on deep time for relevance in the present – strands of a web, swatches of fabric in a timeless grandmother's quilt.

De-Africanisation of indigenous women was and is an epistemicidal act. It calls for a reimagination of an African past through art, literature, music, poetry and the creative engagement with erased and endangered languages (as sources of knowledge). In these creative reimaginations, we are called to engage with the archives as sites of living knowledge production, rather than as a single, static, definitive source. When we reposition *uMakhulu*, *Taras* and *Ausi* (*Ousi*) in the centre in that reimagining process, we get closer to turning the colonial de-Africanisation process on its head through African and indigenous language restoration, knowledge of plants and healing rituals. She is no longer the vacuous body when the ritual archive comes alive – in the space of *ukubuyisa*.

When we reimagine through new methodologies, we invigorate scholarship that helps lift us out of the fatigue and burden of retelling our multigenerational victimhood over and over again. When we reimagine through the *Ausi* (*Ousi*), *Taras* and *uMakhulu* power in the ritual archive, the negating epistemicidal act through the brutalisation of the body of Sarah Baartman is radically negated, confronting also indigenous patriarchy and its now increasingly fashionable fake posturing of 'indigenous tradition' and 'indigenous culture'. This is an important step in decolonising historiography towards herstoriography beyond essentialisms and 'intellectual stagnation' (Keet, 2014). In recognising our maternal ancestors as archives of worthwhile and powerful knowledge, we are rescued from the decolonial curse of irrelevance in Africa. This is something this book argues for current feminist struggles as well; learning from the African metaphoric languages of our grandmothers on how to negotiate power and sometimes how to use it.

And in this process of reimagining a more centred *Ausi* (*Ousi*), *Taras* and *uMakhulu*, we also ask the critical questions of decolonisation beyond frontiers in the global South – what is it that we can share and learn from in a deeper understanding of our indigenous feminist interrelatedness in an ongoing presence that defied attempts at extermination of deep knowledge and deep time?

As authors, we hope that we have begun to provide the new alternatives for these dialogues and circles of conversation for deep listening by presenting this inaugural volume of indigenous women's voices in the Rethinking Africa series.

More volumes in this series are well on their way to you – herstories – as we continue to co-create and rematriate our past, present and future, placing women back where they belong: in the centre of our society. Peace. *Vrede. Uxolo.*

REFERENCES

Freire, P. 1970. *Pedagogy of the Oppressed* (M. Bergman Ramos, trans.). New York: Continuum, pp. 65–80.

Keet, A. 2014. 'Plastic knowledges: Transformations and stagnations in the Humanities', *Alternation*, 21(2): 99–121.

Nyamnjoh, F.B. 2017. 'Incompleteness: Frontier Africa and the currency of conviviality', *Journal of Asian and African Studies*, 52(3): 253–270.

one & many

Bernedette Muthien

With the one in the many,
and the many in the one,
does not mean that one gets eclipsed
or even destroyed
by the many,
as the liberals will have us believe.
Each, one and many,
are important components of the whole and beyond.
Like the many colours that flow into a rainbow
like water into an ocean,
one can see the rainbow,
and the individual colours that create the rainbow,
inseparable and one,
as one can see a drop of water and the infinity of oceans,
one and many,
in an infinite dance,
that defines the essence
of humanity,
of the world,
of the cosmos.

Contributors

ANA LÍGIA LEITE E AGUIAR

Ana Lígia Leite e Aguiar is a professor of Brazilian Literature at the Federal University of Bahia and a post-doctorate at the Federal University of Rio de Janeiro. She specialises in Brazilian literature, biographical criticism, comparative literature, studies on the nation and image studies, and has written many articles on these themes. Currently, she is researching anti-colonial theories and arts in the tropics. Ana is also a visiting professor at the Centre for African Studies under the NIHSS Precolonial Catalytic Project and collaborates in research with the Khoi and San Unit and on the teaching of the African Studies major, Political Economy of Africa.

JUNE BAM

June Bam heads the Khoi and San Unit, Centre for African Studies at the University of Cape Town (UCT). She is an originator, together with fellow indigenous and global South scholars from Africa, Australia, New Zealand, Canada, the United States and the African diaspora, of the Worldwide University Network's *!Gâ re – Rangatiratanga – Dadirri* project on 'deep listening' and decolonising knowledge. As visiting professor with Stanford University's overseas programme, she has directed the 'Sites of Memory' programme from 2014 to 2020. With Lungisile Ntsebeza and Allan Zinn, she co-edited *Whose History Counts* (2018), a finalist for the National Institute for Humanities and Social

Science (NIHSS) inaugural awards of 2020. Her previous work won the UNESCO Peace Education Prize for South Africa in 2008. Co-founder of the A/Xarra Restorative Justice Forum, she led on the historic naming of the Sarah Baartman Hall and the first university certification of foundational erased indigenous Khoekhoegowab at UCT, a historically white university in South Africa, located in the region where the language was once spoken by her maternal family.

SHELLEY BARRY

Award-winning filmmaker, poet and educator, Shelley Barry has worked extensively as a disability rights activist. She teaches film at the University of Johannesburg (UJ), while working towards a Creative PhD in film at the University of the Witwatersrand. She has held positions as media manager in the Office on the Status of Disabled Persons in the Presidency and as the National Parliamentary Policy Co-ordinator for Disabled People South Africa. Shelley is the founder and director of *twospinningwheels*, a production company that aims to explore new languages in cinema and give marginalised voices access to the craft of filmmaking. Her films span genres and are largely experimental in style. She often shoots her own films, exploring the aesthetics of cinematography from the perspective of a wheelchair user. Screenings of her award-winning work have been held at major festivals and events around the world and acquired by television. Her most recent work, *Here*, a virtual reality film, was selected for the Berlinale 2020.

DIANA FERRUS

Diana Ferrus is a writer, poet, performance poet and storyteller. Her work has been published in various collections and some serve as prescribed texts for high school learners. In 2012 Diana received the inaugural Mbokodo Award for poetry. Her third book, *Die Vrede Kom Later*, was launched on 27 July 2019. She is internationally acclaimed for the poem that she wrote for the indigenous South African woman, Sarah Baartman, who was taken away from her country under false pretences and paraded as a sexual freak in Europe. This poem touched the heart of the French Senate and, upon hearing it, they unanimously voted that Baartman's remains should come home. This poem is published in the French Law, a first in French history. Diana's work continues to influence matters of race and ethnicity, sex and gender, and reconciliation.

GERTRUDE FESTER-WICOMB

Cape Town-born gertrude has been involved in anti-Apartheid feminism focusing on women's liberation. She was a founding member of several women's grassroots structures, including the Women's National Coalition, which intervened for a gender-sensitive Constitution (1980s–1990s), and she has published extensively on these struggles. She established the Women's Education and Artistic Voice and Expressions (WEAVE), a black writing collective, to encourage young women's writing, and has conducted many creative writing workshops, including prisoners' workshops. The oppression of women and marginalised groups are key issues in her fiction and non-fiction. Her prison play, *The Spirit Cannot be Caged,* composed in her head during solitary confinement during the Apartheid 1980s, was performed at the Fourth Women's UN Conference in Beijing in 1995. In post-Apartheid South Africa she was a member of Parliament and served as a Constitutional Commissioner for Gender Equality. With a PhD from the London School of Economics, gertrude's academic positions have included the Wynona Lipman Chair for Women Political Leaders at Rutgers University, and Professor of Transitional Justice at the University of Rwanda. Currently she is an honorary professor in the Centre for African Studies at the University of Cape Town, a PhD supervisor at Bishop Stuart University, Uganda, and a member of the A/Xarra Restorative Justice Forum.

SHARON GROENMEYER

Sharon Groenmeyer is a sociologist and development worker with more than 30 years' experience in education and training. She works in a network with other development workers in South Africa as an independent, feminist researcher and gender auditor of non-governmental projects. After completing her doctoral thesis on 'Women and social policy in contemporary post-Apartheid South Africa' at the Norwegian University of Science and Technology in Trondheim, Norway, she continues to write and publish on two main themes in social policy: (1) Women small business (SMME) owners operating in the male-dominated industries of fishing and agriculture; and (2) the role of women in the peace-building process. She is also a paralegal practitioner and continues to contribute knowledge and ideas on monitoring and evaluation. Sharon is a member of the South African Monitoring and Evaluation Association (SAMEA), the South African Sociological Association (SASSA) and CODESRIA, and has presented at various conferences, including the Gender Symposium in Cairo, Egypt.

Khadija Tracey Heeger

Khadija Tracey Carmelita Heeger is a celebrated poet, actor, facilitator, cultural activist, and writer who hails from the Cape Flats. She performs in a number of films and television shows, and other performances. Most recently she appeared in a film on the politics of hair on the Cape Flats. In 2019, Jazzart used Khadija's poetry for their dance drama, *Cape of Ghosts*, during which she narrated the story of land and landlessness on stage with the dancers. She also plays a lead role in a forthcoming film shot on Hangberg in Hout Bay, Cape Town. The Centre for Curating the Archive at the University of Cape Town commissioned Khadija to write the poetic script for their historical film on the washerwoman slaves, and Kirsten Dunbar Chace commissioned her to write a poetic script for her short film on the Cape 'coloured' people. Among others, she has collaborated with the District Six Museum in Cape Town, the Institute for Justice and Reconciliation, Iziko Museums of South Africa, the Cape Town Museum, and other museum services.

Robyn Humphreys

Robyn Humphreys has a BSc in Biochemistry and Development and Genetics (2008), as well as a BSc (Med) Hons in Human Genetics (2010) from the University of Cape Town (UCT). Her honours degree focused on genetic factors affecting the phenotypic outcomes of patients with sickle cell disease. She completed a MSc in Archaeology, also at UCT in 2018, focusing on the effects of hybridisation (between species and subspecies) on coat colour phenotypes in mice to understand the phenotypic patterns in mammalian hybrid offspring. Her current research focuses on how to engage with communities regarding the management of human remains from archaeological sites. Indigenous communities have been and continue to be affected by biological anthropological practices because they have been excluded from research processes. She aims to understand how best to include communities in research agendas to improve biological anthropological research practice. She is currently a PhD candidate in Archaeology and African Studies at UCT.

Babalwa Magoqwana

Babalwa Magoqwana is senior lecturer in Sociology and Anthropology, and interim director for the Centre for Women and Gender Studies, at Nelson Mandela University in Port Elizabeth, South Africa. She is a fellow of the African Humanities Programme; a research associate for the South African Research Chair Initiative (SARChI) Chair in Social Policy at the University of South Africa (UNISA); and former president of the South African Sociological Association (SASA, 2017–2019). She is the recipient of the National Research Foundation/First Rand Foundation Sabbatical Grant for her project on 'Woman-Centred Vernacular Sociology of the Eastern Cape'.

Sarah Malotane Henkeman

Sarah Malotane Henkeman is a transdisciplinary practitioner–scholar who produces knowledge from the standpoint of the oppressed. She is the mother of two adult sons and became aware of the more ubiquitous, invisibilised nature of the criminalisation of blackness (both inside and outside of South Africa) as they grew tall. It is her belief that knowledge produced from the impact side of dehumanisation is first about self-determination, then about a counterpoint to mainstream knowledge and modes of knowledge production. She recognises that she will die structurally oppressed, but that she will do so in the course of decolonising her mind – a lifelong process. And finally, she recognises that inasmuch as oppression is an external force in the lives of the dehumanised, it is also met and matched by an internal, mainly denied force – internalised oppression – that presents in too many masked ways to mention. She has a PhD from the colonial academy, and thus much to disabuse herself of.

Bernedette Muthien

For over 20 years, Bernedette Muthien has held executive and senior management positions in academia, civil society and the public sector in South Africa and abroad. She is an accomplished facilitator, researcher and poet, who designs, implements and evaluates projects for diverse institutions, locally and internationally. She has over 200 publications and conference presentations to her name, some of which have been translated from English into at least 16 other languages. She was the first Fulbright–Amy Biehl fellow at Stanford University, and holds postgraduate degrees in Political Science. She served on the Executive Council of the International Peace Research Association and was co-founder of the African Peace Research and Education Association. She serves on various international advisory boards, including those of two international journals, *Human Security Studies* and *Journal of Human Security*, and the International Institute on Peace Education. She co-founded Women's International Network on Gender and Human Security (WINGHS) in 1998, and Gender Egalitarian, a global indigenous women's network, in 2005. She has chaired and served on a number of constitutional and company boards since 2013.

Sylvia Vollenhoven

Sylvia Vollenhoven is a storyteller, Knight International Journalism Fellow, the University of Johannesburg's first Professor of Practice and winner of the Mbokodo Award for Literature. Her documentary, *Jozi Gold*, has been selected for several international festivals. Sylvia was also winner of the 1st Prize at the Toronto Film Festival's Big Pitch for her feature in development, *Buckingham Palace District Six*. Her play *Krotoa Eva van de Kaap*, premiered in the Netherlands before a sold-out run in South Africa. Her dance drama, *The Keeper of the Kumm* (based on the novel of the same name), opened on the main programme at the South African National Arts Festival (NAF). A play she co-authored, *My Word, Redesigning Buckingham Palace*, was chosen for London's West End, while another of her plays, *Cold Case: Revisiting Dulcie September*, was selected for a Paris arts festival. She was also the only non-Swede ever to be awarded Sweden's main journalism prize.

Captions for images

According to the A/Xarra Restorative Justice Forum, the words 'art' and 'paintings' to describe the San images painted or engraved on rocks are not accurate, since these descriptions may distort the knowledge of indigenous people represented through what has been recorded by the indigenous people. The A/Xarra Restorative Justice Forum therefore speaks of 'sacred scriptures', as these images often depict spirituality and spiritual experiences ('Dialogues on decolonising knowledge', Xarra plenaries, Centre for African Studies Gallery, 2018–2019; see also chapter 4 by June Bam and the discussions on epistemicide and toponymicide). However, for this book to be as accessible as possible for a wide range of readers, the editors will still use the generic language of 'rock art', while critiquing the outdated colonial interpretations from indigenous and women's perspectives.

1. Driekopseiland engraving site on glacial pavement in the bed of the Riet River. *Photo: Jeannette Unite, McGregor Museum Rock Art Collection*
2. The glaciated rock almost resembles the back of a giant mythic snake, which the |xam called !khwa, rising and sinking as the river swells or dries up. *Photo: David Morris, McGregor Museum Rock Art Collection*
3. When the river rises, water flows over the engravings. *Photo: David Morris, McGregor Museum Rock Art Collection*
4. Many of the engraved images are unique compositions – submerged when the river rises. *Photo: David Morris, McGregor Museum Rock Art Collection*
5. A 'powerful place' where part of young women's coming-of-age rites as described in a range of Khoe-San ethnography is hypothesised

to have taken place (Morris, 2002). *Photo: David Morris, McGregor Museum Rock Art Collection*

6. Engravings, perhaps made as part of coming-of-age rites, festooned across the rock. *Photo: David Morris, McGregor Museum Rock Art Collection*
7. Smoothed and striated by glacial action, and situated in the bed of the Riet River, the 'power' of the place is argued (Morris, 2002) to arise from a coincidence of environmental rhythms and phenomena with |xam and other Khoe-San beliefs about water (!khwa) which is synonymous with the snake or rain animal (!khwa-ka-xoro), in turn linked to the menarcheal rites of young women, which would take place in part at the water hole or river. *Photo: David Morris, McGregor Museum Rock Art Collection*
8. Kagga Kamma Nature Reserve, Cederberg. *Photo: Sharon Stanton*
9. Self-representation. Mount Ceder Caves, Cederberg Mountains. The editors acknowledge that rock paintings have been interpreted through particular lenses by various scholars over time. In the past few decades, as especially indigenous scholars seek to decolonise our cultures and research, including interpretations of our peoples' rock and other art, the colonial era and interpretations which still prevail among Eurocentric male anthropologists and other scientists, are recognised as limited, if not outright fallacious, since indigenous intergenerational knowledge still exists of rituals depicted in the art. Hence the art is viewed by indigenous peoples as forms of self-representation, narratives that are especially now being fully explored by descendant communities, and particularly by women. *Photo: June Bam*
10. Sevilla Rock Art Trail, Traveller's Rest Farm, Cederberg Lions. The Sevilla Rock Art Trail is a 5-km walk, which passes nine key sites with extraordinary rock art. See for example, https://www.cederberg.com/places.php?pid=69. *Photo: Sharon Stanton*
11. Lions. Sevilla Rock Art Trail, Traveller's Rest Farm, Cederberg. *Photo: Sharon Stanton*
12. Shaman (healer, visionary). Ceder Valley, Baviaanskloof. This image has been interpreted by descendants of settlers and global North scholars, almost all male, as representing a male healer. In reality, shamans or healers and/or visionaries are often older women, as discussed in Muthien's chapter 2 and elsewhere. What most white male anthropologists personify as male and phallic is characterised

by Yvette Abrahams and Muthien respectively as a loin cloth, a covering of the genitals, since the San did not run around naked, but wore various items of clothing, depending on the weather (a common human practice). Genitalia were never arbitrarily exposed. These white male anthropologists ironically thus define phallogocentrism (centring the phallic). *Photo: Bernedette Muthien and Sharon Stanton*

13. Nieuwoudtville Glacial Pavement. Rock engravings on ancient glacial pavement (plain or bed) south of the town Nieuwoudtville in the Northern Cape (some 350 km north of Cape Town). The glacial pavement which covers the area is dated to 300 million years ago, when it is said to have covered the entire Karoo. The indigenous San engraved the stone that comprises the glacial bed, in particular with geometric designs, including triangles, circles, fish and other symbols.

    There is the most extraordinary rock art in Oorlogskloof Nature Reserve, just outside Nieuwoudtville, and on surrounding farms. Oorlogskloof derives its name from a famous battle between the early European settlers and the indigenous people, led by Jantjie Klipheuwel.

    The Nieuwoudtville region is particularly unique because it is one of the few places in the world that contains all five different soil types within a 20-km radius. It is one of the few places in the world with such natural diversity. There are well over a thousand species of uniquely varied flora. It is the bulb capital of the world, with more bulbs per square metre than anywhere else. It is also a solitary bee hotspot.

    Thus this location would be considered especially sacred by the indigenous people, throughout time. See for example, https://www.nieuwoudtville.com/the-treasure/. *Photo: Bernedette Muthien and Sharon Stanton*.

14. Sevilla Rock Art Trail, Traveller's Rest Farm, Cederberg. *Photo: Sharon Stanton*

15. An illustration of epistemicide in the San landscape, Cederberg mountains. Land dispossession was accompanied by toponymicide (erasure of place names). Graffiti inscribed over ancient, sacred rock art by settlers and their descendants not only deface the sacred symbols, but also re-inscribe colonial desecration, a graphic form of epistemicide, or destruction of knowledge. See discussion in chapter 4 by June Bam. *Photo: June Bam*

16. Self-representation. Cederberg. *Photo: June Bam*

17. Dinosaurs chasing humans. Sevilla Rock Art Trail, Traveller's Rest Farm, Cederberg. *Photo: Sharon Stanton*

18 & 19. Stone wall remnants of the homestead and kraal of Khoe leader, Lang Elsie of the Hessequa, in what is now the Bontebok National Park, near Swellendam. Discussed in Muthien's chapter 2. https://bonteboknationalpark.co.za/. *Photos: Bernedette Muthien*

20 & 21. Marloth Nature Reserve. Depicting the abundance of nature, water and wildlife. The mountain peaks were used to tell time and during colonialism and enslavement were named One O'Clock Peak, etc, to enable the enslaved and/or labourers and the slavers and/or settlers to tell the time. It was in this abundance that the indigenous people thrived, and from which they were so brutally dispossessed by colonialism. Discussed in Muthien's chapter 2. https://www.capenature.co.za/reserves/marloth-nature-reserve/. *Photos: Bernedette Muthien*

22. Open field on site of Hessequa leader Lang Elsie's homestead and village. Wildlife is still abundant. Discussed in Muthien's chapter 2. *Photo: Bernedette Muthien*

23. Cupping, an ancient medicinal practice by Cape Khoe. An illustration of the medicinal practice of cupping by Khoikhoi people at the Cape by Jan Caspar Phillips, Amsterdam, 1727. Alamy (www.alamy.com). Discussed in Bam's chapter 4 and Bam & Humphreys chapter 6.

24. Yacunã Tuxá: A queda do céu II/ Fincar raiz e espalhar a semente (2019). Discussed in Aguiar's chapter 9.

    Yacuña Tuxá is an indigenous artist born in Brazil. She is part of the Tuxá people, who are located in Bahia. In her work she always chooses indigenous women in contact with their roots and ancestry. This image is only on her Instagram, not in any book. She has generously given permission for us to reproduce the image here. (https://www.instagram.com/yacunatuxa/?hl=en).

Index

This index is arranged word by word.

A
aba (carrying of children on the back) 153
abortion 131, 152
Abrahams, Yvette 6
Africa
    diversity 59
    languages 171–172
    spirituality 22
African Charter on Human and Peoples' Rights on the Rights of Women in Africa 9
African Feminist Charter 170, 176
African Feminist Forum 8
African Women's Development Fund 8
Africanders 108
Akan people (West Africa) 13, 98 n.11
alcoholism 46, 47, 142, 155
Amadiume, Ifi 9, 55, 59, 62, 63, 64, 68, 73, 95
Ana (Khoe woman) 131
anarchive 11, 114
Ancestors 43, 44–45, 48, 49, 54, 90–91, 92–93
Angas, George 112
anthropology 87, 91
Apartheid 10, 26, 27, 155, 189, 190, 191, 195
Appollis, Basil 23, 26–27, 30, 31, 37, 39–42, 43–44, 45
archives and libraries 11–12, 30, 47–48, 109, 113, 211. *See also* anarchive; Bleek-Lloyd Archive
    Dutch 106–107
    ritual 12, 93, 210, 211
Argus Group 19 n.2, 30
Atalay, Sonya 62
Ausi-cide 103, 210
Autshumao (Autshumato) 5, 109
A/Xarra Restorative Justice Forum (Centre for African Studies, UCT) 5, 160, 162

B
Baartman, Sarah 1–2, 5, 12, 96 n.7, 108, 112, 115, 197, 198, 209, 211
Banai, Baruch 35
Bantu (concept) 56
Barnard, Ann 110
Basic Conditions of Employment Act (1997/2002, BCEA) 134
Baxter Theatre (Cape Town) 27, 30, 39, 40
Berber people (Kabyle, North Africa) 10
bergies 160
biopiracy 28
birth 153
Bitterputs (Kenhardt) 45
Blanche and Alex La Guma (film, Sylvia Vollenhoven and Basil Appollis) 21
Bleek, Wilhelm 19

Bleek-Lloyd Archive 19, 20, 112–113, 114
blessers 141
blue water lily 105
Bolivia 64–65
'The bones' (poem, Diana Ferrus) 121
botanicide 109
Botswana 56, 59, 175
brainstorming 33
Brazil
    and COVID-19 147, 207
    indigenous people 11, 162, 203–205, 206, 207–208
    literature 201–202
bubonic plague 160
buchu 24, 33, 48, 116
Buckingham Palace, District Six (film and play, Sylvia Vollenhoven) 21, 39–40
Bushmen 19 n.3, 22
    ukubuyisa 12, 90, 91, 92, 211

C

cabbage 152
'call to art' (poem, Shelley Barry) 127
'Camissa' (poem, Khadija Tracey Carmelita Heeger) 123–125
Camissa Africans 106
Campbell, Niall 31–32, 35, 44, 48
Canada 161
Cape Flats 3, 111, 114, 116, 117, 140, 151, 152, 153, 158, 159, 162
Cape Herald (newspaper) 18
Cape Town Castle 43
care work 130, 131, 133–134, 135, 137, 142
Cartesianism 4 –5, 6, 69, 185
caul *see* birth
Cederberg (Western Cape) 28, 45
Chad 150
Charter of Feminist Principles for African Feminists 8–9
China 156
Christianity 25, 112, 113
Coertze, Desiree 35–36
cognitive justice 6, 108, 117
Cold Case, Revisiting Dulcie September (play, Sylvia Vollenhoven) 21, 40–42
collective unconscious 53–54, 66

colonialism 11, 17, 29, 56, 89, 109, 117, 135, 138, 142, 155, 158, 160, 162, 186, 187, 189, 202, 203, 204
compassion 55, 68, 72, 73, 74
conceptual freedom 185
conceptual tools 183, 186
contraception 152
Convention on the Elimination of All Forms of Discrimination against Women (CEDAW) 134
corruption 188, 189
COVID-19
    and African custom 150
    Brazil 207
    cases and deaths 147–148, 149
    and domestic violence 148, 149
    economic impact 133, 136–138, 148
    and education 138–139, 140–141, 149, 150
    and food 140–141, 149–150
    and the homeless 132, 136, 139–140, 159–161
    and indigenous people 158–159, 162
    lockdown 136, 140
    and patriarchy 163–164
    and representation of Cape indigenous women 156–157, 158
    in rural areas 150
    and social grants 140
culturicide 103
cupping 116, 153–154

D

Dadirri (Aboriginal Australian practice and theory) 13, 163, 164
Dagara people (West Africa) 59, 66
dagga 24, 111, 116, 152
Dahomey 94
dance 33, 34
dassiepis see rock rabbit urine
Dausab, Pedro 103 n.3, 153 n.12
decent work 133
decoloniality 7, 10–11, 13, 108
deep listening 11, 13, 14, 164, 209–211
dehumanisation 190, 191, 193–198
diet 33, 70

amadikazi see women, liberated
diplomacy, indigenous 72–73
Disaster Management Act (2002) 135, 136
disciplinary understandings 104
disruption, delinking and dismantling 71, 190, 193
Doctors Without Borders (MSF) 159, 160
domestic violence *see* violence, domestic
domestic workers 132, 136–137, 149
drama 44
dreams and visions 28–29, 32, 33–34, 36, 116, 153
Driekopseiland (Northern Cape) 175–178
Dutch East India Company (VOC) 96, 106, 156

E
Ebola 131, 141
ecocide 4, 11, 103
education with production 142
egalitarianism 57, 65, 66, 69, 187
Einstein, Albert 22
elders *see* Ancestors
Elim 112
Employment Equity Act (1998) 135
enslaved women *see* slavery and women
epidemics 131–133, 134, 141, 142, 147, 156, 157–158, 207
epidemiology 157
epilepsy 116
epistemic disobedience 207
epistemic trauma *see* trauma, epistemic
epistemic violence *see* violence, epistemic
epistemicide 3, 4, 103, 164; *see also* knowledge, erasure
Esau, Katrina *see* Geelmeid, *Grandmother/Ouma*
ethnocide 4
European travellers 110–112, 114, 116, 151, 156, 176
Eve (biblical) 58
Eve's Bayou (film) 29
evictions 137, 158

existential trap 183, 184, 185, 186, 197
Expressen (Swedish newspaper) 26
extinction discourse 3, 156, 157 n.15

F
family constellations 53, 54
farmworkers 137
femicide *see* violence, gender-based
feminism 7, 8–9, 99, 170
    African 52, 73–74, 104, 209
    indigenous 52 n.4, 55
feminism-cide 103, 109, 210
Fester, Christine (*auma/ilnaosa*) 176–178
first contact people 4
first nations (concept) 4, 7, 172

G
gebo aob (seer) 153, 164
Geelmeid, *Grandmother/Ouma* (Katriena Esau) 67, 173
!gei aob (magician) 153, 164
Genadendal (Western Cape) 45, 112
gender 64, 66, 68, 107
gender-based violence *see* violence, gender-based
genocide 4, 5, 7, 173
gentrification of cities 21
Gift Economy/Paradigm 68
Goettner-Abendroth, Heide 58, 62, 64
Goniwe, Mbulelo 97
Goringhaicona people 37, 49, 109
Goringhaiqua people 108, 109
grandmothers see *Ilnaosa /auma/!uiki/ aia; ooMakhulu; Matrutva*
Great Trek 115 116
green kalahari (poem, Bernedette Muthien) 85–86
Grosfoguel, Ramón 206
Guatemala 162

H
Haudenosaunee people (Iroquois, North America) 10, 11, 57 n.12, 72
Hellinger, Bert 53, 54
herbs, medicinal 24, 116, 136, 152, 153; *see also* specific names
herstory 188–189, 198, 211
Hessequa (Western Cape) 67
Hindu religion 174

history 188, 189, 197, 198, 211
  re-enactment of 22–23
  and sensory memory 29
  written 23–24
HIV and AIDS 131, 141
  ukuhlambulula (cleansing) 12, 13, 92, 93–94
Hofmeister, Jeff 42, 43
Hoho (wife of Chief Madoda) 21
hoodia 70, 114
hooks, bell 91–92
human and social sciences 87–88, 91, 92, 98, 99
hypnotherapy 32, 35–36

I

Ilnaosa /auma/!uiki/aia (grandmother) 173–174, 176–179; *see also ooMakhulu*; *Matrutva*
indigeneity 7–8, 129 n.1
indigenous knowledge *see* knowledge, indigenous
indigenous revivalism 163
intergenerational transmission 193–194
International Labour Organisation (ILO) Convention No. 169 (governance of indigenous people) 134
invisibilisation 5, 130, 131
invisible mechanisms 185, 189, 190, 194
Irish people 10, 53
Iroquois people (North America) 54, 55, 66
Isis (deity) 12, 51
'I've come to take you home' (poem, Diana Ferrus) 1–2, 12–13

J

Jansen, Lesle 27
job guarantee schemes 142
Jonker, Ingrid 27
Jotela, Nosuthu 90
journalism 19, 25–26, 30, 49
Jung, Carl 53–54, 66

K

//Kabbo/Uhi-ddoro Jantjie Tooren 5, 19–20, 21, 34, 36, 45–46, 47
Kabyle *see* Berber people

/Kaggen (Mantis figure) 34
Kalahari (Kgalagadi) 45, 46, 56
Kalk Bay (Cape Town) 30
Kedjou, Sogolon 94
The Keeper of the Kumm (novel and dance, Sylvia Vollenhoven) 21, 27, 34, 35, 36, 45, 48
Kenya 149–150, 163
Khayelitsha (Cape Town) 160
Khoe/Khoi (Khoena)
  clan conflict 109
  and colonialism 4, 21, 44, 113, 172 n.7
  economic aspects 135, 136, 151–152
  and egalitarianism 187
  and European travellers 110–111, 116
  geography 3, 12
  health 136, 152–154, 156, 157, 158
  historic representation 154–155, 156–157, 197–198
  land dispossession 134, 154
  languages 173
  and matriarchy 65, 67
  and missionaries 112, 113
  names 153
  scholarship on 5, 115
  social structure 187
  terminology 106
  and wholeness 29
  women 96, 107–108, 111–112, 115, 116, 136, 151, 152–153, 154, 155, 156, 160
khoegoed/kooigoed see sage
Khoekhoegowab language 116
Khoena *see* Khoe/Khoi
Khuzwayo, Ellen 91
Klapmuts (Western Cape) 137
Klein, Claudia 36
Klein, Ernst 26
Knight, Tim 45
knowledge
  democratisation 183–184
  erasure 4–6, 109–110, 112–113, 114
  indigenous 5, 14, 53, 54–55, 72, 104, 105, 108–109, 114–115,

162–163
  intergenerational 4, 110, 210
  production 186–187, 210–211
  women's 88, 89, 90, 91–92, 94, 98–99, 104, 105
Konner, Melvin 69–70, 71, 72
Kopenawa, Davi 204–205, 206
Krotoa (!Goa/gõas) 5, 21, 37–38, 42–43, 44, 96–97, 108, 109, 115, 152
Krotoa Eva van de Kaap (play, Sylvia Vollenhoven) 21, 37–39, 42, 43–44
Kruiper, Dawid 67
kukumakranka 116–117

L

La Guma, Alex 21–22
lactational infertility 70
Lang Elsie (Hessequa leader) 67
language 56, 93, 173
  indigenous 62, 99, 113–114, 164, 171–172
laughter 69
Le Vaillant, François 110, 115
legacies 88, 89, 90, 98
liberated women *see* women, liberated
Lichtenstein, Heinrich 108
linguicide 4, 103
listening 33; *see also* deep listening
Lloyd, Lucy 19
Locke, John 57
Lorde, Audre 71
lotus plant 104–105

M

Maasai 149–150, 163
Madikizela Mandela, Winnie 89
Madoda, *Chief* 21
Mahlangu, Gogo Esther 175
mainstream media 18, 25
Makhanya, Katie 89–90
ooMakhulu (grandmother) 12, 13, 88, 89, 92, 93, 170–171, 174, 211. S*ee also Ilnaosa /auma/!uiki/aia*; *Matrutva*
Malawi 65–66
Mandela, Winnie *see* Madikizela Mandela, Winnie
Mann, Barbara Alice 9, 54, 55, 56–57, 59, 61, 62, 66

Manunga, Ma-Meneputo 66
Maori people 9, 55, 147
Maputo Protocol *see* African Charter on Human and Peoples' Rights on the Rights of Women in Africa
Maracle, Lee 61, 62
Marathi (India) 174
matriarchy 57–58, 65, 93, 94, 174
matricentrism 52–53, 55, 59, 62–63, 65–66, 68, 69, 210
Matrutva (Marathi grandmother) 174
Maxeke, Charlotte 90
Mbeki, Thabo 4, 12–13
meditation 32, 33
Meer, Fatima 91
memory and memories
  access to 35
  cellular 53
  collective 184
  sensory 29
midwifery 152
misogyny 99
Mitchell, Bev 34–35
Mitchells Plain (Cape Town) 160
Mkabayi ka Jama 94
Morales, Evo 64
Morrison, Toni 92
Motherhood Movement 52 n.3 & 4
mothering 63–64
mphepho see sage
Mpondoland 96
My Word! Redesigning Buckingham Palace (play, Sylvia Vollenhoven and Basil Appollis) 20, 26–27

N

Nama language and culture 173–174
Namibia 22–23, 104
Narina (Khoe woman) 110, 115
'native question' 87
Natural Justice (organisation) 28
Ndabeni (Uitvlugt, Cape Town) 160, 161
Nestlé corporation 28
Newman, Denise 41–42
Nisa 69, 70–71
inkulu (first-born male) 95, 98
Nnobi people (Nigeria) 94
Nomawele, Njongo 97
Nouga Saree (Hessequa leader) 67

N|uu language 173
Nzinga, *Queen* 94

O
Omotoso, Timothy 97–98
'one & many' (poem, Bernedette Muthien) 213
online learning 138
Tuxá, Yacuña 224
O'Reilly, Andrea 52
Ouma Geelmeid *see* Geelmeid, Grandmother/Ouma
ousie 105

P
paleolithic diet 70
Palestinians 10
pandemics *see* epidemics
patriarchy 57, 58, 64, 66, 69, 71–72, 73, 99, 113, 131, 170, 174, 210
payment-in-kind (sexual) 138
peace 68, 72
Petersen, Sophia 19, 24–25, 26, 28–29, 49
pharmaceutical companies and pharmaceutics 70, 71, 104, 109, 114, 116
phonemes 56
physical typology 108
Pirates of the Drakensberg (writer and producer Sylvia Vollenhoven) 21
place names 105–107
plants, indigenous 70, 104–105, 108–109, 111, 112, 113–114, 116–117. *See also* herbs, medicinal; and specific names
Platteklip Stream (Table Mountain) 136
postcolonialism 202–203
Public Health Act (1883) 161

Q
quarantine 161

R
rape 96, 97, 132, 139, 151, 159
regression therapy 35, 36
Rematriation 60–62, 63, 64, 65, 73, 74, 212
remedies 111, 152, 194
Re-membering 17–18, 29
repatriation 62
rheumatism 152
ritual 25, 32, 35, 48, 164; *see also* archives and libraries, ritual
Rive, Richard Moore 20–21, 26–27, 30, 39–40
rock art and texts 29, 45, 113, 175–179
rock rabbit urine (*dassiepis*) 116, 152
Römkens, Mories 44
rooibos 21, 24, 27–28, 70
Rooibos Restitution (film, producer Sylvia Vollenhoven) 21, 27–28
Rundganger, *Captain* 113

S
sage (*mphepho, khoegoed/kooigoed*) 53
Salamo, Barend 28
Sami (Saami) people (northern Europe) 10, 11
San
  and colonialism 4, 21, 44, 103, 113, 172 n.7
  and egalitarianism 57, 187
  and European travellers 110–111, 116
  genocide of 173
  geography 3, 7 n.3, 12, 56, 60 n.18
  healing and health 71, 74, 152, 156, 157, 158
  historic representation of 5, 154–155, 156–157
  land loss 134
  languages 56–57, 173
  and matricentrism 57, 66–67
  religion 66
  rock art 175–176
  and wholeness 29
  women 106, 116, 155
sangomas 54
Sara, *Taras* 109
Sarah Baartman Hall (UCT) 13
scarification 153, 154, 176
schools 138, 141
September, Dulcie 21, 41
sexual harassment 97
sexualities 63, 66, 73
shamanic practices and shamans 54, 204, 205, 207

Shostak, Marjorie 69–71, 72, 73
Sierra Leone 141
Slave Emancipation Act (Britain, 1833) 136, 154
slavery 96, 154
  and women 130–131
Slemon, John 26
smallpox 130, 131, 136, 155, 156, 157, 160, 161
smudging 53
social sciences *see* human and social sciences
sociology 91, 92, 93
South African Human Rights Commission 139, 159
Spanish flu pandemic (1918–1920) 147
standpointism 185, 188
Stoffels, Andries 113
storytelling 18–19, 23, 24–25, 30, 31–32, 44, 45, 47–48, 49
Strandfontein camp (Cape Town) 132, 139–140, 159, 160–161
street-based people 139
Strömstedt, Bo 26
Swartberg (Western Cape) 169 n.2
Swellendam (Western Cape) 25, 67, 107

T
Taras see ooMakhulu (grandmother)
Taras-cide 103, 210
teachers 139
Ten Rhijne, Willem 38, 39
terminology 6–7
Thailand 162
ukuthwasa (preparatory tutelage and mentoring for traditional healing) 91
time 22, 36, 184–185
Tisani, Nomathamsanqa 6
tokoloshe 53 n.6
toponymicide 105
traditional healing 114, 115–116; *see also ukuthwasa*
trauma
  epistemic 6
  recovery from 53, 54
  transhistorical 135, 190, 192, 193, 194–197
treaties 72
tribalisation 7

Truth and Reconciliation Commission (TRC) 4, 190
tuberculosis 158, 159
Tupinambá people (Brazil) 207–208

U
ubuntu (*Unhu*, Khoe!Na) 68, 164, 185, 187
!uiki/aia/ Ilnaosa *see* Ilnaosa / auma/!uiki/aia (grandmother)
unemployment 133, 137, 138
United Nations Declaration on the Rights of Indigenous Peoples (UNDRIP) 7–8, 59–60, 129 n.1, 134
Universal Declaration of Human Rights (UDHR) 134, 137
unpaid work 132, 133, 138

V
Vaalbooi, Petrus 45–47
vagrancy laws 160
Van der Stel, Simon 106
Van Meerhoff, Pieter 37, 109
Van Riebeeck, Johan (Jan) 37, 38, 42–43, 44, 96, 97, 109
Van Sitters, Bradley 65
Vaughan, Genevieve 63
venereal disease 111, 156
violence
  domestic 148, 149, 162
  epistemic 191
  gender-based 98, 131, 132, 139, 142, 149, 159; *see also* sexual harassment
  physical 192, 196
  psychological 192–195, 196
  structural 183, 189–190, 192
  symbolic 191
visions *see* dreams and visions
Volkan, Vamik 53, 54

W
Wagenaer, Zacharias 37
washerwomen 136, 156, 157
Watkins, Gloria *see* hooks, bell
wet nurses 130
white episteme 204, 206
Wicomb, Gertrude (*ilnaosa*, née Martinus) 169 n.2, 178–179

Wicomb, Robert 169 n.2
wisdom
   elders' 93
   indigenous 53, 55, 153
   women's 70, 173–174
womb 56, 58
women
   historical trauma 135
   liberated 95–96, 98
   Maori 9
   as property owners 135, 151
   socio-economic status 129–130, 131–133, 134–135, 136–138, 142, 148–149, 162–163
   terms in indigenous languages 169–170
   work *see* socio-economic status
   See also: Khoe/Khoi (Khoena), women; knowledge, women's; San, women
A Writer's Last Word (play, Sylvia Vollenhoven and Basil Appollis) 20, 26–27, 30–31
Wupperthal (Western Cape) 27

X

/Xam people 112, 114
Xhosa people 5, 95, 97
Xipaia, Juma 207, 208
Xri language 173 n.9

Y

Yanomami people (Brazil) 203–205, 206
Yoruba people (Nigeria) 88–89

Z

Zambia 65–66
Zimbabwe 56, 59
Zondi, Cheryl 97
Zondo Commission of Inquiry into State Capture 187–188
Zulu people 94